MORTAL QUESTIONS

Canto is a new imprint offering a range of
titles, classic and more recent, across a
broad spectrum of subject areas and
interests. History, literature, biography,
archaeology, politics, religion, psychology,
philosophy and science are all represented
in Canto's specially selected list of titles,
which now offers some of the best and
most accessible of Cambridge publishing to
a wider readership.

MORTAL QUESTIONS

Thomas Nagel

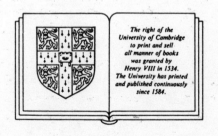

The right of the
University of Cambridge
to print and sell
all manner of books
was granted by
Henry VIII in 1534.
The University has printed
and published continuously
since 1584.

Cambridge University Press

CAMBRIDGE
NEW YORK   PORT CHESTER
MELBOURNE   SYDNEY

Published by the Press Syndicate of the University of Cambridge
The Pitt Building, Trumpington Street, Cambridge CB2 1RP
40 West 20th Street, New York NY 10011-4211, USA
10 Stamford Road, Oakleigh, Melbourne 3166, Australia

First published 1979
Reprinted 1979, 1980, 1981, 1982, 1983 (twice),
1985, 1987, 1988 (twice), 1990
Canto edition 1991

Printed in Great Britain by Billings and Son Ltd, Worcester

British Library cataloguing in publication data
Nagel, Thomas
Mortal questions.
1. Ethics
I. Title
170

Library of Congress cataloguing in publication data
Nagel, Thomas
Mortal questions.
Includes bibliographical references and index.
1. Life-addresses, essays, lectures.
2. Ethics-Addresses, essays, lectures. I.
Title. BD431.N32   170   78-58797

ISBN 0 521 22360 1 hardback
ISBN 0 521 40676 5 paperback

to my father
WALTER NAGEL
pessimist and
skeptic

CONTENTS

PREFACE

Philosophy covers an immense range of topics, but part of its concern has always been with mortal life: how to understand it and how to live it. These essays are about life: about its end, its meaning, its value, and about the metaphysics of consciousness. Some of the topics have not received much attention from analytic philosophers, because it is hard to be clear and precise about them, and hard to separate from a mixture of facts and feelings those questions abstract enough for philosophical treatment. Such problems must be attacked by a philosophical method that aims at personal as well as theoretical understanding, and seeks to combine the two by incorporating theoretical results into the framework of self-knowledge. This involves risk. Large, relevant questions too easily evoke large, wet answers.

Every theoretical field faces a contest between extravagance and repression, imagination and rigor, expansiveness and precision. Fleeing from the excesses of the one, it is easy to fall into the excesses of the other. Attachment to the grand style can produce an impatience with demands for rigor and may lead to a tolerance for the unintelligible. Since the defects of a tradition tend to reflect its virtues, the problem in analytic philosophy has been the reverse. It is not exactly correct to say that Anglo-American philosophy avoids the big questions. For one thing, there are no problems deeper or more important than those in metaphysics, epistemology, and philosophy of language that lie at the center of the field. For another, the analytic establishment has been quite hospitable to recent attempts to explore unfamiliar territory. Nevertheless, the fear of nonsense has had a powerful inhibiting effect. Long after the demise of Logical Positivism, analytic philosophers have tended to proceed with caution and to load themselves with the latest technical equipment.

It is understandable that an attachment to certain standards and methods should lead to a concentration on problems amenable to those methods. This can be a perfectly rational strategic choice. But it is often accompanied by a tendency to define the legitimate questions in terms of the available methods of solution. This habit appears not only in academic subjects but also in discussion of political and social questions – where it goes under the name of Realism or Pragmatism. It insures comfort of a sort – one is saved from the possibility that one may be ignoring real and important problems – but it is insane in any field, and especially in philosophy. Interesting things happen when new methods and their appropriate standards have to be developed to deal with questions that cannot be posed in terms of the already existing procedures of inquiry. Sometimes the questions cannot be fully understood until the methods have been developed. It is important to try to avoid making claims that are vague, obscure, or unfounded, and to maintain high standards of evidence and argument. But other values are also important, some of which make it difficult to keep things neat.

My own philosophical sympathies and antipathies are easily stated. I believe one should trust problems over solutions, intuition over arguments, and pluralistic discord over systematic harmony. Simplicity and elegance are never reasons to think that a philosophical theory is true: on the contrary, they are usually grounds for thinking it false. Given a knockdown argument for an intuitively unacceptable conclusion, one should assume there is probably something wrong with the argument that one cannot detect – though it is also possible that the source of the intuition has been misidentified. If arguments or systematic theoretical considerations lead to results that seem intuitively not to make sense, or if a neat solution to a problem does not remove the conviction that the problem is still there, or if a demonstration that some question is unreal leaves us still wanting to ask it, then something is wrong with the argument and more work needs to be done. Often the problem has to be reformulated, because an adequate answer to the original formulation fails to make the *sense* of the problem disappear. It is always reasonable in philosophy to have great respect for the intuitive sense of an unsolved problem, because in philosophy our methods are always themselves in question, and this is one way of being prepared to abandon them at any point.

What ties these views about philosophical practice together is the assumption that to create understanding, philosophy must *convince*. That means it must produce or destroy belief, rather than merely provide us with a consistent set of things to say. And belief, unlike utterance, should not be under the control of the will, however motivated. It should be involuntary.

Of course belief is often controlled by the will; it can even be coerced. The obvious examples are political and religious. But the captive mind is found in subtler forms in purely intellectual contexts. One of its strongest motives is the simple hunger for belief itself. Sufferers from this condition find it difficult to tolerate having no opinion for any length of time on a subject that interests them. They may change their opinions easily, when there is an alternative that can be adopted without discomfort, but they do not like to be in a condition of suspended judgment.

This can express itself in different ways, all of them well represented in the subject. One is an attachment to systematic theories that produce conclusions about everything. Another is the penchant for clearcut dichotomies that force a choice between the right alternative and the wrong one. Another is the disposition to adopt a view because all the other views one can think of on the topic have been refuted. Only an intemperate appetite for belief will motivate its adoption on such grounds. As a last resort, those who are uncomfortable without convictions but who also cannot manage to figure out what is true may escape by deciding that there is no right or wrong in the area of dispute, so that we need not decide what to believe, but can simply decide to say what we like so long as it is consistent, or else float above the battle of deluded theoretical opponents, observant but detached.

Superficiality is as hard to avoid in philosophy as it is anywhere else. It is too easy to reach solutions that fail to do justice to the difficulty of the problems. All one can do is try to maintain a desire for answers, a tolerance for long periods without any, an unwillingness to brush aside unexplained intuitions, and an adherence to reasonable standards of clear expression and cogent argument.

It may be that some philosophical problems have no solutions. I suspect this is true of the deepest and oldest of them. They show us the limits of our understanding. In that case such insight as we can achieve depends on maintaining a strong grasp of the problem instead of abandoning it, and coming to understand the failure of each new attempt at a solution, and of earlier attempts. (That is why we study the works of philosophers like Plato and Berkeley, whose views are accepted by no one.) Unsolvable problems are not for that reason unreal.

These essays have both internal and external sources. Disparate as they are, they are held together by an interest in the point of view of individual human life and the problem of its relation to more impersonal conceptions of reality. This problem, which receives a general discussion in chapter 14, arises across the board in philosophy, from ethics to metaphysics. The same concern with the place of subjectivity in an objective world motivates the essays on philosophy of mind, on the absurd, on moral luck, and others. It has been at the center of my interests since I began to think about philosophy, determining the problems I work on and the kind of understanding I want to reach.

Some of these essays were written while the United States was engaged in a criminal war, criminally conducted. This produced a heightened sense of the absurdity of my theoretical pursuits. Citizenship is a surprisingly strong bond, even for those of us whose patriotic feelings are weak. We read the newspaper every day with rage and horror, and it was different from reading about the crimes of another country. Those feelings led to the growth in the late 1960s of serious professional work by philosophers on public issues.

But a different kind of absurdity attaches to the production of philosophical criticism of public policy. Moral judgment and moral theory certainly apply to public questions, but they are notably ineffective. When powerful interests are involved it is very difficult to change anything by arguments, however cogent, which appeal to decency, humanity, compassion, or fairness. These considerations also have to compete with the more primitive moral sentiments of honor and retribution and respect for strength. The importance of these in our time makes it unwise in a political argument to condemn aggression and urge altruism or humanity, since the preservation of honor usually demands a capacity for aggression and resistance to humanity. Of course the notion is flexible, and may eventually expand to include certain requirements of decency. But that is not the general form of moral consciousness in this time and place.

So I am pessimistic about ethical theory as a form of public service. The conditions under which moral argument can have an influence on what is done are rather special, and not very well understood by me. (They need to be investigated through the history and psychology of morals, important but undeveloped subjects much neglected by philosophers since Nietzsche.) It certainly is not enough that the injustice of a practice or the wrongness of a policy should be made glaringly evident. People have to be ready to listen, and that is not determined by argument. I say this only to emphasize that philosophical writing on even the most current public issues remains theoretical, and cannot be measured by its practical effects. It is likely to be ineffective; and if it is theoretically less deep than work that is irrelevant to the problems of society, it cannot claim superior importance merely by virtue of the publicity of its concerns. I do not know whether it is more important to change the world or to understand it, but philosophy is best judged by its contribution to the understanding, not to the course of events.

SOURCES

Chapters 13 and 14 are published here for the first time. Original versions of chapters 1–12 appeared in the places listed below. There have been various revisions, including some changes of title.

1 *Nous*, IV, no. 1 (February, 1970). Reprinted by permission of the Wayne State University Press
2 *Journal of Philosophy*, LXVIII, no. 20 (October 21, 1971)
3 *Proceedings of the Aristotelian Society*, supplementary vol. L (1976). This was a reply to Bernard Williams' paper of the same name
4 *Journal of Philosophy*, LXVI, no. 1 (January 16, 1969)
5 *Philosophy & Public Affairs*, I, no. 2 (Winter, 1972), with replies by R. B. Brandt and R. M. Hare
6 *Public and Private Morality*, ed. Stuart Hampshire (Cambridge: Cambridge University Press, 1978)
7 *Philosophy & Public Affairs*, II, no. 4 (Summer, 1973)
8 Delivered as the Tanner Lecture at Stanford University in 1977, and published in *Critica* (1978). Published by permission of the Tanner Lecture Trust
9 *Knowledge, Value and Belief,* ed. H. Tristram Engelhardt Jr and Daniel Callahan (Hastings-on-Hudson, N.Y.: Institute of Society, Ethics and the Life sciences, 1977)
10 *Morality as a Biological Phenomenon*, ed. G. S. Stent (Berlin: Dahlem Konferenzen, 1978)
11 *Synthese*, XX (1971)
12 *Philosophical Review*, LXXXIII (October, 1974)

1

Death

If death is the unequivocal and permanent end of our existence, the question arises whether it is a bad thing to die.

There is conspicuous disagreement about the matter: some people think death is dreadful; others have no objection to death *per se*, though they hope their own will be neither premature nor painful. Those in the former category tend to think those in the latter are blind to the obvious, while the latter suppose the former to be prey to some sort of confusion. On the one hand it can be said that life is all we have and the loss of it is the greatest loss we can sustain. On the other hand it may be objected that death deprives this supposed loss of its subject, and that if we realize that death is not an unimaginable condition of the persisting person, but a mere blank, we will see that it can have no value whatever, positive or negative.

Since I want to leave aside the question whether we are, or might be, immortal in some form, I shall simply use the word 'death' and its cognates in this discussion to mean *permanent* death, unsupplemented by any form of conscious survival. I want to ask whether death is in itself an evil; and how great an evil, and of what kind, it might be. The question should be of interest even to those who believe in some form of immortality, for one's attitude toward immortality must depend in part on one's attitude toward death.

If death is an evil at all, it cannot be because of its positive features, but only because of what it deprives us of. I shall try to deal with the difficulties surrounding the natural view that death is an evil because it brings to an end all the goods that life contains. We need not give an account of these goods here, except to observe that some of them, like perception, desire, activity, and thought, are so general as to be constitutive of human life. They are widely regarded as formidable benefits in themselves, despite the fact that they are conditions of misery as well as of happiness, and that a sufficient quantity of more particular evils can perhaps outweigh them. That is what is meant, I think, by the allegation that it is good simply to be alive, even if one is undergoing terrible experiences. The situation is roughly this: There are elements which, if added to one's experience, make life better; there are other elements which, if added to one's experience, make life worse. But what remains when these are set aside is not merely *neutral*: it is emphatically positive. Therefore life is worth living even when the bad elements of experience are plentiful, and the good ones too meager to outweigh the bad ones on their own. The additional positive weight is supplied by experience itself, rather than by any of its contents.

I shall not discuss the value that one person's life or death may have for others, or its objective value, but only the value it has for the person who is its subject. That seems to me the primary case, and the case which presents the greatest difficulties. Let me add only two observations. First, the value of life and its contents does not attach to mere organic survival: almost everyone would be indifferent (other things equal) between immediate death and immediate coma followed by death twenty years later without reawakening. And second, like most goods, this can be multiplied by time: more is better than less. The added quantities need not be temporally continuous (though continuity has its social advantages). People are attracted to the possibility of long-term suspended animation or freezing, followed by the resumption of conscious life, because they can regard it from within simply as a *continuation* of their present life. If these techniques are ever perfected, what from outside appeared as a dormant interval of three hundred years could be experienced by the subject as nothing more than a sharp discontinuity in the character of his experiences. I do not deny, of course, that this has its own disadvantages. Family and friends may have died in the meantime; the language may have changed; the comforts of social, geographical, and cultural familiarity would be lacking. Nevertheless these inconveniences would not obliterate the basic advantage of continued, though discontinuous, existence.

If we turn from what is good about life to what is bad about death, the case is completely different. Essentially, though there may be problems about their specification, what we find desirable in life are certain states, conditions, or types of activity. It is *being* alive, *doing* certain things, having certain experiences, that we consider good. But if death is an evil, it is the *loss of life*, rather than the state of being dead, or nonexistent, or unconscious, that is objectionable.[1] This asymmetry is important. If it is good to be alive, that advantage can be attributed to a person at each point of his life. It is a good of which Bach had more than Schubert, simply because he lived longer. Death, however, is not an evil of which Shakespeare has so far received a larger portion than Proust. If death is a disadvantage, it is not easy to say when a man suffers it.

There are two other indications that we do not object to death merely because it involves long periods of nonexistence. First, as has been mentioned, most of us would not regard the *temporary* suspension of life, even for substantial intervals, as in itself a misfortune. If it ever happens that people can be frozen without reduction of the conscious lifespan, it will be inappropriate to pity those who are temporarily out of circulation. Second, none of us existed before we were born (or conceived), but few regard that as a misfortune. I shall have more to say about this later.

The point that death is not regarded as an unfortunate *state* enables us to refute a curious but very common suggestion about the origin of the fear of death. It is often said that those who object to death have made the mistake of trying to imagine what it is like to *be* dead. It is alleged that the failure to realize that this task is logically impossible (for the banal reason that there is nothing to imagine) leads to the conviction that death is a mysterious and therefore terrifying prospective *state*. But this diagnosis is evidently false, for it is just as impossible to imagine being totally unconscious as to imagine being dead (though it is easy enough to imagine oneself, from the outside, in either of those conditions). Yet people who are averse to death are not

---

[1] It is sometimes suggested that what we really mind is the process of *dying*. But I should not really object to dying if it were not followed by death.

usually averse to unconsciousness (so long as it does not entail a substantial cut in the total duration of waking life).

If we are to make sense of the view that to die is bad, it must be on the ground that life is a good and death is the corresponding deprivation or loss, bad not because of any positive features but because of the desirability of what it removes. We must now turn to the serious difficulties which this hypothesis raises, difficulties about loss and privation in general, and about death in particular.

Essentially, there are three types of problem. First, doubt may be raised whether *anything* can be bad for a man without being positively unpleasant to him: specifically, it may be doubted that there are any evils which consist merely in the deprivation or absence of possible goods, and which do not depend on someone's *minding* that deprivation. Second, there are special difficulties, in the case of death, about how the supposed misfortune is to be assigned to a subject at all. There is doubt both as to *who* its subject is, and as to *when* he undergoes it. So long as a person exists, he has not yet died, and once he has died, he no longer exists; so there seems to be no time when death, if it is a misfortune, can be ascribed to its unfortunate subject. The third type of difficulty concerns the asymmetry, mentioned above, between our attitudes to posthumous and prenatal nonexistence. How can the former be bad if the latter is not?

It should be recognized that if these are valid objections to counting death as an evil, they will apply to many other supposed evils as well. The first type of objection is expressed in general form by the common remark that what you don't know can't hurt you. It means that even if a man is betrayed by his friends, ridiculed behind his back, and despised by people who treat him politely to his face, none of it can be counted as a misfortune for him so long as he does not suffer as a result. It means that a man is not injured if his wishes are ignored by the executor of his will, or if, after his death, the belief becomes current that all the literary works on which his fame rests were really written by his brother, who died in Mexico at the age of 28. It seems to me worth asking what assumptions about good and evil lead to these drastic restrictions.

All the questions have something to do with time. There certainly are goods and evils of a simple kind (including some pleasures and pains) which a person possesses at a given time simply in virtue of his condition at that time. But this is not true of all the things we regard as good or bad for a man. Often we need to know his history to tell whether something is a misfortune or not; this applies to ills like deterioration, depriva- tion, and damage. Sometimes his experiential *state* is relatively unimportant – as in the case of a man who wastes his life in the cheerful pursuit of a method of communicating with asparagus plants. Someone who holds that all goods and evils must be temporally assignable states of the person may of course try to bring difficult cases into line by pointing to the pleasure or pain that more complicated goods and evils cause. Loss, betrayal, deception, and ridicule are on this view bad because people suffer when they learn of them. But it should be asked how our ideas of human value would have to be constituted to accom- modate these cases directly instead. One advantage of such an account might be that it would enable us to explain *why* the discovery of these misfortunes causes suffering – in a way that makes it reasonable. For the natural view is that the discovery of betrayal makes us unhappy because it is bad to be betrayed – not that betrayal is bad because its discovery makes us unhappy.

It therefore seems to me worth exploring the position that most good and ill fortune has as its subject a person identified by his history and his possibilities, rather than merely by his categorical state of the moment – and that while this subject can be exactly located in a sequence of places and times, the same is not necessarily true of the goods and ills that befall him.[2]

These ideas can be illustrated by an example of deprivation whose severity approaches that of death. Suppose an intelligent person receives a brain injury that reduces him to the mental condition of a contented infant, and that such desires as remain to him can be satisfied by a custodian, so that he is free from care. Such a development would be widely regarded as a severe misfortune, not only for his friends and relations, or for society, but also, and primarily, for the person himself. This does not mean that a contented infant is unfortunate. The intelligent adult who has been *reduced* to this condition is the subject of the misfortune. He is the one we pity, though of course he does not

[2] It is certainly not true in general of the things that can be said of him. For example, Abraham Lincoln was taller than Louis XIV. But when?

mind his condition – there is some doubt, in fact, whether he can
be said to exist any longer.

The view that such a man has suffered a misfortune is open to
the same objections which have been raised in regard to death.
He does not mind his condition. It is in fact the same condition
he was in at the age of three months, except that he is bigger. If
we did not pity him then, why pity him now; in any case, who
is there to pity? The intelligent adult has disappeared, and for a
creature like the one before us, happiness consists in a full
stomach and a dry diaper.

If these objections are invalid, it must be because they rest on a
mistaken assumption about the temporal relation between the
subject of a misfortune and the circumstances which constitute
it. If, instead of concentrating exclusively on the oversized baby
before us, we consider the person he was, and the person he *could*
be now, then his reduction to this state and the cancellation of his
natural adult development constitute a perfectly intelligible
catastrophe.

This case should convince us that it is arbitrary to restrict the
goods and evils that can befall a man to nonrelational properties
ascribable to him at particular times. As it stands, that restriction
excludes not only such cases of gross degeneration, but also a
good deal of what is important about success and failure, and
other features of a life that have the character of processes. I
believe we can go further, however. There are goods and evils
which are irreducibly relational; they are features of the relations
between a person, with spatial and temporal boundaries of the
usual sort, and circumstances which may not coincide with him
either in space or in time. A man's life includes much that does
not take place within the boundaries of his body and his mind,
and what happens to him can include much that does not take
place within the boundaries of his life. These boundaries are
commonly crossed by the misfortunes of being deceived, or
despised, or betrayed. (If this is correct, there is a simple account
of what is wrong with breaking a deathbed promise. It is an
injury to the dead man. For certain purposes it is possible to
regard time as just another type of distance.). The case of mental
degeneration shows us an evil that depends on a contrast
between the reality and the possible alternatives. A man is the
subject of good and evil as much because he has hopes which

may or may not be fulfilled, or possibilities which may or may not be realized, as because of his capacity to suffer and enjoy. If death is an evil, it must be accounted for in these terms, and the impossibility of locating it within life should not trouble us.

When a man dies we are left with his corpse, and while a corpse can suffer the kind of mishap that may occur to an article of furniture, it is not a suitable object for pity. The man, however, is. He has lost his life, and if he had not died, he would have continued to live it, and to possess whatever good there is in living. If we apply to death the account suggested for the case of dementia, we shall say that although the spatial and temporal locations of the individual who suffered the loss are clear enough, the misfortune itself cannot be so easily located. One must be content just to state that his life is over and there will never be any more of it. That *fact*, rather than his past or present condition, constitutes his misfortune, if it is one. Nevertheless if there is a loss, someone must suffer it, and *he* must have existence and specific spatial and temporal location even if the loss itself does not. The fact that Beethoven had no children may have been a cause of regret to him, or a sad thing for the world, but it cannot be described as a misfortune for the children that he never had. All of us, I believe, are fortunate to have been born. But unless good and ill can be assigned to an embryo, or even to an unconnected pair of gametes, it cannot be said that not to be born is a misfortune. (That is a factor to be considered in deciding whether abortion and contraception are akin to murder.)

This approach also provides a solution to the problem of temporal asymmetry, pointed out by Lucretius. He observed that no one finds it disturbing to contemplate the eternity preceding his own birth, and he took this to show that it must be irrational to fear death, since death is simply the mirror image of the prior abyss. That is not true, however, and the difference between the two explains why it is reasonable to regard them differently. It is true that both the time before a man's birth and the time after his death are times when he does not exist. But the time after his death is time of which his death deprives him. It is time in which, had he not died then, he would be alive. Therefore any death entails the loss of *some* life that its victim would have led had he not died at that or any earlier point. We know perfectly well what it would be for him to have had it instead of losing it, and there is no difficulty in identifying the loser.

But we cannot say that the time prior to a man's birth is time in which he would have lived had he been born not then but earlier. For aside from the brief margin permitted by premature labor, he *could* not have been born earlier: anyone born substantially earlier than he was would have been someone else. Therefore the time prior to his birth is not time in which his subsequent birth prevents him from living. His birth, when it occurs, does not entail the loss to him of any life whatever.

The direction of time is crucial in assigning possibilities to people or other individuals. Distinct possible lives of a single person can diverge from a common beginning, but they cannot converge to a common conclusion from diverse beginnings. (The latter would represent not a set of different possible lives of one individual, but a set of distinct possible individuals, whose lives have identical conclusions.) Given an identifiable individual, countless possibilities for his continued existence are imaginable, and we can clearly conceive of what it would be for him to go on existing indefinitely. However inevitable it is that this will not come about, its possibility is still that of the continuation of a good for him, if life is the good we take it to be.[3]

---

[3] I confess to being troubled by the above argument, on the ground that it is too sophisticated to explain the simple difference between our attitudes to prenatal and posthumous nonexistence. For this reason I suspect that something essential is omitted from the account of the badness of death by an analysis which treats it as a deprivation of possibilities. My suspicion is supported by the following suggestion of Robert Nozick. We could imagine discovering that people developed from individual spores that had existed indefinitely far in advance of their birth. In this fantasy, birth never occurs naturally more than a hundred years before the permanent end of the spore's existence. But then we discover a way to trigger the premature hatching of these spores, and people are born who have thousands of years of active life before them. Given such a situation, it would be possible to imagine *oneself* having come into existence thousands of years previously. If we put aside the question whether this would really be the same person, even given the identity of the spore, then the consequence appears to be that a person's birth at a given time *could* deprive him of many earlier years of possible life. Now while it would be cause for regret that one had been deprived of all those possible years of life by being born too late, the feeling would differ from that which many people have about death. I conclude that something about the future

We are left, therefore, with the question whether the nonrealization of this possibility is in every case a misfortune, or whether it depends on what can naturally be hoped for. This seems to me the most serious difficulty with the view that death is always an evil. Even if we can dispose of the objections against admitting misfortune that is not experienced, or cannot be assigned to a definite time in the person's life, we still have to set some limits on *how* possible a possibility must be for its nonrealization to be a misfortune (or good fortune, should the possibility be a bad one). The death of Keats at 24 is generally regarded as tragic; that of Tolstoy at 82 is not. Although they will both be dead for ever, Keats' death deprived him of many years of life which were allowed to Tolstoy; so in a clear sense Keats' loss was greater (though not in the sense standardly employed in mathematical comparison between infinite quantities). However, this does not prove that Tolstoy's loss was insignificant. Perhaps we record an objection only to evils which are gratuitously added to the inevitable; the fact that it is worse to die at 24 than at 82 does not imply that it is not a terrible thing to die at 82, or even at 806. The question is whether we can regard as a misfortune any limitation, like mortality, that is normal to the species. Blindness or near-blindness is not a misfortune for a mole, nor would it be for a man, if that were the natural condition of the human race.

The trouble is that life familiarizes us with the goods of which death deprives us. We are already able to appreciate them, as a mole is not able to appreciate vision. If we put aside doubts about their status as goods and grant that their quantity is in part a function of their duration, the question remains whether death, no matter when it occurs, can be said to deprive its victim of what is in the relevant sense a possible continuation of life.

The situation is an ambiguous one. Observed from without, human beings obviously have a natural lifespan and cannot live much longer than a hundred years. A man's sense of his own

---

prospect of permanent nothingness is not captured by the analysis in terms of denied possibilities. If so, then Lucretius' argument still awaits an answer. I suspect that it requires a general treatment of the difference between past and future in our attitudes toward our own lives. Our attitudes toward past and future pain are very different, for example. Derek Parfit's unpublished writings on this topic have revealed its difficulty to me.

experience, on the other hand, does not embody this idea of a natural limit. His existence defines for him an essentially open-ended possible future, containing the usual mixture of goods and evils that he has found so tolerable in the past. Having been gratuitously introduced to the world by a collection of natural, historical, and social accidents, he finds himself the subject of a *life*, with an indeterminate and not essentially limited future. Viewed in this way, death, no matter how inevitable, is an abrupt cancellation of indefinitely extensive possible goods. Normality seems to have nothing to do with it, for the fact that we will all inevitably die in a few score years cannot by itself imply that it would not be good to live longer. Suppose that we were all inevitably going to die in *agony* – physical agony lasting six months. Would inevitability make *that* prospect any less unpleasant? And why should it be different for a deprivation? If the normal lifespan were a thousand years, death at 80 would be a tragedy. As things are, it may just be a more widespread tragedy. If there is no limit to the amount of life that it would be good to have, then it may be that a bad end is in store for us all.

2

The Absurd

Most people feel on occasion that life is absurd, and some feel it vividly and continually. Yet the reasons usually offered in defense of this conviction are patently inadequate: they *could* not really explain why life is absurd. Why then do they provide a natural expression for the sense that it is?

I

Consider some examples. It is often remarked that nothing we do now will matter in a million years. But if that is true, then by the same token, nothing that will be the case in a million years matters now. In particular, it does not matter now that in a million years nothing we do now will matter. Moreover, even if what we did now *were* going to matter in a million years, how could that keep our present concerns from being absurd? If their mattering now is not enough to accomplish that, how would it help if they mattered a million years from now?

Whether what we do now will matter in a million years could make the crucial difference only if its mattering in a million years depended on its mattering, period. But then to deny that whatever happens now will matter in a million years is to beg the question against its mattering, period; for in that sense one cannot know that it will not matter in a million years whether (for example) someone now is happy or miserable, without knowing that it does not matter, period.

What we say to convey the absurdity of our lives often has to do with space or time: we are tiny specks in the infinite vastness of the universe; our lives are mere instants even on a geological time scale, let alone a cosmic one; we will all be dead any minute. But of course none of these evident facts can be what *makes* life absurd, if it is absurd. For suppose we lived for ever; would not a life that is absurd if it lasts seventy years be infinitely absurd if it lasted through eternity? And if our lives are absurd given our present size, why would they be any less absurd if we filled the universe (either because we were larger or because the universe was smaller)? Reflection on our minuteness and brevity appears to be intimately connected with the sense that life is meaningless; but it is not clear what the connection is.

Another inadequate argument is that because we are going to die, all chains of justification must leave off in mid-air: one studies and works to earn money to pay for clothing, housing, entertainment, food, to sustain oneself from year to year, perhaps to support a family and pursue a career – but to what final end? All of it is an elaborate journey leading nowhere. (One will also have some effect on other people's lives, but that simply reproduces the problem, for they will die too.)

There are several replies to this argument. First, life does not consist of a sequence of activities each of which has as its purpose some later member of the sequence. Chains of justification come repeatedly to an end within life, and whether the process as a whole can be justified has no bearing on the finality of these end-points. No further justification is needed to make it reasonable to take aspirin for a headache, attend an exhibition of the work of a painter one admires, or stop a child from putting his hand on a hot stove. No larger context or further purpose is needed to prevent these acts from being pointless.

Even if someone wished to supply a further justification for pursuing all the things in life that are commonly regarded as self-justifying, that justification would have to end somewhere too. If *nothing* can justify unless it is justified in terms of something outside itself, which is also justified, then an infinite regress results, and no chain of justification can be complete. Moreover, if a finite chain of reasons cannot justify anything, what could be accomplished by an infinite chain, each link of which must be justified by something outside itself?

Since justifications must come to an end somewhere, nothing is gained by denying that they end where they appear to, within life – or by trying to subsume the multiple, often trivial ordinary justifications of action under a single, controlling life scheme. We can be satisfied more easily than that. In fact, through its misrepresentation of the process of justification, the argument makes a vacuous demand. It insists that the reasons available within life are incomplete, but suggests thereby that all reasons that come to an end are incomplete. This makes it impossible to supply any reasons at all.

The standard arguments for absurdity appear therefore to fail as arguments. Yet I believe they attempt to express something that is difficult to state, but fundamentally correct.

II

In ordinary life a situation is absurd when it includes a conspicuous discrepancy between pretension or aspiration and reality: someone gives a complicated speech in support of a motion that has already been passed; a notorious criminal is made president of a major philanthropic foundation; you declare your love over the telephone to a recorded announcement; as you are being knighted, your pants fall down.

When a person finds himself in an absurd situation, he will usually attempt to change it, by modifying his aspirations, or by trying to bring reality into better accord with them, or by removing himself from the situation entirely. We are not always willing or able to extricate ourselves from a position whose absurdity has become clear to us. Nevertheless, it is usually possible to imagine some change that would remove the absurdity – whether or not we can or will implement it. The sense that life as a whole is absurd arises when we perceive, perhaps dimly, an inflated pretension or aspiration which is inseparable from the continuation of human life and which makes its absurdity inescapable, short of escape from life itself.

Many people's lives are absurd, temporarily or permanently, for conventional reasons having to do with their particular ambitions, circumstances, and personal relations. If there is a philosophical sense of absurdity, however, it must arise from the perception of something universal – some respect in which pretension and reality inevitably clash for us all. This condition is supplied, I shall argue, by the collison between the seriousness with which we take our lives and the perpetual possibility of regarding everything about which we are serious as arbitrary, or open to doubt.

We cannot live human lives without energy and attention, nor without making choices which show that we take some things more seriously than others. Yet we have always available a point of view outside the particular form of our lives, from which the seriousness appears gratuitous. These two inescapable viewpoints collide in us, and that is what makes life absurd. It is absurd because we ignore the doubts that we know cannot be settled, continuing to live with nearly undiminished seriousness in spite of them.

This analysis requires defense in two respects: first as regards the unavoidability of seriousness; second as regards the inescapability of doubt.

We take ourselves seriously whether we lead serious lives or not and whether we are concerned primarily with fame, pleasure, virtues, luxury, triumph, beauty, justice, knowledge, salvation, or mere survival. If we take other people seriously and devote ourselves to them, that only multiplies the problem. Human life is full of effort, plans, calculation, success and failure: we *pursue* our lives, with varying degrees of sloth and energy.

It would be different if we could not step back and reflect on the process, but were merely led from impulse to impulse without self-consciousness. But human beings do not act solely on impulse. They are prudent, they reflect, they weigh consequences, they ask whether what they are doing is worth while. Not only are their lives full of particular choices that hang together in larger activities with temporal structure: they also decide in the broadest terms what to pursue and what to avoid, what the priorities among their various aims should be, and what kind of people they want to be or become. Some men are faced with such choices by the large decisions they make from time to time; some merely by reflection on the course their lives are taking as the product of countless small decisions. They decide whom to marry, what profession to follow, whether to join the Country Club, or the Resistance; or they may just wonder why they go on being salesmen or academics or taxi drivers, and then stop thinking about it after a certain period of inconclusive reflection.

Although they may be motivated from act to act by those immediate needs with which life presents them, they allow the process to continue by adhering to the general system of habits and the form of life in which such motives have their place – or perhaps only by clinging to life itself. They spend enormous quantities of energy, risk, and calculation on the details. Think of how an ordinary individual sweats over his appearance, his health, his sex life, his emotional honesty, his social utility, his self-knowledge, the quality of his ties with family, colleagues, and friends, how well he does his job, whether he understands the world and what is going on in it. Leading a human life is a full-time occupation, to which everyone devotes decades of intense concern.

This fact is so obvious that it is hard to find it extraordinary and important. Each of us lives his own life – lives with himself twenty-four hours a day. What else is he supposed to do – live someone else's life? Yet humans have the special capacity to step back and survey themselves, and the lives to which they are committed, with that detached amazement which comes from watching an ant struggle up a heap of sand. Without developing the illusion that they are able to escape from their highly specific and idiosyncratic position, they can view it *sub specie aeternitatis* – and the view is at once sobering and comical.

The crucial backward step is not taken by asking for still another justification in the chain, and failing to get it. The objections to that line of attack have already been stated; justifications come to an end. But this is precisely what provides universal doubt with its object. We step back to find that the whole system of justification and criticism, which controls our choices and supports our claims to rationality, rests on responses and habits that we never question, that we should not know how to defend without circularity, and to which we shall continue to adhere even after they are called into question.

The things we do or want without reasons, and without requiring reasons – the things that define what is a reason for us and what is not – are the starting points of our skepticism. We see ourselves from outside, and all the contingency and specificity of our aims and pursuits become clear. Yet when we take this view and recognize what we do as arbitrary, it does not disengage us from life, and there lies our absurdity: not in the fact that such an external view can be taken of us, but in the fact that we ourselves can take it, without ceasing to be the persons whose ultimate concerns are so coolly regarded.

III

One may try to escape the position by seeking broader ultimate concerns, from which it is impossible to step back – the idea being that absurdity results because what we take seriously is something small and insignificant and individual. Those seeking to supply their lives with meaning usually envision a role or function in something larger than themselves. They therefore seek fulfillment in service to society, the state, the revolution, the progress of history, the advance of science, or religion and the glory of God.

But a role in some larger enterprise cannot confer significance unless that enterprise is itself significant. And its significance must come back to what we can understand, or it will not even appear to give us what we are seeking. If we learned that we were being raised to provide food for other creatures fond of human flesh, who planned to turn us into cutlets before we got too stringy – even if we learned that the human race had been developed by animal breeders precisely for this purpose – that would still not give our lives meaning, for two reasons. First, we would still be in the dark as to the significance of the lives of those other beings; second, although we might acknowledge that this culinary role would make our lives meaningful to them, it is not clear how it would make them meaningful to us.

Admittedly, the usual form of service to a higher being is different from this. One is supposed to behold and partake of the glory of God, for example, in a way in which chickens do not share in the glory of coq au vin. The same is true of service to a state, a movement, or a revolution. People can come to feel, when they are part of something bigger, that it is part of them too. They worry less about what is peculiar to themselves, but identify enough with the larger enterprise to find their role in it fulfilling.

However, any such larger purpose can be put in doubt in the same way that the aims of an individual life can be, and for the same reasons. It is as legitimate to find ultimate justification there as to find it earlier, among the details of individual life. But this does not alter the fact that justifications come to an end when we are content to have them end -- when we do not find it necessary to look any further. If we can step back from the purposes of individual life and doubt their point, we can step back also from the progress of human history, or of science, or the success of a society, or the kingdom, power, and glory of God, and put all these things into question in the same way. What seems to us to confer meaning, justification, significance, does so in virtue of the fact that we need no more reasons after a certain point.

What makes doubt inescapable with regard to the limited aims of individual life also makes it inescapable with regard to any larger purpose that encourages the sense that life is meaningful. Once the fundamental doubt has begun, it cannot be laid to rest.

Camus maintains in *The Myth of Sisyphus* that the absurd arises because the world fails to meet our demands for meaning. This suggests that the world might satisfy those demands if it were different. But now we can see that this is not the case. There does not appear to be any conceivable world (containing us) about which unsettlable doubts could not arise. Consequently the absurdity of our situation derives not from a collison between our expectations and the world, but from a collision within ourselves.

IV

It may be objected that the standpoint from which these doubts are supposed to be felt does not exist – that if we take the recommended backward step we will land on thin air, without any basis for judgment about the natural responses we are supposed to be surveying. If we retain our usual standards of what is important, then questions about the significance of what we are doing with our lives will be answerable in the usual way. But if we do not, then those questions can mean nothing to us, since there is no longer any content to the idea of what matters, and hence no content to the idea that nothing does.

But this objection misconceives the nature of the backward step. It is not supposed to give us an understanding of what is *really* important, so that we see by contrast that our lives are insignificant. We never, in the course of these reflections, abandon the ordinary standards that guide our lives. We merely observe them in operation, and recognize that if they are called into question we can justify them only by reference to themselves, uselessly. We adhere to them because of the way we are put together; what seems to us important or serious or valuable would not seem so if we were differently constituted.

In ordinary life, to be sure, we do not judge a situation absurd unless we have in mind some standards of seriousness, significance, or harmony with which the absurd can be contrasted. This contrast is not implied by the philosophical judgment of absurdity, and that might be thought to make the concept unsuitable for the expression of such judgments. This is not so, however, for the philosophical judgment depends on another contrast which makes it a natural extension from more ordinary cases. It departs from them only in contrasting the pretensions of life with a larger context in which *no* standards can be discovered, rather than with a context from which alternative, overriding standards may be applied.

V

In this respect, as in others, philosophical perception of the absurd resembles epistemological skepticism. In both cases the final, philosophical doubt is not contrasted with any unchallenged certainties, though it is arrived at by extrapolation from examples of doubt within the system of evidence or justification, where a contrast with other certainties *is* implied. In both cases our limitedness joins with a capacity to transcend those limitations in thought (thus seeing them as limitations, and as inescapable).

Skepticism begins when we include ourselves in the world about which we claim knowledge. We notice that certain types of evidence convince us, that we are content to allow justifications of belief to come to an end at certain points, that we feel we know many things even without knowing or having grounds for believing the denial of others which, if true, would make what we claim to know false.

For example, I know that I am looking at a piece of paper, although I have no adequate grounds for claiming I know that I am not dreaming; and if I am dreaming then I am not looking at a piece of paper. Here an ordinary conception of how appearance may diverge from reality is employed to show that we take our world largely for granted; the certainty that we are not dreaming cannot be justified except circularly, in terms of those very appearances which are being put in doubt. It is somewhat far-fetched to suggest I may be dreaming; but the possibility is only illustrative. It reveals that our claims to knowledge depend on our not feeling it necessary to exclude certain incompatible alternatives, and the dreaming possibility or the total-hallucination possibility are just representatives for limitless possibilities most of which we cannot even conceive.[1]

Once we have taken the backward step to an abstract view of our whole system of beliefs, evidence, and justification, and seen that it works only, despite its pretensions, by taking the world largely for granted, we are *not* in a position to contrast all these appearances with an alternative reality. We cannot shed our ordinary responses, and if we could it would leave us with no means of conceiving a reality of any kind.

It is the same in the practical domain. We do not step outside our lives to a new vantage point from which we see what is really, objectively significant. We continue to take life largely for granted while seeing that all our decisions and certainties are possible only because there is a great deal we do not bother to rule out.

Both epistemological skepticism and a sense of the absurd can be reached via initial doubts posed within systems of evidence and justification that we accept, and can be stated without violence to our ordinary concepts. We can ask not only why we should believe there is a floor under us, but also why we should believe the evidence of our senses at all – and at some point the framable questions will have outlasted the answers. Similarly, we can ask not only why we should take aspirin, but why we should take trouble over our own comfort at all. The fact that we shall take the aspirin without waiting for an answer to this last question does not show that it is an unreal question. We shall also continue to believe there is a floor under us without waiting for an answer to the other question. In both cases it is this unsupported natural confidence that generates skeptical doubts; so it cannot be used to settle them.

Philosophical skepticism does not cause us to abandon our ordinary beliefs, but it lends them a peculiar flavor. After

---

[1] I am aware that skepticism about the external world is widely thought to have been refuted, but I have remained convinced of its irrefutability since being exposed at Berkeley to Thompson Clarke's largely unpublished ideas on the subject.

acknowledging that their truth is incompatible with possibilities that we have no grounds for believing do not obtain – apart from grounds in those very beliefs which we have called into question – we return to our familiar convictions with a certain irony and resignation. Unable to abandon the natural responses on which they depend, we take them back, like a spouse who has run off with someone else and then decided to return; but we regard them differently (not that the new attitude is necessarily inferior to the old, in either case).

The same situation obtains after we have put in question the seriousness with which we take our lives and human life in general and have looked at ourselves without presuppositions. We then return to our lives, as we must, but our seriousness is laced with irony. Not that irony enables us to escape the absurd. It is useless to mutter: 'Life is meaningless; life is meaning-less . . .' as an accompaniment to everything we do. In continu-ing to live and work and strive, we take ourselves seriously in action no matter what we say.

What sustains us, in belief as in action, is not reason or justification, but something more basic than these – for we go on in the same way even after we are convinced that the reasons have given out.[2] If we tried to rely entirely on reason, and pressed it hard, our lives and beliefs would collapse – a form of madness that may actually occur if the inertial force of taking the world and life for granted is somehow lost. If we lose our grip on that, reason will not give it back to us.

VI

In viewing ourselves from a perspective broader than we can occupy in the flesh, we become spectators of our own lives. We cannot do very much as pure spectators of our own lives, so we continue to lead them, and devote ourselves to what we are able

---

[2] As Hume says in a famous passage of the *Treatise*: 'Most fortunately it happens, that since reason is incapable of dispelling these clouds, nature herself suffices to that purpose, and cures me of this philosophical melancholy and delirium, either by relaxing this bent of mind, or by some avocation, and lively impression of my senses, which obliterate all these chimeras. I dine, I play a game of backgammon, I converse, and am merry with my friends; and when after three or four hours' amusement, I would return to these speculations, they appear so cold, and strain'd, and ridiculous, that I cannot find in my heart to enter into them any farther' (bk I, pt IV, sect. 7; Selby-Bigge, p. 269).

at the same time to view as no more than a curiosity, like the ritual of an alien religion.

This explains why the sense of absurdity finds its natural expression in those bad arguments with which the discussion began. Reference to our small size and short lifespan and to the fact that all of mankind will eventually vanish without a trace are metaphors for the backward step which permits us to regard ourselves from without and to find the particular form of our lives curious and slightly surprising. By feigning a nebula's-eye view, we illustrate the capacity to see ourselves without presuppositions, as arbitrary, idiosyncratic, highly specific occupants of the world, one of countless possible forms of life.

Before turning to the question whether the absurdity of our lives is something to be regretted and if possible escaped, let me consider what would have to be given up in order to avoid it.

Why is the life of a mouse not absurd? The orbit of the moon is not absurd either, but that involves no strivings or aims at all. A mouse, however, has to work to stay alive. Yet he is not absurd, because he lacks the capacities for self-consciousness and self-transcendence that would enable him to see that he is only a mouse. If that *did* happen, his life would become absurd, since self-awareness would not make him cease to be a mouse and would not enable him to rise above his mousely strivings. Bringing his new-found self-consciousness with him, he would have to return to his meager yet frantic life, full of doubts that he was unable to answer, but also full of purposes that he was unable to abandon.

Given that the transcendental step is natural to us humans, can we avoid absurdity by refusing to take that step and remaining entirely within our sublunar lives? Well, we cannot refuse consciously, for to do that we would have to be aware of the viewpoint we were refusing to adopt. The only way to avoid the relevant self-consciousness would be either never to attain it or to forget it – neither of which can be achieved by the will.

On the other hand, it is possible to expend effort on an attempt to destroy the other component of the absurd – abandoning one's earthly, individual, human life in order to identify as completely as possible with that universal viewpoint from which human life seems arbitrary and trivial. (This appears to be the ideal of certain Oriental religions.) If one succeeds, then one will not have to drag the superior awareness through a strenuous mundane life, and absurdity will be diminished.

However, insofar as this self-etiolation is the result of effort, will-power, asceticism, and so forth, it requires that one take oneself seriously as an individual – that one be willing to take considerable trouble to avoid being creaturely and absurd. Thus one may undermine the aim of unworldliness by pursuing it too vigorously. Still, if someone simply allowed his individual, animal nature to drift and respond to impulse, without making the pursuit of its needs a central conscious aim, then he might, at considerable dissociative cost, achieve a life that was less absurd than most. It would not be a meaningful life either, of course; but it would not involve the engagement of a transcendent awareness in the assiduous pursuit of mundane goals. And that is the main condition of absurdity – the dragooning of an unconvinced transcendent consciousness into the service of an immanent, limited enterprise like a human life.

The final escape is suicide; but before adopting any hasty solutions, it would be wise to consider carefully whether the absurdity of our existence truly presents us with a *problem*, to which some solution must be found – a way of dealing with *prima facie* disaster. That is certainly the attitude with which Camus approaches the issue, and it gains support from the fact that we are all eager to escape from absurd situations on a smaller scale.

Camus – not on uniformly good grounds – rejects suicide and the other solutions he regards as escapist. What he recommends is defiance or scorn. We can salvage our dignity, he appears to believe, by shaking a fist at the world which is deaf to our pleas, and continuing to live in spite of it. This will not make our lives un-absurd, but it will lend them a certain nobility.[3]

This seems to me romantic and slightly self-pitying. Our absurdity warrants neither that much distress nor that much defiance. At the risk of falling into romanticism by a different

---

[3] 'Sisyphus, proletarian of the gods, powerless and rebellious, knows the whole extent of his wretched condition: it is what he thinks of during his descent. The lucidity that was to constitute his torture at the same time crowns his victory. There is no fate that cannot be surmounted by scorn' (*The Myth of Sisyphus*, trans. Justin O'Brien (New York: Vintage, 1959), p. 90; first published, Paris: Gallimard, 1942).

route, I would argue that absurdity is one of the most human things about us: a manifestation of our most advanced and interesting characteristics. Like skepticism in epistemology, it is possible only because we possess a certain kind of insight – the capacity to transcend ourselves in thought.

If a sense of the absurd is a way of perceiving our true situation (even though the situation is not absurd until the perception arises), then what reason can we have to resent or escape it? Like the capacity for epistemological skepticism, it results from the ability to understand our human limitations. It need not be a matter for agony unless we make it so. Nor need it evoke a defiant contempt of fate that allows us to feel brave or proud. Such dramatics, even if carried on in private, betray a failure to appreciate the cosmic unimportance of the situation. If *sub specie aeternitatis* there is no reason to believe that anything matters, then that does not matter either, and we can approach our absurd lives with irony instead of heroism or despair.

3

Moral Luck

Kant believed that good or bad luck should influence neither our moral judgment of a person and his actions, nor his moral assessment of himself.

> The good will is not good because of what it effects or accomplishes or because of its adequacy to achieve some proposed end; it is good only because of its willing, i.e., it is good of itself. And, regarded for itself, it is to be esteemed incomparably higher than anything which could be brought about by it in favor of any inclination or even of the sum total of all inclinations. Even if it should happen that, by a particularly unfortunate fate or by the niggardly provision of a stepmotherly nature, this will should be wholly lacking in power to accomplish its purpose, and if even the greatest effort should not avail it to achieve anything of its end, and if there remained only the good will (not as a mere wish but as the summoning of all the means in our power), it would sparkle like a jewel in its own right, as something that had its full worth in itself. Usefulness or fruitlessness can neither diminish nor augment this worth.[1]

He would presumably have said the same about a bad will: whether it accomplishes its evil purposes is morally irrelevant. And a course of action that would be condemned if it had a bad outcome cannot be vindicated if by luck it turns out well. There cannot be moral risk. This view seems to be wrong, but it arises

[1] *Foundations of the Metaphysics of Morals*, first section, third paragraph.

in response to a fundamental problem about moral responsibility to which we possess no satisfactory solution.

The problem develops out of the ordinary conditions of moral judgment. Prior to reflection it is intuitively plausible that people cannot be morally assessed for what is not their fault, or for what is due to factors beyond their control. Such judgment is different from the evaluation of something as a good or bad thing, or state of affairs. The latter may be present in addition to moral judgment, but when we blame someone for his actions we are not merely saying it is bad that they happened, or bad that he exists: we are judging *him*, saying he is bad, which is different from his being a bad thing. This kind of judgment takes only a certain kind of object. Without being able to explain exactly why, we feel that the appropriateness of moral assessment is easily undermined by the discovery that the act or attribute, no matter how good or bad, is not under the person's control. While other evaluations remain, this one seems to lose its footing. So a clear absence of control, produced by involuntary movement, physical force, or ignorance of the circumstances, excuses what is done from moral judgment. But what we do depends in many more ways than these on what is not under our control – what is not produced by a good or a bad will, in Kant's phrase. And external influences in this broader range are not usually thought to excuse what is done from moral judgment, positive or negative.

Let me give a few examples, beginning with the type of case Kant has in mind. Whether we succeed or fail in what we try to do nearly always depends to some extent on factors beyond our control. This is true of murder, altruism, revolution, the sacrifice of certain interests for the sake of others – almost any morally important act. What has been done, and what is morally judged, is partly determined by external factors. However jewel-like the good will may be in its own right, there is a morally significant difference between rescuing someone from a burning building and dropping him from a twelfth-storey window while trying to rescue him. Similarly, there is a morally significant difference between reckless driving and manslaughter. But whether a reckless driver hits a pedestrian depends on the presence of the pedestrian at the point where he recklessly passes a red light. What we do is also limited by the opportunities and choices with which we are faced, and these are largely determined by factors beyond our control. Someone who was an officer in a concentration camp might have led a quiet and harmless life if the Nazis had never come to power in Germany. And someone who led a quiet and harmless life in Argentina might have become an officer in a concentration camp if he had not left Germany for business reasons in 1930.

I shall say more later about these and other examples. I introduce them here to illustrate a general point. Where a significant aspect of what someone does depends on factors beyond his control, yet we continue to treat him in that respect as an object of moral judgment, it can be called moral luck. Such luck can be good or bad. And the problem posed by this phenomenon, which led Kant to deny its possibility, is that the broad range of external influences here identified seems on close examination to undermine moral assessment as surely as does the narrower range of familiar excusing conditions. If the condition of control is consistently applied, it threatens to erode most of the moral assessments we find it natural to make. The things for which people are morally judged are determined in more ways than we at first realize by what is beyond their control. And when the seemingly natural requirement of fault or responsibility is applied in light of these facts, it leaves few pre-reflective moral judgments intact. Ultimately, nothing or almost nothing about what a person does seems to be under his control.

Why not conclude, then, that the condition of control is false – that it is an initially plausible hypothesis refuted by clear counter-examples? One could in that case look instead for a more refined condition which picked out the *kinds* of lack of control that really undermine certain moral judgments, without yielding the unacceptable conclusion derived from the broader condition, that most or all ordinary moral judgments are illegitimate.

What rules out this escape is that we are dealing not with a theoretical conjecture but with a philosophical problem. The condition of control does not suggest itself merely as a generalization from certain clear cases. It seems *correct* in the further cases to which it is extended beyond the original set. When we undermine moral assessment by considering new ways in which control is absent, we are not just discovering what *would* follow given the general hypothesis, but are actually being persuaded that in itself the absence of control is relevant in these cases too. The erosion of moral judgment emerges not as the absurd consequence of an over-simple theory, but as a natural consequence of the ordinary idea of moral assessment, when it is applied in view of a more complete and precise account of the facts. It would therefore be a mistake to argue from the unacceptability of the conclusions to the need for a different account of the conditions of moral responsibility. The view that moral luck is paradoxical is not a *mistake*, ethical or logical, but a perception of one of the ways in which the intuitively acceptable conditions of moral judgment threaten to undermine it all.

It resembles the situation in another area of philosophy, the theory of knowledge. There too conditions which seem perfectly natural, and which grow out of the ordinary procedures for challenging and defending claims to knowledge, threaten to undermine all such claims if consistently applied. Most skeptical arguments have this quality: they do not depend on the imposition of arbitrarily stringent standards of knowledge, arrived at by misunderstanding, but appear to grow inevitably from the consistent application of ordinary standards.[2] There is a substantive parallel as well, for epistemological skepticism arises from consideration of the respects in which our beliefs and their relation to reality depend on factors beyond our control. External and internal causes produce our beliefs. We may subject these processes to scrutiny in an effort to avoid error, but our conclusions at this next level also result, in part, from influences which we do not control directly. The same will be true no matter how far we carry the investigation. Our beliefs are always, ultimately, due to factors outside our control, and the impossibility of encompassing those factors without being at the mercy of others leads us to doubt whether we know anything. It looks as though, if any of our beliefs are true, it is pure biological luck rather than knowledge.

Moral luck is like this because while there are various respects in which the natural objects of moral assessment are out of our control or influenced by what is out of our control, we cannot

[2] See Thompson Clarke, 'The Legacy of Skepticism', *Journal of Philosophy*, LXIX, no. 20 (November 9, 1972), 754-69.

reflect on these facts without losing our grip on the judgments.

There are roughly four ways in which the natural objects of moral assessment are disturbingly subject to luck. One is the phenomenon of constitutive luck – the kind of person you are, where this is not just a question of what you deliberately do, but of your inclinations, capacities, and temperament. Another category is luck in one's circumstances – the kind of problems and situations one faces. The other two have to do with the causes and effects of action: luck in how one is determined by antecedent circumstances, and luck in the way one's actions and projects turn out. All of them present a common problem. They are all opposed by the idea that one cannot be more culpable or estimable for anything than one is for that fraction of it which is under one's control. It seems irrational to take or dispense credit or blame for matters over which a person has no control, or for their influence on results over which he has partial control. Such things may create the conditions for action, but action can be judged only to the extent that it goes beyond these conditions and does not just result from them.

Let us first consider luck, good and bad, in the way things turn out. Kant, in the above-quoted passage, has one example of this in mind, but the category covers a wide range. It includes the truck driver who accidentally runs over a child, the artist who abandons his wife and five children to devote himself to painting,[3] and other cases in which the possibilities of success and failure are even greater. The driver, if he is entirely without fault, will feel terrible about his role in the event, but will not

---

[3] Such a case, modelled on the life of Gauguin, is discussed by Bernard Williams in 'Moral Luck' *Proceedings of the Aristotelian Society*, supplementary vol. L (1976), 115–35 (to which the original version of this essay was a reply). He points out that though success or failure cannot be predicted in advance, Gauguin's most basic retrospective feelings about the decision will be determined by the development of his talent. My disagreement with Williams is that his account fails to explain why such retrospective attitudes can be called moral. If success does not permit Gauguin to justify himself to others, but still determines his most basic feelings, that shows only that his most basic feelings need not be moral. It does not show that morality is subject to luck. If the restrospective judgment were moral, it would imply the truth of a hypothetical judgment made in advance, of the form 'If I leave my family and become a great painter, I will be justified by success; if I don't become a great painter, the act will be unforgivable.'

have to reproach himself. Therefore this example of agent-regret[4] is not yet a case of *moral* bad luck. However, if the driver was guilty of even a minor degree of negligence – failing to have his brakes checked recently, for example – then if that negligence contributes to the death of the child, he will not merely feel terrible. He will blame himself for the death. And what makes this an example of moral luck is that he would have to blame himself only slightly for the negligence itself if no situation arose which required him to brake suddenly and violently to avoid hitting a child. Yet the *negligence* is the same in both cases, and the driver has no control over whether a child will run into his path.

The same is true at higher levels of negligence. If someone has had too much to drink and his car swerves on to the sidewalk, he can count himself morally lucky if there are no pedestrians in its path. If there were, he would be to blame for their deaths, and would probably be prosecuted for manslaughter. But if he hurts no one, although his recklessness is exactly the same, he is guilty of a far less serious legal offence and will certainly reproach himself and be reproached by others much less severely. To take another legal example, the penalty for attempted murder is less than that for successful murder – however similar the intentions and motives of the assailant may be in the two cases. His degree of culpability can depend, it would seem, on whether the victim happened to be wearing a bullet-proof vest, or whether a bird flew into the path of the bullet – matters beyond his control.

Finally, there are cases of decision under uncertainty – common in public and in private life. Anna Karenina goes off with Vronsky, Gauguin leaves his family, Chamberlain signs the Munich agreement, the Decembrists persuade the troops under their command to revolt against the czar, the American colonies declare their independence from Britain, you introduce two people in an attempt at match-making. It is tempting in all such cases to feel that some decision must be possible, in the light of what is known at the time, which will make reproach unsuitable no matter how things turn out. But this is not true; when someone acts in such ways he takes his life, or his moral position, into his hands, because how things turn out determines

---

[4] Williams' term (*ibid.*).

what he has done. It is possible *also* to assess the decision from the point of view of what could be known at the time, but this is not the end of the story. If the Decembrists had succeeded in overthrowing Nicholas I in 1825 and establishing a constitutional regime, they would be heroes. As it is, not only did they fail and pay for it, but they bore some responsibility for the terrible punishments meted out to the troops who had been persuaded to follow them. If the American Revolution had been a bloody failure resulting in greater repression, then Jefferson, Franklin and Washington would still have made a noble attempt, and might not even have regretted it on their way to the scaffold, but they would also have had to blame themselves for what they had helped to bring on their compatriots. (Perhaps peaceful efforts at reform would eventually have succeeded.) If Hitler had not overrun Europe and exterminated millions, but instead had died of a heart attack after occupying the Sudetenland, Chamberlain's action at Munich would still have utterly betrayed the Czechs, but it would not be the great moral disaster that has made his name a household word.[5]

In many cases of difficult choice the outcome cannot be foreseen with certainty. One kind of assessment of the choice is possible in advance, but another kind must await the outcome, because the outcome determines what has been done. The same degree of culpability or estimability in intention, motive, or concern is compatible with a wide range of judgments, positive or negative, depending on what happened beyond the point of decision. The *mens rea* which could have existed in the absence of any consequences does not exhaust the grounds of moral judgment. Actual results influence culpability or esteem in a large class of unquestionably ethical cases ranging from negligence through political choice.

That these are genuine moral judgments rather than expressions of temporary attitude is evident from the fact that one can say *in advance* how the moral verdict will depend on the results. If one negligently leaves the bath running with the baby in it, one will realize, as one bounds up the stairs toward the bath-

---

[5] For a fascinating but morally repellent discussion of the topic of justification by history, see Maurice Merleau-Ponty, *Humanisme et Terreur* (Paris: Gallimard, 1947), translated as *Humanism and Terror* (Boston: Beacon Press, 1969).

room, that if the baby has drowned one has done something awful, whereas if it has not one has merely been careless. Someone who launches a violent revolution against an authoritarian regime knows that if he fails he will be responsible for much suffering that is in vain, but if he succeeds he will be justified by the outcome. I do not mean that *any* action can be retroactively justified by history. Certain things are so bad in themselves, or so risky, that no results can make them all right. Nevertheless, when moral judgment does depend on the outcome, it is objective and timeless and not dependent on a change of standpoint produced by success or failure. The judgment after the fact follows from an hypothetical judgment that can be made beforehand, and it can be made as easily by someone else as by the agent.

From the point of view which makes responsibility dependent on control, all this seems absurd. How is it possible to be more or less culpable depending on whether a child gets into the path of one's car, or a bird into the path of one's bullet? Perhaps it is true that what is done depends on more than the agent's state of mind or intention. The problem then is, why is it not irrational to base moral assessment on what people do, in this broad sense? It amounts to holding them responsible for the contributions of fate as well as for their own – provided they have made some contribution to begin with. If we look at cases of negligence or attempt, the pattern seems to be that overall culpability corresponds to the product of mental or intentional fault and the seriousness of the outcome. Cases of decision under uncertainty are less easily explained in this way, for it seems that the overall judgment can even shift from positive to negative depending on the outcome. But here too it seems rational to subtract the effects of occurrences subsequent to the choice, that were merely possible at the time, and concentrate moral assessment on the actual decision in light of the probabilities. If the object of moral judgment is the *person*, then to hold him accountable for what he has done in the broader sense is akin to strict liability, which may have its legal uses but seems irrational as a moral position.

The result of such a line of thought is to pare down each act to its morally essential core, an inner act of pure will assessed by motive and intention. Adam Smith advocates such a position in *The Theory of Moral Sentiments*, but notes that it runs contrary to our actual judgments.

> But how well soever we may seem to be persuaded of the
> truth of this equitable maxim, when we consider it after
> this manner, in abstract, yet when we come to particular
> cases, the actual consequences which happen to proceed
> from any action, have a very great effect upon our
> sentiments concerning its merit or demerit, and almost
> always either enhance or diminish our sense of both.
> Scarce, in any one instance, perhaps, will our sentiments be
> found, after examination, to be entirely regulated by this
> rule, which we all acknowledge ought entirely to regulate
> them.[6]

Joel Feinberg points out further that restricting the domain of
moral responsibility to the inner world will not immunize it to
luck. Factors beyond the agent's control, like a coughing fit, can
interfere with his decisions as surely as they can with the path of
a bullet from his gun.[7] Nevertheless the tendency to cut down
the scope of moral assessment is pervasive, and does not limit
itself to the influence of effects. It attempts to isolate the will
from the other direction, so to speak, by separating out constitutive luck. Let us consider that next.

Kant was particularly insistent on the moral irrelevance of
qualities of temperament and personality that are not under the
control of the will. Such qualities as sympathy or coldness might
provide the background against which obedience to moral
requirements is more or less difficult, but they could not be
objects of moral assessment themselves, and might well interfere
with confident assessment of its proper object – the determination of the will by the motive of duty. This rules out moral
judgment of many of the virtues and vices, which are states of
character that influence choice but are certainly not exhausted by
dispositions to act deliberately in certain ways. A person may be
greedy, envious, cowardly, cold, ungenerous, unkind, vain, or
conceited, but *behave* perfectly by a monumental effort of will.
To possess these vices is to be unable to help having certain
feelings under certain circumstances, and to have strong spon-

---

[6] Pt II, sect. 3, Introduction, para. 5.

[7] 'Problematic Responsibility in Law and Morals', in Joel Feinberg, *Doing
and Deserving* (Princeton: Princeton University Press, 1970).

taneous impulses to act badly. Even if one controls the impulses, one still has the vice. An envious person hates the greater success of others. He can be morally condemned as envious even if he congratulates them cordially and does nothing to denigrate or spoil their success. Conceit, likewise, need not be displayed. It is fully present in someone who cannot help dwelling with secret satisfaction on the superiority of his own achievements, talents, beauty, intelligence, or virtue. To some extent such a quality may be the product of earlier choices; to some extent it may be amenable to change by current actions. But it is largely a matter of constitutive bad fortune. Yet people are morally condemned for such qualities, and esteemed for others equally beyond control of the will: they are assessed for what they are *like*.

To Kant this seems incoherent because virtue is enjoined on everyone and therefore must in principle be possible for everyone. It may be easier for some than for others, but it must be possible to achieve it by making the right choices, against whatever temperamental background.[8] One may want to have a generous spirit, or regret not having one, but it makes no sense to condemn oneself or anyone else for a quality which is not within the control of the will. Condemnation implies that you should not be like that, not that it is unfortunate that you are.

Nevertheless, Kant's conclusion remains intuitively unacceptable. We may be persuaded that these moral judgments are irrational, but they reappear involuntarily as soon as the argument is over. This is the pattern throughout the subject.

The third category to consider is luck in one's circumstances, and I shall mention it briefly. The things we are called upon to do, the moral tests we face, are importantly determined by factors beyond our control. It may be true of someone that in a dangerous situation he would behave in a cowardly or heroic fashion, but if the situation never arises, he will never have the

---

[8] 'if nature has put little sympathy in the heart of a man, and if he, though an honest man, is by temperament cold and indifferent to the sufferings of others, perhaps because he is provided with special gifts of patience and fortitude and expects or even requires that others should have the same – and such a man would certainly not be the meanest product of nature – would not he find in himself a source from which to give himself a far higher worth than he could have got by having a good-natured temperament?' (*Foundations of the Metaphysics of Morals*, first section, eleventh paragraph).

chance to distinguish or disgrace himself in this way, and his moral record will be different.[9]

A conspicuous example of this is political. Ordinary citizens of Nazi Germany had an opportunity to behave heroically by opposing the regime. They also had an opportunity to behave badly, and most of them are culpable for having failed this test. But it is a test to which the citizens of other countries were not subjected, with the result that even if they, or some of them, would have behaved as badly as the Germans in like circumstances, they simply did not and therefore are not similarly culpable. Here again one is morally at the mercy of fate, and it may seem irrational upon reflection, but our ordinary moral attitudes would be unrecognizable without it. We judge people for what they actually do or fail to do, not just for what they would have done if circumstances had been different.[10]

This form of moral determination by the actual is also paradoxical, but we can begin to see how deep in the concept of responsibility the paradox is embedded. A person can be morally responsible only for what he does; but what he does results from a great deal that he does not do; therefore he is not morally responsible for what he is and is not responsible for. (This is not a contradiction, but it is a paradox.)

[9] Cf. Thomas Gray, 'Elegy Written in a Country Churchyard':
> Some mute inglorious Milton here may rest,
> Some Cromwell, guiltless of his country's blood.

An unusual example of circumstantial moral luck is provided by the kind of moral dilemma with which someone can be faced through no fault of his own, but which leaves him with nothing to do which is not wrong. See chapter 5; and Bernard Williams, 'Ethical Consistency', *Proceedings of the Aristotelian Society*, supplementary vol. xxxix (1965), reprinted in *Problems of the Self* (Cambridge: Cambridge University Press, 1973), pp. 166–86.

[10] Circumstantial luck can extend to aspects of the situation other than individual behavior. For example, during the Vietnam War even U.S. citizens who had opposed their country's actions vigorously from the start often felt compromised by its crimes. Here they were not even responsible; there was probably nothing they could do to stop what was happening, so the feeling of being implicated may seem unintelligible. But it is nearly impossible to view the crimes of one's own country in the same way that one views the crimes of another country, no matter how equal one's lack of power to stop them in the two cases. One *is* a citizen of one of them, and has a connexion with its actions (even if only through taxes that cannot be withheld) – that one does not have with the other's. This makes it possible to be ashamed of one's country, and to feel a victim of moral bad luck that one was an American in the 1960s.

It should be obvious that there is a connection between these problems about responsibility and control and an even more familiar problem, that of freedom of the will. That is the last type of moral luck I want to take up, though I can do no more within the scope of this essay than indicate its connection with the other types.

If one cannot be responsible for consequences of one's acts due to factors beyond one's control, or for antecedents of one's acts that are properties of temperament not subject to one's will, or for the circumstances that pose one's moral choices, then how can one be responsible even for the stripped-down acts of the will itself, if *they* are the product of antecedent circumstances outside of the will's control?

The area of genuine agency, and therefore of legitimate moral judgment, seems to shrink under this scrutiny to an extension-less point. Everything seems to result from the combined influence of factors, antecedent and posterior to action, that are not within the agent's control. Since he cannot be responsible for them, he cannot be responsible for their results – though it may remain possible to take up the aesthetic or other evaluative analogues of the moral attitudes that are thus displaced.

It is also possible, of course, to brazen it out and refuse to accept the results, which indeed seem unacceptable as soon as we stop thinking about the arguments. Admittedly, if certain surrounding circumstances had been different, then no unfortunate consequences would have followed from a wicked intention, and no seriously culpable act would have been performed; but since the circumstances were *not* different, and the agent *in fact* succeeded in perpetrating a particularly cruel murder, *that* is what he did, and that is what he is responsible for. Similarly, we may admit that if certain antecedent circumstances had been different, the agent would never have developed into the sort of person who would do such a thing; but since he *did* develop (as the inevitable result of those antecedent circumstances) into the sort of swine he is, and into the person who committed such a murder, *that* is what he is blameable for. In both cases one is responsible for what one actually does – even if what one actually does depends in important ways on what is not within one's control. This compatibilist account of our moral judgments would leave room for the ordinary conditions of responsibility – the absence of coercion, ignorance, or involuntary movement – as part of the determination of what someone has done – but it is understood not to exclude the influence of a great deal that he has not done.[11]

The only thing wrong with this solution is its failure to explain how skeptical problems arise. For they arise not from the imposition of an arbitrary external requirement, but from the nature of moral judgment itself. Something in the ordinary idea of what someone does must explain how it can seem necessary to subtract from it anything that merely happens – even though the ultimate consequence of such subtraction is that nothing remains. And something in the ordinary idea of knowledge must explain why it seems to be undermined by any influences on belief not within the control of the subject – so that knowledge seems impossible without an impossible foundation in autonomous reason. But let us leave epistemology aside and concentrate on action, character, and moral assessment.

The problem arises, I believe, because the self which acts and is the object of moral judgment is threatened with dissolution by the absorption of its acts and impulses into the class of events. Moral judgment of a person is judgment not of what happens to him, but of him. It does not say merely that a certain event or state of affairs is fortunate or unfortunate or even terrible. It is not an evaluation of a state of the world, or of an individual as part of the world. We are not thinking just that it would be better if he were different, or did not exist, or had not done some of the things he has done. We are judging *him*, rather than his existence or characteristics. The effect of concentrating on the influence of what is not under his control is to make this responsible self seem to disappear, swallowed up by the order of mere events.

What, however, do we have in mind that a person must *be* to be the object of these moral attitudes? While the concept of agency is easily undermined, it is very difficult to give it a

---

11 The corresponding position in epistemology would be that knowledge consists of true beliefs formed in certain ways, and that it does not require all aspects of the process to be under the knower's control, actually or potentially. Both the correctness of these beliefs and the process by which they are arrived at would therefore be importantly subject to luck. The Nobel Prize is not awarded to people who turn out to be wrong, no matter how brilliant their reasoning.

positive characterization. That is familiar from the literature on Free Will.

I believe that in a sense the problem has no solution, because something in the idea of agency is incompatible with actions being events, or people being things. But as the external determinants of what someone has done are gradually exposed, in their effect on consequences, character, and choice itself, it becomes gradually clear that actions are events and people things. Eventually nothing remains which can be ascribed to the responsible self, and we are left with nothing but a portion of the larger sequence of events, which can be deplored or celebrated, but not blamed or praised.

Though I cannot define the idea of the active self that is thus undermined, it is possible to say something about its sources. There is a close connexion between our feelings about ourselves and our feelings about others. Guilt and indignation, shame and contempt, pride and admiration are internal and external sides of the same moral attitudes. We are unable to view ourselves simply as portions of the world, and from inside we have a rough idea of the boundary between what is us and what is not, what we do and what happens to us, what is our personality and what is an accidental handicap. We apply the same essentially internal conception of the self to others. About ourselves we feel pride, shame, guilt, remorse – and agent-regret. We do not regard our actions and our characters merely as fortunate or unfortunate episodes – though they may also be that. We cannot *simply* take an external evaluative view of ourselves – of what we most essentially are and what we do. And this remains true even when we have seen that we are not responsible for our own existence, or our nature, or the choices we have to make, or the circumstances that give our acts the consequences they have. Those acts remain ours and we remain ourselves, despite the persuasiveness of the reasons that seem to argue us out of existence.

It is this internal view that we extend to others in moral judgment – when we judge *them* rather than their desirability or utility. We extend to others the refusal to limit ourselves to external evaluation, and we accord to them selves like our own. But in both cases this comes up against the brutal inclusion of humans and everything about them in a world from which they cannot be separated and of which they are nothing but contents. The external view forces itself on us at the same time that we resist it. One way this occurs is through the gradual erosion of what we do by the subtraction of what happens.[12]

The inclusion of consequences in the conception of what we have done is an acknowledgment that we are parts of the world, but the paradoxical character of moral luck which emerges from this acknowledgment shows that we are unable to operate with such a view, for it leaves us with no one to be. The same thing is revealed in the appearance that determinism obliterates responsibility. Once we see an aspect of what we or someone else does as something that happens, we lose our grip on the idea that it has been done and that we can judge the doer and not just the happening. This explains why the absence of determinism is no more hospitable to the concept of agency than is its presence – a point that has been noticed often. Either way the act is viewed externally, as part of the course of events.

The problem of moral luck cannot be understood without an account of the internal conception of agency and its special connection with the moral attitudes as opposed to other types of value. I do not have such an account. The degree to which the problem has a solution can be determined only by seeing whether in some degree the incompatibility between this conception and the various ways in which we do not control what we do is only apparent. I have nothing to offer on that topic either. But it is not enough to say merely that our basic moral attitudes toward ourselves and others are determined by what is actual; for they are also threatened by the sources of that actuality, and by the external view of action which forces itself on us when we see how everything we do belongs to a world that we have not created.

---

[12] See P. F. Strawson's discussion of the conflict between the objective attitude and personal reactive attitudes in 'Freedom and Resentment', *Proceedings of the British Academy*, 1962, reprinted in *Studies in the Philosophy of Thought and Action*, ed. P. F. Strawson (London: Oxford University Press, 1968), and in P. F. Strawson, *Freedom and Resentment and Other Essays* (London: Methuen, 1974).

4

Sexual Perversion

There is something to be learned about sex from the fact that we possess a concept of sexual perversion. I wish to examine the idea, defending it against the charge of unintelligibility and trying to say exactly what about human sexuality qualifies it to admit of perversions. Let me begin with some general conditions that the concept must meet if it is to be viable at all. These can be accepted without assuming any particular analysis.

First, if there are any sexual perversions, they will have to be sexual desires or practices that are in some sense unnatural, though the explanation of this natural/unnatural distinction is of course the main problem. Second, certain practices will be perversions if anything is, such as shoe fetishism, bestiality, and sadism; other practices, such as unadorned sexual intercourse, will not be; about still others there is controversy. Third, if there are perversions, they will be unnatural sexual *inclinations* rather than just unnatural practices adopted not from inclination but for other reasons. Thus contraception, even if it is thought to be a deliberate perversion of the sexual and reproductive functions, cannot be significantly described as a *sexual* perversion. A sexual perversion must reveal itself in conduct that expresses an unnatural *sexual* preference. And although there might be a form of fetishism focused on the employment of contraceptive devices, that is not the usual explanation for their use.

The connection between sex and reproduction has no bearing on sexual perversion. The latter is a concept of psychological, not physiological, interest, and it is a concept that we do not apply to the lower animals, let alone to plants, all of which have reproductive functions that can go astray in various ways. (Think of seedless oranges.) Insofar as we are prepared to regard higher animals as perverted, it is because of their psychological, not their anatomical, similarity to humans. Furthermore, we do not regard as a perversion every deviation from the reproductive function of sex in humans: sterility, miscarriage, contraception, abortion.

Nor can the concept of sexual perversion be defined in terms of social disapprobation or custom. Consider all the societies that have frowned upon adultery and fornication. These have not been regarded as unnatural practices, but have been thought objectionable in other ways. What is regarded as unnatural admittedly varies from culture to culture, but the classification is not a pure expression of disapproval or distaste. In fact it is often regarded as a *ground* for disapproval, and that suggests that the classification has independent content.

I shall offer a psychological account of sexual perversion that depends on a theory of sexual desire and human sexual interactions. To approach this solution I shall first consider a contrary position that would justify skepticism about the existence of any sexual perversions at all, and perhaps even about the significance of the term. The skeptical argument runs as follows:

'Sexual desire is simply one of the appetites, like hunger and thirst. As such it may have various objects, some more common than others perhaps, but none in any sense "natural". An appetite is identified as sexual by means of the organs and erogenous zones in which its satisfaction can be to some extent localized, and the special sensory pleasures which form the core of that satisfaction. This enables us to recognize widely divergent goals, activities, and desires as sexual, since it is conceivable in principle that anything should produce sexual pleasure and that a nondeliberate, sexually charged desire for it should arise (as a result of conditioning, if nothing else). We may fail to empathize with some of these desires, and some of them, like sadism, may be objectionable on extraneous grounds, but once we have observed that they meet the criteria for being sexual, there is nothing more to be said on *that* score. Either they are sexual or they are not: sexuality does not admit of imperfection, or perversion, or any other such qualification – it is not that sort of affection.'

This is probably the received radical position. It suggests that the cost of defending a psychological account may be to deny that sexual desire is an appetite. But insofar as that line of defense is plausible, it should make us suspicious of the simple picture of appetites on which the skepticism depends. Perhaps the standard appetites, like hunger, cannot be classed as pure appetites in that sense either, at least in their human versions.

Can we imagine anything that would qualify as a gastronomical perversion? Hunger and eating, like sex, serve a biological function and also play a significant role in our inner lives. Note that there is little temptation to describe as perverted an appetite for substances that are not nourishing: we should probably not consider someone's appetites *perverted* if he liked to eat paper, sand, wood, or cotton. Those are merely rather odd and very unhealthy tastes: they lack the psychological complexity that we expect of perversions. (Coprophilia, being already a sexual perversion, may be disregarded.) If on the other hand someone liked to eat cookbooks, or magazines with pictures of food in them, and preferred these to ordinary food – or if when hungry he sought satisfaction by fondling a napkin or ashtray from his favorite restaurant – then the concept of perversion might seem appropriate (it would be natural to call it gastronomical fetishism). It would be natural to describe as gastronomically perverted someone who could eat only by having food forced down his throat through a funnel, or only if the meal were a living animal. What helps is the peculiarity of the desire itself, rather than the inappropriateness of its object to the biological function that the desire serves. Even an appetite can have perversions if in addition to its biological function it has a significant psychological structure.

In the case of hunger, psychological complexity is provided by the activities that give it expression. Hunger is not merely a disturbing sensation that can be quelled by eating; it is an attitude toward edible portions of the external world, a desire to treat them in rather special ways. The method of ingestion: chewing, savoring, swallowing, appreciating the texture and smell, all are important components of the relation, as is the passivity and controllability of the food (the only animals we eat live are helpless mollusks). Our relation to food depends also on our size: we do not live upon it or burrow into it like aphids or worms. Some of these features are more central than others, but an adequate phenomenology of eating would have to treat it as a relation to the external world and a way of appropriating bits of that world, with characteristic affection. Displacements or serious restrictions of the desire to eat could then be described as perversions, if they undermined that direct relation between man and food which is the natural expression of hunger. This explains why it is easy to imagine gastronomical fetishism, voyeurism, exhibitionism, or even gastronomical sadism and Masochism. Some of these perversions are fairly common.

If we can imagine perversions of an appetite like hunger, it should be possible to make sense of the concept of sexual perversion. I do not wish to imply that sexual desire is an appetite – only that being an appetite is no bar to admitting of perversions. Like hunger, sexual desire has as its characteristic object a certain relation with something in the external world; only in this case it is usually a person rather than an omelet, and the relation is considerably more complicated. This added complication allows scope for correspondingly complicated perversions.

The fact that sexual desire is a feeling about other persons may encourage a pious view of its psychological content – that it is properly the expression of some other attitude, like love, and that when it occurs by itself it is incomplete or subhuman. (The extreme Platonic version of such a view is that sexual practices are all vain attempts to express something they cannot in principle achieve: this makes them all perversions, in a sense.) But sexual desire is complicated enough without having to be linked to anything else as a condition for phenomenological analysis. Sex may serve various functions – economic, social, altruistic – but it also has its own content as a relation between persons.

The object of sexual attraction is a particular individual, who transcends the properties that make him attractive. When different persons are attracted to a single person for different reasons – eyes, hair, figure, laugh, intelligence – we nevertheless feel that the object of their desire is the same. There is even an inclination to feel that this is so if the lovers have different sexual aims, if they include both men and women, for example. Different specific attractive characteristics seem to provide enabling conditions for the operation of a single basic feeling, and the different aims all provide expressions of it. We approach the sexual attitude toward the person through the features that we find attractive, but these features are not the objects of that attitude.

This is very different from the case of an omelet. Various people may desire it for different reasons, one for its fluffiness, another for its mushrooms, another for its unique combination of aroma and visual aspect; yet we do not enshrine the transcendental omelet as the true common object of their affections. Instead we might say that several desires have accidentally converged on the same object: any omelet with the crucial characterstics would do as well. It is not similarly true that any person with the same flesh distribution and way of smoking can be substituted as object for a particular sexual desire that has been elicited by those characteristics. It may be that they recur, but it will be a new sexual attraction with a new particular object, not merely a transfer of the old desire to someone else. (This is true even in cases where the new object is unconsciously identified with a former one.)

The importance of this point will emerge when we see how complex a psychological interchange constitutes the natural development of sexual attraction. This would be incomprehensible if its object were not a particular person, but rather a person of a certain *kind*. Attraction is only the beginning, and fulfillment does not consist merely of behaviour and contact expressing this attraction, but involves much more.

The best discussion of these matters that I have seen appears in part III of Sartre's *Being and Nothingness*.[1] Sartre's treatment of sexual desire and of love, hate, sadism, masochism, and further attitudes toward others, depends on a general theory of consciousness and the body which we can neither expound nor assume here. He does not discuss perversion, and this is partly because he regards sexual desire as one form of the perpetual attempt of an embodied consciousness to come to terms with the existence of others, an attempt that is as doomed to fail in this

---

[1] *L'Etre et le Néant* (Paris: Gallimand, 1943), translated by Hazel E. Barnes (New York: Philosophical Library, 1956).

form as it is in any of the others, which include sadism and masochism (if not certain of the more impersonal deviations) as well as several nonsexual attitudes. According to Sartre, all attempts to incorporate the other into my world as another subject, i.e. to apprehend him at once as an object for me and as a subject for whom I am an object, are unstable and doomed to collapse into one or other of the two aspects. Either I reduce him entirely to an object, in which case his subjectivity escapes the possession or appropriation I can extend to that object; or I become merely an object for him, in which case I am no longer in a position to appropriate his subjectivity. Moreover, neither of these aspects is stable; each is continually in danger of giving way to the other. This has the consequence that there can be no such thing as a *successful* sexual relation, since the deep aim of sexual desire cannot in principle be accomplished. It seems likely, therefore, that the view will not permit a basic distinction between successful or complete and unsuccessful or incomplete sex, and therefore cannot admit the concept of perversion.

I do not adopt this aspect of the theory, nor many of its metaphysical underpinnings. What interests me is Sartre's picture of the attempt. He says that the type of possession that is the object of sexual desire is carried out by 'a double reciprocal incarnation' and that this is accomplished, typically in the form of a caress, in the following way: 'I make myself flesh in order to impel the Other to realize *for herself* and *for me* her own flesh, and my caresses cause my flesh to be born for me in so far as it is for the Other *flesh causing her to be born as flesh*' (*Being and Nothingness*, p. 391; Sartre's italics). The incarnation in question is described variously as a clogging or troubling of consciousness, which is inundated by the flesh in which it is embodied.

The view I am going to suggest, I hope in less obscure language, is related to this one, but it differs from Sartre's in allowing sexuality to achieve its goal on occasion and thus in providing the concept of perversion with a foothold.

Sexual desire involves a kind of perception, but not merely a single perception of its object, for in the paradigm case of mutual desire there is a complex system of superimposed mutual perceptions – not only perceptions of the sexual object, but perceptions of oneself. Moreover, sexual awareness of another involves considerable self-awareness to begin with – more than is involved in ordinary sensory perception. The experience is felt as an assault on oneself by the view (or touch, or whatever) of the sexual object.

Let us consider a case in which the elements can be separated. For clarity we will restrict ourselves initially to the somewhat artificial case of desire at a distance. Suppose a man and a woman, whom we may call Romeo and Juliet, are at opposite ends of a cocktail lounge, with many mirrors on the walls which permit unobserved observation, and even mutual unobserved observation. Each of them is sipping a martini and studying other people in the mirrors. At some point Romeo notices Juliet. He is moved, somehow, by the softness of her hair and the diffidence with which she sips her martini, and this arouses him sexually. Let us say that *X senses Y* whenever *X* regards *Y* with sexual desire. (*Y* need not be a person, and *X*'s apprehension of *Y* can be visual, tactile, olfactory, etc., or purely imaginary; in the present example we shall concentrate on vision.) So Romeo senses Juliet, rather than merely noticing her. At this stage he is aroused by an unaroused object, so he is more in the sexual grip of his body than she of hers.

Let us suppose, however, that Juliet now senses Romeo in another mirror on the opposite wall, though neither of them yet knows that he is seen by the other (the mirror angles provide three-quarter views). Romeo then begins to notice in Juliet the subtle signs of sexual arousal, heavy-lidded stare, dilating pupils, faint flush, etc. This of course intensifies her bodily presence, and he not only notices but senses this as well. His arousal is nevertheless still solitary. But now, cleverly calculating the line of her stare without actually looking her in the eyes, he realizes that it is directed at him through the mirror on the opposite wall. That is, he notices, and moreover senses, Juliet sensing him. This is definitely a new development, for it gives him a sense of embodiment not only through his own reactions but through the eyes and reactions of another. Moreover, it is separable from the initial sensing of Juliet; for sexual arousal might begin with a person's sensing that he is sensed and being assailed by the perception of the other person's desire rather than merely by the perception of the person.

But there is a further step. Let us suppose that Juliet, who is a little slower than Romeo, now senses that he senses her. This puts Romeo in a position to notice, and be aroused by, her arousal at being sensed by him. He senses that she senses that he senses her. This is still another level of arousal, for he becomes conscious of his sexuality through his awareness of its effect on her and of her awareness that this effect is due to him. Once she takes the same step and senses that he senses her sensing him, it becomes difficult to state, let alone imagine, further iterations, though they may be logically distinct. If both are alone, they will presumably turn to look at each other directly, and the proceedings will continue on another plane. Physical contact and intercourse are natural extensions of this complicated visual exchange, and mutual touch can involve all the complexities of awareness present in the visual case, but with a far greater range of subtlety and acuteness.

Ordinarily, of course, things happen in a less orderly fashion – sometimes in a great rush – but I believe that some version of this overlapping system of distinct sexual perceptions and interactions is the basic framework of any full-fledged sexual relation and that relations involving only part of the complex are significantly incomplete. The account is only schematic, as it must be to achieve generality. Every real sexual act will be psychologically far more specific and detailed, in ways that depend not only on the physical techniques employed and on anatomical details, but also on countless features of the participants' conceptions of themselves and of each other, which become embodied in the act. (It is familiar enough fact, for example, that people often take their social roles and the social roles of their partners to bed with them.)

The general schema is important, however, and the proliferation of levels of mutual awareness it involves is an example of a type of complexity that typifies human interactions. Consider aggression, for example. If I am angry with someone, I want to make him feel it, either to produce self-reproach by getting him to see himself through the eyes of my anger, and to dislike what he sees – or else to produce reciprocal anger or fear, by getting him to perceive my anger as a threat or attack. What I want will depend on the details of my anger, but in either case it will involve a desire that the object of that anger be aroused. This accomplishment constitutes the fulfillment of my emotion, through domination of the object's feelings.

Another example of such reflexive mutual recognition is to be found in the phenomenon of meaning, which appears to involve an intention to produce a belief or other effect in another by bringing about his recognition of one's intention to produce that effect. (That result is due to H. P. Grice,[2] whose position I shall not attempt to reproduce in detail.) Sex has a related structure: it involves a desire that one's partner be aroused by the recognition of one's desire that he or she be aroused.

It is not easy to define the basic types of awareness and arousal of which these complexes are composed, and that remains a lacuna in this discussion. In a sense, the object of awareness is the same in one's own case as it is in one's sexual awareness of another, although the two awarenesses will not be the same, the difference being as great as that between feeling angry and experiencing the anger of another. All stages of sexual perception are varieties of identification of a person with his body. What is perceived is one's own or another's *subjection* to or *immersion* in his body, a phenomenon which has been recognized with loathing by St Paul and St Augustine, both of whom regarded 'the law of sin which is in my members' as a grave threat to the dominion of the holy will.[3] In sexual desire and its expression the blending of involuntary response with deliberate control is extremely important. For Augustine, the revolution launched against him by his body is symbolized by erection and the other involuntary physical components of arousal. Sartre too stresses the fact that the penis is not a prehensile organ. But mere involuntariness characterizes other bodily processes as well. In sexual desire the involuntary responses are combined with submission to spontaneous impulses: not only one's pulse and secretions but one's actions are taken over by the body; ideally, deliberate control is needed only to guide the expression of those impulses. This is to some extent also true of an appetite like hunger, but the takeover there is more localized, less pervasive, less extreme. One's whole body does not become saturated with hunger as it can with desire. But the most characteristic feature of a specifically sexual immersion in the body is its ability to fit into the complex of mutual perceptions that we have described.

[2] 'Meaning'. *Philosophical Review*, LXVI, no. 3 (July, 1957), 377–88.
[3] See Romans, VII, 23; and the *Confessions*, bk VIII, pt V.

Hunger leads to spontaneous interactions with food; sexual desire leads to spontaneous interactions with other persons, whose bodies are asserting their sovereignty in the same way, producing involuntary reactions and spontaneous impulses in *them*. These reactions are perceived, and the perception of them is perceived, and that perception is in turn perceived; at each step the domination of the person by his body is reinforced, and the sexual partner becomes more possessible by physical contact, penetration, and envelopment.

Desire is therefore not merely the perception of a pre-existing embodiment of the other, but ideally a contribution to his further embodiment which in turn enhances the original subject's sense of himself. This explains why it is important that the partner be aroused, and not merely aroused, but aroused by the awareness of one's desire. It also explains the sense in which desire has unity and possession as its object: physical possession must eventuate in creation of the sexual object in the image of one's desire, and not merely in the object's recognition of that desire, or in his or her own private arousal.

Even if this is a correct model of the adult sexual capacity, it is not plausible to describe as perverted every deviation from it. For example, if the partners in heterosexual intercourse indulge in private heterosexual fantasies, thus avoiding recognition of the real partner, that would, on this model, constitute a defective sexual relation. It is not, however, generally regarded as a perversion. Such examples suggest that a simple dichotomy between perverted and unperverted sex is too crude to organize the phenomena adequately.

Still, various familiar deviations constitute truncated or incomplete versions of the complete configuration, and may be regarded as perversions of the central impulse. If sexual desire is prevented from taking its full interpersonal form, it is likely to find a different one. The concept of perversion implies that a normal sexual development has been turned aside by distorting influences. I have little to say about this causal condition. But if perversions are in some sense unnatural, they must result from interference with the development of a capacity that is there potentially.

It is difficult to apply this condition, because environmental factors play a role in determining the precise form of anyone's sexual impulse. Early experiences in particular seem to determine the choice of a sexual object. To describe some causal influences as distorting and others as merely formative is to imply that certain general aspects of human sexuality realize a definite potential whereas many of the details in which people differ realize an indeterminate potential, so that they cannot be called more or less natural. What is included in the definite potential is therefore very important, although the distinction between definite and indeterminate potential is obscure. Obviously a creature incapable of developing the levels of interpersonal sexual awareness I have described could not be deviant in virtue of the failure to do so. (Though even a chicken might be called perverted in an extended sense if it had been conditioned to develop a fetishistic attachment to a telephone.) But if humans will tend to develop some version of reciprocal interpersonal sexual awareness unless prevented, then cases of blockage can be called unnatural or perverted.

Some familiar deviations can be described in this way. Narcissistic practices and intercourse with animals, infants, and inanimate objects seem to be stuck at some primitive version of the first stage of sexual feeling. If the object is not alive, the experience is reduced entirely to an awareness of one's own sexual embodiment. Small children and animals permit awareness of the embodiment of the other, but present obstacles to reciprocity, to the recognition by the sexual object of the subject's desire as the source of his (the object's) sexual self-awareness. Voyeurism and exhibitionism are also incomplete relations. The exhibitionist wishes to display his desire without needing to be desired in return; he may even fear the sexual attentions of others. A voyeur, on the other hand, need not require any recognition by his object at all: certainly not a recognition of the voyeur's arousal.

On the other hand, if we apply our model to the various forms that may be taken by two-party heterosexual intercourse, none of them seem clearly to qualify as perversions. Hardly anyone can be found these days to inveigh against oral–genital contact, and the merits of buggery are urged by such respectable figures as D. H. Lawrence and Norman Mailer. In general, it would appear that any bodily contact between a man and a woman that

gives them sexual pleasure is a possible vehicle for the system of
multi-level interpersonal awareness that I have claimed is the
basic psychological content of sexual interaction. Thus a liberal
platitude about sex is upheld.

The really difficult cases are sadism, masochism, and
homosexuality. The first two are widely regarded as perversions
and the last is controversial. In all three cases the issue depends
partly on causal factors: do these dispositions result only when
normal development has been prevented? Even the form in
which this question has been posed is circular, because of the
word 'normal'. We appear to need an independent criterion for a
distorting influence, and we do not have one.

It may be possible to class sadism and masochism as perversions because they fall short of interpersonal reciprocity. Sadism
concentrates on the evocation of passive self-awareness in
others, but the sadist's engagement is itself active and requires a
retention of deliberate control which may impede awareness of
himself as a bodily subject of passion in the required sense. De
Sade claimed that the object of sexual desire was to evoke
involuntary responses from one's partner, especially audible
ones. The infliction of pain is no doubt the most efficient way to
accomplish this, but it requires a certain abrogation of one's own
exposed spontaneity. A masochist on the other hand imposes the
same disability on his partner as the sadist imposes on himself.
The masochist cannot find a satisfactory embodiment as the
object of another's sexual desire, but only as the object of his
control. He is passive not in relation to his partner's passion but
in relation to his nonpassive agency. In addition, the subjection
to one's body characteristic of pain and physical restraint is of a
very different kind from that of sexual excitement: pain causes
people to contract rather than dissolve. These descriptions may
not be generally accurate. But to the extent that they are, sadism
and masochism would be disorders of the second stage of
awareness – the awareness of oneself as an object of desire.

Homosexuality cannot similarly be classed as a perversion on
phenomenological grounds. Nothing rules out the full range of
interpersonal perceptions between persons of the same sex. The
issue then depends on whether homosexuality is produced by
distorting influences that block or displace a natural tendency to
heterosexual development. And the influences must be more

distorting than those which lead to a taste for large breasts or fair hair or dark eyes. These also are contingencies of sexual preference in which people differ, without being perverted.

The question is whether heterosexuality is the natural expression of male and female sexual dispositions that have not been distorted. It is an unclear question, and I do not know how to approach it. There is much support for an aggressive–passive distinction between male and female sexuality. In our culture the male's arousal tends to initiate the perceptual exchange, he usually makes the sexual approach, largely controls the course of the act, and of course penetrates whereas the woman receives. When two men or two women engage in intercourse they cannot both adhere to these sexual roles. But a good deal of deviation from them occurs in heterosexual intercourse. Women can be sexually aggressive and men passive, and temporary reversals of role are not uncommon in heterosexual exchanges of reasonable length. For these reasons it seems to be doubtful that homosexuality must be a perversion, though like heterosexuality it has perverted forms.

Let me close with some remarks about the relation of perversion to good, bad, and morality. The concept of perversion can hardly fail to be evaluative in some sense, for it appears to involve the notion of an ideal or at least adequate sexuality which the perversions in some way fail to achieve. So, if the concept is viable, the judgment that a person or practice or desire is perverted will constitute a sexual evaluation, implying that better sex, or a better specimen of sex, is possible. This in itself is a very weak claim, since the evaluation might be in a dimension that is of little interest to us. (Though, if my account is correct, that will not be true.)

Whether it is a moral evaluation, however, is another question entirely – one whose answer would require more understanding of both morality and perversion than can be deployed here. Moral evaluation of acts and of persons is a rather special and very complicated matter, and by no means all our evaluations of persons and their activities are moral evaluations. We make judgments about people's beauty or health or intelligence which are evaluative without being moral. Assessments of their sexuality may be similar in that respect.

Furthermore, moral issues aside, it is not clear that unperverted sex is necessarily *preferable* to the perversions. It may be that sex which receives the highest marks for perfection *as sex* is less enjoyable than certain perversions; and if enjoyment is considered very important, that might outweigh considerations of sexual perfection in determining rational preference.

That raises the question of the relation between the evaluative content of judgments of perversion and the rather common *general* distinction between good and bad sex. The latter distinction is usually confined to sexual acts, and it would seem, within limits, to cut across the other: even someone who believed, for example, that homosexuality was a perversion could admit a distinction between better and worse homosexual sex, and might even allow that good homosexual sex could be better *sex* than not very good unperverted sex. If this is correct, it supports the position that, if judgments of perversion are viable at all, they represent only one aspect of the possible evaluation of sex, even *qua sex*. Moreover it is not the only important aspect: sexual deficiencies that evidently do not constitute perversions can be the object of great concern.

Finally, even if perverted sex is to that extent not so good as it might be, bad sex is generally better than none at all. This should not be controversial: it seems to hold for other important matters, like food, music, literature, and society. In the end, one must choose from among the available alternatives, whether their availability depends on the environment or on one's own constitution. And the alternatives have to be fairly grim before it becomes rational to opt for nothing.

5

War and Massacre

From the apathetic reaction to atrocities committed in Vietnam by the United States and its allies, one may conclude that moral restrictions on the conduct of war command almost as little sympathy among the general public as they do among those charged with the formation of U.S. military policy.[1] Even when restrictions on the conduct of warfare are defended, it is usually on legal grounds alone: their moral basis is often poorly understood. I wish to argue that certain restrictions are neither arbitrary nor merely conventional, and that their validity does not depend simply on their usefulness. There is, in other words, a moral basis for the rules of war, even though the conventions now officially in force are far from giving it perfect expression.

I

No elaborate moral theory is required to account for what is wrong in cases like the Mylai massacre, since it did not serve, and was not intended to serve, any strategic purpose. Moreover, if the participation of the United States in the Indo-Chinese war is entirely wrong to begin with, then that engagement is incapable of providing a justification for *any* measures taken in its pursuit – not only for the measures which are atrocities in every war, however just its aims.

But this war has revealed attitudes of a more general kind, which influenced the conduct of earlier wars as well. After it has ended, we shall still be faced with the problem of how warfare

---

[1] This essay was completed in 1971. Direct U.S. military involvement in the Vietnam War lasted from 1961 to 1973. Hence the present tense.

may be conducted, and the attitudes that have resulted in the specific conduct of this war will not have disappeared. Moreover, similar problems can arise in wars or rebellions fought for very different reasons, and against very different opponents. It is not easy to keep a firm grip on the idea of what is not permissible in warfare, because while some military actions are obvious atrocities, other cases are more difficult to assess, and the general principles underlying these judgments remain obscure. Such obscurity can lead to the abandonment of sound intuitions in favor of criteria whose rationale may be more obvious. If such a tendency is to be resisted, it will require a better understanding of the restrictions than we now have.

I propose to discuss the most general moral problem raised by the conduct of warfare: the problem of means and ends. In one view, there are limits on what may be done even in the service of an end worth pursuing – and even when adherence to the restriction may be very costly. A person who acknowledges the force of such restrictions can find himself in acute moral dilemmas. He may believe, for example, that by torturing a prisoner he can obtain information necessary to prevent a disaster, or that by obliterating one village with bombs he can halt a campaign of terrorism. If he believes that the gains from a certain measure will clearly outweigh its costs, yet still supects that he ought not to adopt it, then he is in a dilemma produced by the conflict between two disparate categories of moral reason: categories that may be called *utilitarian* and *absolutist*.

Utilitarianism gives primacy to a concern with what will *happen*. Absolutism gives primacy to a concern with what one is *doing*. The conflict between them arises because the alternatives we face are rarely just choices between *total outcomes*: they are also choices between alternative pathways or measures to be taken. When one of the choices is to do terrible things to another person, the problem is altered fundamentally; it is no longer merely a question of which outcome would be worse.

Few of us are completely immune to either of these types of moral intuition, though in some people, either naturally or for doctrinal reasons, one type will be dominant and the other suppressed or weak. But it is perfectly possible to feel the force of both types of reason very strongly; in that case the moral dilemma in certain situations of crisis will be acute, and it may appear that every possible course of action or inaction is unacceptable for one reason or another.

II

Although it is this dilemma that I propose to explore, most of the discussion will be devoted to its absolutist component. The utilitarian component is straightforward by comparison, and has a natural appeal to anyone who is not a complete skeptic about ethics. Utilitarianism says that one should try, either individually or through institutions, to maximize good and minimize evil (the definition of these categories need not enter into the schematic formulation of the view), and that if faced with the possibility of preventing a great evil by producing a lesser, one should choose the lesser evil. There are certainly problems about the formulation of utilitarianism, and much has been written about it, but its intent is morally transparent. Nevertheless, despite the additions and refinements, it continues to leave large portions of ethics unaccounted for. I do not suggest that some form of absolutism can account for them all, only that an examination of absolutism will lead us to see the complexity, and perhaps the incoherence, of our moral ideas.

Utilitarianism certainly justifies *some* restrictions on the conduct of warfare. There are strong utilitarian reasons for adhering to any limitation which seems natural to most people – particularly if the limitation is widely accepted already. An exceptional measure which seems to be justified by its results in a particular conflict may create a precedent with disastrous long-term effects.[2] It may even be argued that war involves violence on such a scale that it is never justified on utilitarian grounds – the consequences of refusing to go to war will never be as bad as the war itself would be, even if atrocities were not committed. Or in a more sophisticated vein it might be claimed that a uniform policy of never resorting to military force would do less harm in the long run, if followed consistently, than a policy of deciding each case on utilitarian grounds (even though on occasion particular applications of the pacifist policy might have worse results than a specific utilitarian decision). But I shall not

---

[2] Straightforward considerations of national interest often tend in the same direction: the inadvisability of using nuclear weapons seems to be overdetermined in this way.

consider these arguments, for my concern is with reasons of a different kind, which may remain when reasons of utility and interest fail.[3]

In the final analysis, I believe that the dilemma cannot always be resolved. While not every conflict between absolutism and utilitarianism creates an insoluble dilemma, and while it seems to me certainly right to adhere to absolutist restrictions unless the utilitarian considerations favoring violation are overpoweringly weighty and extremely certain – nevertheless, when that special condition is met, it may become impossible to adhere to an absolutist position. What I shall offer, therefore, is a somewhat qualified defense of absolutism. I believe it underlies a valid and fundamental type of moral judgment – which cannot be reduced to or overridden by other principles. And while there may be other principles just as fundamental, it is particularly important not to lose confidence in our absolutist intuitions, for they are often the only barrier before the abyss of utilitarian apologetics for large-scale murder.

III

One absolutist position that creates no problems of interpretation is pacifism: the view that one may not kill another person under any circumstances, no matter what good would be achieved or evil averted thereby. The type of absolutist position that I am going to discuss is different. Pacifism draws the conflict with utilitarian considerations very starkly. But there are other views according to which violence may be undertaken, even on a large scale, in a clearly just cause, so long as certain absolute restrictions on the character and direction of that violence are observed. The line is drawn somewhat closer to the bone, but it exists.

The philosopher who has done most to advance contemporary philosophical discussion of such a view, and to explain it to those unfamiliar with its extensive treatment in Roman Catholic

---

[3] These reasons, moreover, have special importance in that they are available even to one who denies the appropriateness of utilitarian considerations in international matters. He may acknowledge limitations on what may be done to the soldiers and civilians of other countries in pursuit of his nation's military objectives, while denying that one country should in general consider the interests of nationals of other countries in determining its policies.

moral theology, is G.E.M. Anscombe. In 1958 Miss Anscombe published a pamphlet entitled *Mr. Truman's Degree*,[4] on the occasion of the award by Oxford University of an honorary doctorate to Harry Truman. The pamphlet explained why she had opposed the decision to award that degree, recounted the story of her unsuccessful opposition, and offered some reflections on the history of Truman's decision to drop atom bombs on Hiroshima and Nagasaki, and on the difference between murder and allowable killing in warfare. She pointed out that the policy of deliberately killing large numbers of civilians either as a means or as an end in itself did not originate with Truman, and was common practice among all parties during World War II for some time before Hiroshima. The Allied area bombings of German cities by conventional explosives included raids which killed more civilians than did the atomic attacks; the same is true of certain fire-bomb raids on Japan.

The policy of attacking the civilian population in order to induce an enemy to surrender, or to damage his morale, seems to have been widely accepted in the civilized world, and seems to be accepted still, at least if the stakes are high enough. It gives evidence of a moral conviction that the deliberate killi.ig of noncombatants–women, children, old people–is permissible if enough can be gained by it. This follows from the more general position that any means can in principle be justified if it leads to a sufficiently worthy end. Such an attitude is evident not only in the more spectacular current weapons systems but also in the day-to-day conduct of the nonglobal war in Indo-China: the indiscriminate destructiveness of antipersonnel weapons, napalm, and aerial bombardment; cruelty to prisoners; massive relocation of civilians; destruction of crops; and so forth. An absolutist position opposes to this the view that certain acts

---

[4] (Privately printed.) See also her essay 'War and Murder', in *Nuclear Weapons and Christian Conscience*, ed. Walter Stein (London: The Merlin Press, 1961). The present paper is much indebted to these two essays throughout. These and related subjects are extensively treated by Paul Ramsey in *The Just War* (New York: Scribners, 1968). Among recent writings that bear on the moral problem are Jonathan Bennett, 'Whatever the Consequences', *Analysis*, xxvi, no. 3 (1966), 83–102; and Philippa Foot, 'The Problem of Abortion and the Doctrine of the Double Effect', *Oxford Review*, v (1967), 5–15. Miss Anscombe's replies are 'A Note on Mr. Bennett', *Analysis*, xxvi, no. 3 (1966), 208 and 'Who is Wronged?', *Oxford Review*, v (1967), 16–17.

cannot be justified no matter what the consequences. Among those acts is murder – the deliberate killing of the harmless: civilians, prisoners of war, and medical personnel.

In the present war such measures are sometimes said to be regrettable, but they are generally defended by reference to military necessity and the importance of the long-term consequences of success or failure in the war. I shall pass over the inadequacy of this consequentialist defense in its own terms. (That is the dominant form of moral criticism of the war, for it is part of what people mean when they ask, 'Is it worth it?') I am concerned rather to account for the inappropriateness of offering any defense of that kind for such actions.

Many people feel, without being able to say much more about it, that something has gone seriously wrong when certain measures are admitted into consideration in the first place. The fundamental mistake is made there, rather than at the point where the overall benefit of some monstrous measure is judged to outweigh its disadvantages, and it is adopted. An account of absolutism might help us to understand this. If it is not allowable to *do* certain things, such as killing unarmed prisoners or civilians, then no argument about what will happen if one does not do them can show that doing them would be all right.

Absolutism does not, of course, require one to ignore the consequences of one's acts. It operates as a limitation on utilitarian reasoning, not as a substitute for it. An absolutist can be expected to try to maximize good and minimize evil, so long as this does not require him to transgress an absolute prohibition like that against murder. But when such a conflict occurs, the prohibition takes complete precedence over any consideration of consequences. Some of the results of this view are clear enough. It requires us to forgo certain potentially useful military measures, such as the slaughter of hostages and prisoners or indiscriminate attempts to reduce the enemy civilian population by starvation, epidemic infectious diseases like anthrax and bubonic plague, or mass incineration. It means that we cannot deliberate on whether such measures are justified by the fact that they will avert still greater evils, for as intentional measures they cannot be justified in terms of any consequences whatever.

Someone unfamiliar with the events of this century might imagine that utilitarian arguments, or arguments of national interest, would suffice to deter measures of this sort. But it has become evident that such considerations are insufficient to prevent the adoption and employment of enormous antipopulation weapons once their use is considered a serious moral possibility. The same is true of the piecemeal wiping out of rural civilian populations in airborne antiguerrilla warfare. Once the door is opened to calculations of utility and national interest, the usual speculations about the future of freedom, peace, and economic prosperity can be brought to bear to ease the consciences of those responsible for a certain number of charred babies.

For this reason alone it is important to decide what is wrong with the frame of mind which allows such arguments to begin. But it is also important to understand absolutism in the cases where it genuinely conflicts with utility. Despite its appeal, it is a paradoxical position, for it can require that one refrain from choosing the lesser of two evils when that is the only choice one has. And it is additionally paradoxical because, unlike pacifism, it permits one to do horrible things to people in some circumstances but not in others.

IV

Before going on to say what, if anything, lies behind the position, there remain a few relatively technical matters which are best discussed at this point.

First, it is important to specify as clearly as possible the kind of thing to which absolutist prohibitions can apply. We must take seriously the proviso that they concern what we deliberately do to people. There could not, for example, without incoherence, be an absolute prohibition against *bringing about* the death of an innocent person. For one may find oneself in a situation in which, no matter what one does, some innocent people will die as a result. I do not mean just that there are cases in which someone will die no matter what one does, because one is not in a position to affect the outcome one way or the other. That, it is to be hoped, is one's relation to the deaths of most innocent people. I have in mind, rather, a case in which someone is bound to die, but who it is will depend on what one does. Sometimes these situations have natural causes, as when too few resources (medicine, lifeboats) are available to rescue everyone threatened with a certain catastrophe. Sometimes the situations are man-made, as when the only way to control a campaign of terrorism is to to employ terrorist tactics against the community from which it has arisen. Whatever one does in cases such as these, some innocent people will die as a result. If the absolutist prohibition forbade doing what would result in the deaths of innocent people, it would have the consequence that in such cases nothing one could do would be morally permissible.

This problem is avoided, however, because what absolutism forbids is *doing* certain things to people, rather than bringing about certain *results*. Not everything that happens to others as a result of what one does is something that one has *done* to them. Catholic moral theology seeks to make this distinction precise in a doctrine known as the law of double effect, which asserts that there is a morally relevant distinction between bringing about or permitting the death of an innocent person deliberately, either as an end in itself or as a means, and bringing it about or permitting it as a side effect of something else one does deliberately. In the latter case, even if the outcome is foreseen, it is not murder, and does not fall under the absolute prohibition, though of course it may still be wrong for other reasons (reasons of utility, for example). Briefly, the principle states that one is sometimes permitted knowingly to bring about or permit as a side-effect of one's actions something which it would be absolutely impermissible to bring about or permit deliberately as an end or as a means. In application to war or revolution, the law of double effect permits a certain amount of civilian carnage as a side-effect of bombing munitions plants or attacking enemy soldiers. And even this is permissible only if the cost is not too great to be justified by one's objectives.

However, despite its importance and its usefulness in accounting for certain plausible moral judgments, I do not believe that the law of double effect is a generally applicable test for the consequences of an absolutist position. Its own application is not always clear, so that it introduces uncertainty where there need not be uncertainty.

In Indo-China, for example, there is a great deal of aerial bombardment, strafing, spraying of napalm, and employment of pellet- or needle-spraying antipersonnel weapons against rural villages in which guerrillas are suspected to be hiding, or from which small-arms fire has been received. The majority of those killed and wounded in these aerial attacks are reported to be women and children, even when some combatants are caught as well. However, the government regards these civilian casualties as a regrettable side-effect of what is a legitimate attack against an armed enemy.

It might be thought easy to dismiss this as sophistry: if one bombs, burns, or strafes a village containing a hundred people, twenty of whom one believes to be guerrillas, so that by killing most of them one will be statistically likely to kill most of the guerrillas, then is not one's attack on the group of one hundred a *means* of destroying the guerrillas, pure and simple? If one makes no attempt to discriminate between guerrillas and civilians, as is impossible in an aerial attack on a small village, then one cannot regard as a mere side-effect the deaths of those in the group that one would not have bothered to kill if more selective means had been available.

The difficulty is that this argument depends on one particular description of the act, and the reply might be that the means used against the guerrillas is not: killing everybody in the village – but rather: obliteration bombing of the *area* in which the twenty guerrillas are known to be located. If there are civilians in the area as well, they will be killed as a side-effect of such action.[5]

Because of casuistical problems like this, I prefer to stay with the original, unanalyzed distinction between what one does to people and what merely happens to them as a result of what one does. The law of double effect provides an approximation to that distinction in many cases, and perhaps it can be sharpened to the point where it does better than that. Certainly the original distinction itself needs clarification, particularly since some of the things we do to people involve things happening to them as a result of other things we do. In a case like the one discussed, however, it is clear that by bombing the village one slaughters and maims the civilians in it. Whereas by giving the only available medicine to one of two sufferers from a disease, one does not kill the other or deliberately allow him to die, even if he dies as a result.

The second technical point is this. The absolutist focus on actions rather than outcomes does not merely introduce a new, outstanding item into the catalogue of evils. That is, it does not

---

[5] This counter-argument was suggested by Rogers Albritton.

say that the worst thing in the world is the deliberate murder of an innocent person. For if that were all, then one could presumably justify one such murder on the ground that it would prevent several others, or ten thousand on the ground that they would prevent a hundred thousand more. That is a familiar argument. But if this is allowable, then there is no absolute prohibition against murder after all. Absolutism requires that we *avoid* murder at all costs, not that we *prevent* it at all costs.

It would also be possible to adopt a deontological position less stringent than absolutism, without falling into utilitarianism. There are two ways in which someone might acknowledge the moral relevance of the distinction between deliberate and nondeliberate killing, without being an absolutist. One would be to count murder as a specially bad item in the catalogue of evils, much worse than accidental death or nondeliberate killing. But the other would be to say that deliberately killing an innocent is impermissible unless it is the only way to prevent some very large evil (say the deaths of fifty innocent people). Call this the *threshold* at which the prohibition against murder is overridden. The position is not absolutist, obviously, but it is also not equivalent to an assignment of utilitarian disvalue to murder equal to the disvalue of the threshold. This is easily seen. If a murder had the disvalue of fifty accidental deaths, it would still be permissible on utilitarian grounds to commit a murder to prevent one other murder, plus some lesser evil like a broken arm. Worse still, we would be required on utilitarian grounds to prevent one murder even at the cost of forty-nine accidental deaths that we could otherwise have prevented. These are not in fact consequences of a deontological prohibition against murder with a threshold, because it does not say that the occurrence of a certain kind of act is a bad thing, and therefore to be prevented, but rather tells everyone to *refrain* from such acts, except under certain conditions. In fact, it is perfectly compatible with a deontological prohibition against murder to hold that, considered as an outcome, a murder has *no* more disvalue than an accidental death. While the admission of thresholds would reduce the starkness of the conflicts discussed here, I do not think it would make them disappear, or change their basic character. They would persist in the clash between any deontological requirement and utilitarian values somewhat lower than its threshold.

Finally, let me remark on a frequent criticism of absolutism that depends on a misunderstanding. It is sometimes suggested that such prohibitions depend on a kind of moral self-interest, a primary obligation to preserve one's own moral purity, to keep one's hands clean no matter what happens to the rest of the world. If this were the position, it might be exposed to the charge of self-indulgence. After all, what gives one man a right to put the purity of his soul or the cleanness of his hands above the lives or welfare of large numbers of other people? It might be argued that a public servant like Truman has no right to put himself first in that way; therefore if he is convinced that the alternatives would be worse, he must give the order to drop the bombs, and take the burden of those deaths on himself, as he must do other distasteful things for the general good.

But there are two confusions behind the view that moral self-interest underlies moral absolutism. First, it is a confusion to suggest that the need to preserve one's moral purity might be the *source* of an obligation. For if by committing murder one sacrifices one's moral purity or integrity, that can only be because there is *already* something wrong with murder. The general reason against committing murder cannot therefore be merely that it makes one an immoral person. Secondly, the notion that one might sacrifice one's moral integrity justifiably, in the service of a sufficiently worthy end, is an incoherent notion. For if one were justified in making such a sacrifice (or even morally required to make it), then one would not be sacrificing one's moral integrity by adopting that course: one would be preserving it.

Moral absolutism is not unique among moral theories in requiring each person to do what will preserve his own moral purity in all circumstances. This is equally true of utilitarianism, or of any other theory which distinguishes between right and wrong. Any theory which defines the right course of action in various circumstances and asserts that one should adopt that course, *ipso facto* asserts that one should do what will preserve one's moral purity, simply because the right course of action *is* what will preserve one's moral purity in those circumstances. Of course utilitarianism does not assert that this is *why* one should adopt that course, but we have seen that the same is true of absolutism.

V

It is easier to dispose of false explanations of absolutism than to produce a true one. A positive account of the matter must begin with the observation that war, conflict, and aggression are relations between persons. The view that it can be wrong to consider merely the overall effect of one's action on the general welfare comes into prominence when those actions involve relations with others. A man's acts usually affect more people than he deals with directly, and those effects must naturally be considered in his decisions. But if there are special principles governing the manner in which he should *treat* people, that will require special attention to the particular persons toward whom the act is directed, rather than just to its total effect.

Absolutist restrictions in warfare appear to be of two types: restrictions on the class of persons at whom aggression or violence may be directed and restrictions on the manner of attack, given that the object falls within that class. These can be combined, however, under the principle that hostile treatment of any person must be justified in terms of something *about that person* which makes the treatment appropriate. Hostility is a personal relation, and it must be suited to its target. One consequence of this condition will be that certain persons may not be subjected to hostile treatment in war at all, since nothing about them justifies such treatment. Others will be proper objects of hostility only in certain circumstances, or when they are engaged in certain pursuits. And the appropriate manner and extent of hostile treatment will depend on what is justified by the particular case.

A coherent view of this type will hold that extremely hostile behavior toward another is compatible with treating him as a person – even perhaps as an end in himself. This is possible only if one has not automatically stopped treating him as a person as soon as one starts to fight with him. If hostile, aggressive, or combative treatment of others always violated the condition that they be treated as human beings, it would be difficult to make further distinctions on that score *within* the class of hostile actions. That point of view, on the level of international relations, leads to the position that if complete pacifism is not accepted, no holds need be barred at all, and we may slaughter and massacre to our hearts' content, if it seems advisable. Such a position is often expressed in discussions of war crimes.

But the fact is that ordinary people do not believe this about conflicts, physical or otherwise, between individuals, and there is no more reason why it should be true of conflicts between nations. There seems to be a perfectly natural conception of the distinction between fighting clean and fighting dirty. To fight dirty is to direct one's hostility or aggression not at its proper object, but at a peripheral target which may be more vulnerable, and through which the proper object can be attacked indirectly. This applies in a fist fight, an election campaign, a duel, or a philosophical argument. If the concept is general enough to apply to all these matters, it should apply to war – both to the conduct of individual soldiers and to the conduct of nations.

Suppose that you are a candidate for public office, convinced that the election of your opponent would be a disaster, that he is an unscrupulous demagogue who will serve a narrow range of interests and seriously infringe the rights of those who disagree with him; and suppose you are convinced that you cannot defeat him by conventional means. Now imagine that various unconventional means present themselves as possibilities: you possess information about his sex life which would scandalize the electorate if made public; or you learn that his wife is an alcoholic or that in his youth he was associated for a brief period with a proscribed political party, and you believe that this information could be used to blackmail him into withdrawing his candidacy; or you can have a team of your supporters flatten the tires of a crucial subset of his supporters on election day; or you are in a position to stuff the ballot boxes; or, more simply, you can have him assassinated. What is wrong with these methods, given that they will achieve an overwhelmingly desirable result?

There are, of course, many things wrong with them: some are against the law; some infringe the procedures of an electoral process to which you are presumably committed by taking part in it; very importantly, some may backfire, and it is in the interest of all political candidates to adhere to an unspoken agreement not to allow certain personal matters to intrude into a campaign. But that is not all. We have in addition the feeling that these measures, these methods of attack, are *irrelevant* to the issue between you and your opponent, that in taking them up you would not be directing yourself to that which makes him an object of your opposition. You would be directing your attack not at the true target of your hostility, but at peripheral targets that happen to be vulnerable.

The same is true of a fight or argument outside the framework of any system of regulations or law. In an altercation with a taxi driver over an excessive fare, it is inappropriate to taunt him about his accent, flatten one of his tires, or smear chewing gum on his windshield; and it remains inappropriate even if he casts aspersions on your race, politics, or religion, or dumps the contents of your suitcase into the street.[6]

The importance of such restrictions may vary with the seriousness of the case; and what is unjustifiable in one case may be justified in a more extreme one. But they all derive from a single principle: that hostility or aggression should be directed at its true object. This means both that it should be directed at the person or persons who provoke it and that it should aim more specifically at what is provocative about them. The second condition will determine what form the hostility may appropriately take.

It is evident that some idea of the relation in which one should stand to other people underlies this principle, but the idea is difficult to state. I believe it is roughly this: whatever one does to another person intentionally must be aimed at him as a subject, with the intention that he receive it as a subject. It should manifest an attitude to *him* rather than just to the situation, and he should be able to recognize it and identify himself as its object. The procedures by which such an attitude is manifested need not be addressed to the person directly. Surgery, for example, is not a form of personal confrontation but part of a medical treatment that can be offered to a patient face to face and received by him as a response to his needs and the natural outcome of an attitude toward *him*.

---

[6] Why, on the other hand, does it seem appropriate, rather than irrelevant, to punch someone in the mouth if he insults you? The answer is that in our culture it is an insult to punch someone in the mouth, and not just an injury. This reveals, by the way, a perfectly unobjectionable sense in which convention may play a part in determining exactly what falls under an absolutist restriction and what does not. I am indebted to Robert Fogelin for this point.

Hostile treatment, unlike surgery, is already addressed *to* a person, and does not take its interpersonal meaning from a wider context. But hostile acts can serve as the expression or implementation of only a limited range of attitudes to the person who is attacked. Those attitudes in turn have as objects certain real or presumed characteristics or activities of the person which are thought to justify them. When this background is absent, hostile or aggressive behavior can no longer be intended for the reception of the victim as a subject. Instead it takes on the character of a purely bureaucratic operation. This occurs when one attacks someone who is not the true object of one's hostility – the true object may be someone else, who can be attacked through the victim; or one may not be manifesting a hostile attitude toward anyone, but merely using the easiest available path to some desired goal. One finds oneself not facing or addressing the victim at all, but operating on him – without the larger context of personal interaction that surrounds a surgical operation.

If absolutism is to defend its claim to priority over considerations of utility, it must hold that the maintenance of a direct interpersonal response to the people one deals with is a requirement which no advantages can justify one in abandoning. The requirement is absolute only if it rules out any calculation of what would justify its violation. I have said earlier that there may be circumstances so extreme that they render an absolutist position untenable. One may find then that one has no choice but to do something terrible. Nevertheless, even in such cases absolutism retains its force in that one cannot claim *justification* for the violation. It does not become *all right*.

As a tentative effort to explain this, let me try to connect absolutist limitations with the possibility of justifying *to the victim* what is being done to him. If one abandons a person in the course of rescuing several others from a fire or a sinking ship, one *could* say to him, 'You understand, I have to leave you to save the others.' Similarly, if one subjects an unwilling child to a painful surgical procedure, one can say to him, 'If you could understand, you would realize that I am doing this to help you.' One could *even* say, as one bayonets an enemy soldier, 'It's either you or me.' But one cannot really say while torturing a prisoner, 'You understand, I have to pull out your finger-nails because it is

absolutely essential that we have the names of your confeder-
ates'; nor can one say to the victims of Hiroshima, 'You
understand, we have to incinerate you to provide the Japanese
government with an incentive to surrender.'

This does not take us very far, of course, since a utilitarian
would presumably be willing to offer justifications of the latter
sort to his victims, in cases where he thought they were
sufficient. They are really justifications to the world at large,
which the victim, as a reasonable man, would be expected to
appreciate. However, there seems to me something wrong with
this view, for it ignores the possibility that to treat someone else
horribly puts you in a special relation to him, which may have to
be defended in terms of other features of your relation to him.
The suggestion needs much more development; but it may help
us to understand how there may be requirements which are
absolute in the sense that there can be no justification for
violating them. If the justification for what one did to another
person had to be such that it could be offered to him specifically,
rather than just to the world at large, that would be a significant
source of restraint.

If the account is to be deepened, I would hope for some results
along the following lines. Absolutism is associated with a view
of oneself as a small being interacting with others in a large
world. The justifications it requires are primarily interpersonal.
Utilitarianism is associated with a view of oneself as a benevo-
lent bureaucrat distributing such benefits as one can control to
countless other beings, with whom one may have various
relations or none. The justifications it requires are primarily
administrative. The argument between the two moral attitudes
may depend on the relative priority of these two conceptions.[7]

VI

Some of the restrictions on methods of warfare which have been
adhered to from time to time are to be explained by the mutual
interests of the involved parties: restrictions on weaponry,

[7] Finally, I should mention a different possibility, suggested by Robert
Nozick: that there is a strong general presumption against benefiting from
the calamity of another, whether or not it has been deliberately inflicted
for that or any other reason. This broader principle may well lend its force
to the absolutist position.

treatment of prisoners, etc. But that is not all there is to it. The conditions of directness and relevance which I have argued apply to relations of conflict and aggression apply to war as well. I have said that there are two types of absolutist restrictions on the conduct of war: those that limit the legitimate targets of hostility and those that limit its character, even when the target is acceptable. I shall say something about each of these. As will become clear, the principle I have sketched does not yield an unambiguous answer in every case.

First let us see how it implies that attacks on some people are allowed, but not attacks on others. It may seem paradoxical to assert that to fire a machine gun at someone who is throwing hand grenades at your emplacement is to treat him as a human being. Yet the relation with him is direct and straightforward.[8] The attack is aimed specifically against the threat presented by a dangerous adversary, and not against a peripheral target through which he happens to be vulnerable but which has nothing to do with that threat. For example, you might stop him by machine-gunning his wife and children, who are standing nearby, thus distracting him from his aim of blowing you up and enabling you to capture him. But if his wife and children are not threatening your life, that would be to treat them as means with a vengeance.

This, however, is just Hiroshima on a smaller scale. One objection to weapons of mass annihilation – nuclear, thermonuclear, biological, or chemical – is that their indiscriminateness disqualifies them as direct instruments for the expression of hostile relations. In attacking the civilian population, one treats neither the military enemy nor the civilians with that minimal respect which is owed to them as human beings. This is clearly true of the direct attack on people who present no threat at all. But it is also true of the character of the attack on those who *are* threatening you, i.e., the government and military forces of the enemy. Your aggression is directed against an area of vulnerability quite distinct from any threat presented by them which you may be justified in meeting. You are taking aim at them through the mundane life and survival of their countrymen, instead of

---

[8] Marshall Cohen once remarked that, according to my view, shooting at someone establishes an I–thou relationship.

aiming at the destruction of their military capacity. And of course it does not require hydrogen bombs to commit such crimes.

This way of looking at the matter also helps us to understand the importance of the distinction between combatants and noncombatants, and the irrelevance of much of the criticism offered against its intelligibility and moral significance. According to an absolutist position, deliberate killing of the innocent is murder, and in warfare the role of the innocent is filled by noncombatants. This has been thought to raise two sorts of problems: first, the widely imagined difficulty of making a division, in modern warfare, between combatants and noncombatants; second, problems deriving from the connotation of the word 'innocence'.

Let me take up the latter question first.[9] In the absolutist position, the operative notion of innocence is not moral innocence, and it is not opposed to moral guilt. If it were, then we would be justified in killing a wicked but noncombatant hairdresser in an enemy city who supported the evil policies of his government, and unjustified in killing a morally pure conscript who was driving a tank toward us with the profoundest regrets and nothing but love in his heart. But moral innocence has very little to do with it, for in the definition of murder 'innocent' means 'currently harmless', and it is opposed not to 'guilty' but to 'doing harm'. It should be noted that such an analysis has the consequence that in war we may often be justified in killing people who do not deserve to die, and unjustified in killing people who do deserve to die, if anyone does.

So we must distinguish combatants from noncombatants on the basis of their immediate threat or harmfulness. I do not claim that the line is a sharp one, but it is not so difficult as is often supposed to place individuals on one side of it or the other. Children are not combatants even though they may join the armed forces if they are allowed to grow up. Women are not combatants just because they bear children or offer comfort to the soldiers. More problematic are the supporting personnel, whether in or out of uniform, from drivers of munitions trucks and army cooks to civilian munitions workers and farmers. I

[9] What I say on this subject derives from Anscombe.

believe they can be plausibly classified by applying the condition that the prosecution of conflict must direct itself to the cause of danger, and not to what is peripheral. The threat presented by an army and its members does not consist merely in the fact that they are men, but in the fact that they are armed and are using their arms in the pursuit of certain objectives. Contributions to their arms and logistics are contributions to this threat; contributions to their mere existence as men are not. It is therefore wrong to direct an attack against those who merely serve the combatants' needs as human beings, such as farmers and food suppliers, even though survival as a human being is a necessary condition of efficient functioning as a soldier.

This brings us to the second group of restrictions: those that limit what may be done even to combatants. These limits are harder to explain clearly. Some of them may be arbitrary or conventional, and some may have to be derived from other sources; but I believe that the condition of directness and relevance in hostile relations accounts for them to a considerable extent.

Consider first a case which involves both a protected class of noncombatants and a restriction on the measures that may be used against combatants. One provision of the rules of war which is universally recognized, though it seems to be turning into a dead letter in Vietnam, is the special status of medical personnel and the wounded in warfare. It might be more efficient to shoot medical officers on sight and to let the enemy wounded die rather than be patched up to fight another day. But someone with medical insignia is supposed to be left alone and permitted to tend and retrieve the wounded. I believe this is because medical attention is a species of attention to completely general human needs, not specifically the needs of a combat soldier, and our conflict with the soldier is not with his existence as a human being.

By extending the application of this idea, one can justify prohibitions against certain particularly cruel weapons: starvation, poisoning, infectious diseases (supposing they could be inflicted on combatants only), weapons designed to maim or disfigure or torture the opponent rather than merely to stop him. It is not, I think, mere casuistry to claim that such weapons attack the men, not the soldiers. The effect of dum-dum bullets.

for example, is much more extended than necessary to cope with the combat situation in which they are used. They abandon any attempt to discriminate in their effects between the combatant and the human being. For this reason the use of flamethrowers and napalm is an atrocity in all circumstances that I can imagine, whoever the target may be. Burns are both extremely painful and extremely disfiguring – far more than any other category of wound. That this well-known fact plays no (inhibiting) part in the determination of U.S. weapons policy suggests that moral sensitivity among public officials has not increased markedly since the Spanish Inquisition.[10]

Finally, the same condition of appropriateness to the true object of hostility should limit the scope of attacks on an enemy country: its economy, agriculture, transportation system, and so forth. Even if the parties to a military conflict are considered to be not armies or governments but entire nations (which is usually a grave error), that does not justify one nation in warring against every aspect or element of another nation. That is not justified in a conflict between individuals, and nations are even more complex than individuals, so the same reasons apply. Like a human being, a nation is engaged in countless other pursuits while waging war, and it is not in those respects that it is an enemy.

The burden of the argument has been that absolutism about murder has a foundation in principles governing all one's relations to other persons, whether aggressive or amiable, and that these principles and that absolutism, apply to warfare as well, with the result that certain measures are impermissible no matter

10 Beyond this I feel uncertain. Ordinary bullets, after all, can cause death, and nothing is more permanent than that. I am not at all sure why we are justified in trying to kill those who are trying to kill us (rather than merely in trying to stop them with force which may also result in their deaths). It is often argued that incapacitating gases are a relatively humane weapon (when not used, as in Vietnam, merely to make people easier to shoot). Perhaps the legitimacy of restrictions against them must depend on the dangers of escalation, and the great utility of maintaining *any* conventional category of restriction so long as nations are willing to adhere to it.
Let me make clear that I do not regard my argument as a defense of the moral immutability of the Hague and Geneva Conventions. Rather, I believe that they rest partly on a moral foundation, and that modifications of them should also be assessed on moral grounds.

what the consequences.[11] I do not mean to romanticize war. It is sufficiently utopian to suggest that when nations conflict they might rise to the level of limited barbarity that typically characterizes violent conflict between individuals, rather than wallowing in the moral pit where they appear to have settled, surrounded by enormous arsenals.

VI

Having described the elements of the absolutist position, we must now return to the conflict between it and utilitarianism. Even if certain types of dirty tactics become acceptable when the stakes are high enough, the most serious of the prohibited acts, like murder and torture, are not just supposed to require unusually strong justification. They are supposed *never* to be done, because no quantity of resulting benefit is thought capable of *justifying* such treatment of a person.

The fact remains that when an absolutist knows or believes that the utilitarian cost of refusing to adopt a prohibited course will be very high, he may hold to his refusal to adopt it, but he will find it difficult to feel that a moral dilemma has been satisfactorily resolved. The same may be true of someone who rejects an absolutist requirement and adopts instead the course yielding the most acceptable consequences. In either case, it is possible to feel that one has acted for reasons insufficient to justify violation of the opposing principle. In situations of deadly conflict, particularly where a weaker party is threatened with annihilation or enslavement by a stronger one, the argument for resorting to atrocities can be powerful, and the dilemma acute.

There may exist principles, not yet codified, which would enable us to resolve such dilemmas. But then again there may not. We must face the pessimistic alternative that these two forms of moral intuition are not capable of being brought together into a single, coherent moral system, and that the world can present us with situations in which there is no honorable or

---

[11] It is possible to draw a more radical conclusion, which I shall not pursue here. Perhaps the technology and organization of modern war are such as to make it impossible to wage as an acceptable form of interpersonal or even international hostility. Perhaps it is too impersonal and large-scale for that. If so, then absolutism would in practice imply pacifism, given the present state of things. On the other hand, I am skeptical about the unstated assumption that a technology dictates its own use.

moral course for a man to take, no course free of guilt and responsibility for evil.[12]

The idea of a moral blind alley is a perfectly intelligible one. It is possible to get into such a situation by one's own fault, and people do it all the time. If, for example, one makes two incompatible promises or commitments – becomes engaged to two people, for example – then there is no course one can take which is not wrong, for one must break one's promise to at least one of them. Making a clean breast of the whole thing will not be enough to remove one's reprehensibility. The existence of such cases is not morally disturbing, however, because we feel that the situation was not unavoidable: one had to do something wrong in the first place to get into it. But what if the world itself, or someone else's actions, could face a previously innocent person with a choice between morally abominable courses of action, and leave him no way to escape with his honor? Our intuitions rebel at the idea, for we feel that the constructibility of such a case must show a contradiction in our moral views. But it is not in itself a contradiction to say that someone can do X or not do X, and that for him to take either course would be wrong. It merely contradicts the supposition that *ought* implies *can* – since presumably one ought to refrain from what is wrong, and in such a case it is impossible to do so.[13] Given the limitations on human action, it is naïve to suppose that there is a solution to every moral problem with which the world can face us. We have always known that the world is a bad place. It appears that it may be an evil place as well.

---

[12] In his reply to this essay ('Rules of War and Moral Reasoning', *Philosophy & Public Affairs*, I, no. 2 (Winter, 1972), 167), R. M. Hare pointed out the apparent discrepancy between my acceptance of such a possibility here and my earlier claim in section IV that absolutism must be formulated so as to avoid the consequence that in certain cases nothing one could do would be morally permissible. The difference is that in those cases the moral incoherence would result from the application of a single principle, whereas the dilemmas described here result from a conflict between two fundamentally different types of principle.

[13] This was first pointed out to me by Christopher Boorse. The point is also made in E. J. Lemmon's 'Moral Dilemmas', *Philosophical Review*, LXXI (April, 1962), 150.

6

Ruthlessness in Public Life

I

The great modern crimes are public crimes. To a degree the same can be said of the past, but the growth of political power has introduced a scale of massacre and despoliation that makes the efforts of private criminals, pirates, and bandits seem truly modest.

Public crimes are committed by individuals who play roles in political, military, and economic institutions. (Because religions are politically weak, crimes committed on their behalf are now rare.) Yet unless the offender has the originality of Hitler, Stalin, or Amin, the crimes do not seem to be fully attributable to the individual himself. Famous political monsters have moral personalities large enough to transcend the boundaries of their public roles; they take on the full weight of their deeds as personal moral property. But they are exceptional. Not only are ordinary soldiers, executioners, secret policemen, and bombardiers morally encapsulated in their roles, but so are most secretaries of defense or state, and even many presidents and prime ministers. They act as office-holders or functionaries, and thereby as individuals they are insulated in a puzzling way from what they do: insulated both in their own view and in the view of most observers. Even if one is in no doubt about the merits of the acts in question, the agents seem to have a slippery moral surface, produced by their roles or offices.

This is certainly true of several American statesmen responsible for the more murderous aspects of policy during the Vietnam War. Robert McNamara is president of the World

Bank. McGeorge Bundy is president of the Ford Foundation. Elliot Richardson was secretary of defense under Nixon during the completely illegal bombing of Cambodia which went on *after* the Vietnam peace agreements were signed. He then became attorney general and was widely acclaimed for resigning that office rather than comply with Nixon's request that he fire Archibald Cox for demanding the White House tapes. His highly selective sense of honor has served him well: he has since been ambassador to Britain, secretary of commerce and ambassador at large, and we shall hear more of him. Kissinger is of course a highly esteemed figure, despite the Christmas bombing of 1972 and all that preceded it.

The judgments I am presupposing are controversial: not everyone agrees that American policy during the Vietnam War was criminal. But even those who do think so may find it hard to attach the crimes to the criminals, in virtue of the official role in which they were committed. Few old anti-war demonstrators would feel more than mildly uncomfortable about meeting one of these distinguished figures, unless it was just because we were unaccustomed to personal contract with anyone as powerful as the president of the World Bank.

There is, I think, a problem about the moral effects of public roles and offices. Certainly they have a profound effect on the behavior of the individuals who fill them, an effect partly restrictive but significantly liberating. Sometimes they confer great power, but even where they do not, as in the case of an infantryman or police interrogator, they can produce a feeling of moral insulation that has strong attractions. The combination of special requirements and release from some of the usual restrictions, the ability to say that one is only following orders or doing one's job or meeting one's responsibilities, the sense that one is the agent of vast impersonal forces or the servant of institutions larger than any individual – all these ideas form a heady and sometimes corrupting brew.

But this would not be so unless there were something to the special status of action in a role. If roles encourage illegitimate release from moral restraints it is because their moral effect has been distorted. It will help to understand the distortion if we consider another curiosity of current moral discourse about public life: the emphasis placed on those personal restrictions that complement the lack of official restraint – the other side of the coin of public responsibility and irresponsibility. Public figures are not supposed to use their power openly to enrich themselves and their families, or to obtain sexual favors. Such primitive indulgences are generally hidden or denied, and stress is laid on the personal probity and disinterest of public figures. This kind of personal detachment in the exercise of official functions is thought to guarantee their good moral standing, and it leaves them remarkably free in the public arena. No doubt private transgressions are widespread, but when they are inescapably exposed the penalty can be severe, for a delicate boundary of moral restraint that sets off the great body of public power and freedom has been breached. Spiro Agnew will never be head of the Ford Foundation.

The exchange seems fairly straightforward. The exercise of public power is to be liberated from certain constraints by the imposition of others, which are primarily personal. Because the office is supposedly shielded from the personal interests of the one who fills it, what he does in his official capacity seems also to be depersonalized. This nourishes the illusion that personal morality does not apply to it with any force, and that it cannot be strictly assigned to his moral account. The office he occupies gets between him and his depersonalized acts.

Among other things, such a picture disguises the fact that the exercise of power, in whatever role, is one of the most personal forms of individual self-expression, and a rich source of purely personal pleasure. The pleasure of power is not easily acknowledged, but it is one of the most primitive human feelings – probably one with infantile roots. Those who have had it for years sometimes realize its importance only when they have to retire. Despite their grave demeanor, impersonal diction, and limited physical expression, holders of public power are personally involved to an intense degree and probably enjoying it immensely. But whether or not it is consciously enjoyed, the exercise of power is a primary form of individual expression, not diminished but enhanced by the institutions and offices on which it depends.

When we try, therefore, to say what is morally special about public roles and public action, we must concentrate on how they alter the demands on the individual. The actions are his, whether

they consist of planning to obliterate a city or only firing in
response to an order. So if the moral situation is different from
the case where he acts in no official capacity, it must be because
the requirements are different.

II

It is hard to discuss this subject in general terms, since roles and
offices differ so widely. Nevertheless, the question of the nature
of the discontinuity between individual morality and public
morality is in part a general one, because the answer must take
one of two forms. Either public morality will be derivable from
individual morality or it will not. The answer will vary greatly
in detail from case to case, but if a significant element of public
morality is not derivable from the moral requirements that apply
to private individuals, it is probably a common feature of many
different examples.

To give the question content, it is necessary to say more about
derivability. The interesting question is whether the special
features of public morality can be explained in terms of principles already present at the individual level, which yield apparent
moral discontinuities when applied to the special circumstances
of public life. If so, then public morality is in a substantive and
not merely trivial sense derivable from private morality.[1] It
emerges naturally from individual morality under the conditions
that define the individual's public role.

This could still yield different moral requirements in two
ways. Either the general principles could imply additional
constraints on public action; or the principles could be such that
certain requirements would cease to apply once one assumed a
public role, because the conditions for their application would
have disappeared. Or the change might involve some combination
of the two. In view of the second kind of change, even if public
morality is derivable from private, it is possible that the moral
restraints on public action are weaker than those on individual
action.

The alternative to derivability is that public morality is not

---

[1] Public morality becomes trivially derivable from individual morality if
individual morality is extended to include all true propositions of the
form, 'if the individual is acting in public role X, he may (or must) do Y',
and so forth. This is compatible, however, with there being no connection
between the grounds of the public and private requirements.

grounded on individual morality, and that therefore people acting in certain official roles or capacities are required or permitted to do things that cannot be accounted for on that basis. This also might take two forms. They might come under restrictions in areas left free by individual morality: public officials might be held to higher standards of concern for the general welfare, for example, than ordinary people. Or else those acting in official roles might be permitted or even required to do things which, considered from the point of view of individual morality, would be impermissible.

Both derivability and non-derivability are formally suited to explain either the addition or the removal of restrictions in public morality; both can therefore explain the appearance of discontinuity. The only way to decide between them is to see which form of explanation can be more plausibly filled out. I shall begin with a version of the derivability hypothesis, based on familiar concepts of individual morality. But while this can explain a good deal, it also leaves something out. I shall therefore go on to say what seems to me true in the nonderivability hypothesis, and this will involve giving an account of the alternative basis on which special conditions of public morality depend.

Even if public morality is not derivable from private, however, it does not mean that they are independent of one another. Both may derive from a common source that yields different results when applied to the generation of principles for action in the widely differing circumstances of private and public life. Neither private morality nor public morality is ultimate. Both result when the general constraints of morality are applied to certain types of action. Public morality would be derivable from private only if those constraints had to be applied first to the development of principles governing the conduct of persons acting individually, and could not be applied directly to public life. In that case one would have to reach the private principles from the general constraints of morality, and the public principles only from the private ones, as applied to public circumstances. But there is no *a priori* reason to think that ethics has this structure. If it does not, then public and private morality may share a common basis without one being derived from the other. I shall say more about this later. First I want to explore the more direct connexions between them.

Part of my aim is to give a correct account of facts that are easily distorted by those defenders of political, diplomatic or military license who cloak themselves in the responsibilities of office. Whoever denies the application of moral restraints to certain public decisions is making a moral claim, and a very strong one. But there is something to the idea of a moral discontinuity between private and public, and to understand the distortions we must know what this is.

III

Some of the moral peculiarity of official roles can be explained by the theory of obligation. Whoever takes on a public or official role assumes the obligation to serve a special function and often the interests of a special group. Like more personal obligations, this limits the claim that other sorts of reasons can make on him. Recall E. M. Forster's remark: 'I hate the idea of causes, and if I had to choose between betraying my country and betraying my friend, I hope I should have the courage to betray my country.'[2] He was not talking about public office, but similar problems can arise there. In a rigidly defined role like that of a soldier or judge or prison guard, only a very restricted set of considerations is supposed to bear on what one decides to do, and nearly all general considerations are excluded. With less definition, other public offices limit their occupants to certain considerations and free them from others, such as the good of mankind. Public figures sometimes even say and believe that they are obliged to consider only the national or state interest in arriving at their decisions as if it would be a breach of responsibility for them to consider anything else.

This apparent restriction on choice is easy to accept partly because, looked at from the other direction, it lifts restraints that might otherwise be burdensome. But any view as absolute as this is mistaken: there are no such extreme obligations or offices to which they attach. One cannot, by joining the army, undertake an obligation to obey any order whatever from one's commanding officer. It is not possible to acquire an obligation to

---

[2] 'What I Believe', in *Two Cheers for Democracy* (London: Edward Arnold, 1939).

kill indebted gamblers by signing a contract as a Mafia hit man. It is not even possible to undertake a commitment to serve the interests of one's children in complete disregard of the interests of everyone else. Obligations to the state also have limits, which derive from their moral context.

Every obligation or commitment reserves some portion of the general pool of motivated action for a special purpose. Life being what it is, each person's supply of time, power, and energy is limited. The kinds of obligations one may undertake, and their limits, depend on how it is reasonable to allocate this pool, and how much liberty individuals should have to allocate it in radically uneven ways. This is true for personal obligations. It applies to public ones as well.

In private life some exclusivity is necessary if we are to allow people to form special relations and attachments, and to make special arrangements with each other on which they can rely. For similar reasons larger groups should be able to cooperate for mutual benefit, or to form social units that may have a geographical definition. And it is natural that the organization of such cooperative units will include institutions, roles, and offices and that the individuals in them will undertake obligations to serve the interests of the group in special ways – by promoting its prosperity, defending it against enemies, etc. To a degree, large-scale social arrangements can be seen as extensions of more individual obligations and commitments.

It may be that the added power conferred by an institutional role should be used primarily for the benefit of that institution and its constituents. The interests of mankind in general have a lesser claim on it. But this does not mean that prohibitions against harming others, directly or indirectly, are correspondingly relaxed. Just because the power to kill thousands of people is yours only because you are the secretary of defense of a certain country, it does not follow that you should be under no restrictions on the use of that power which do not derive specifically from your obligations to serve that country. The same reasoning that challenges private obligations that imply too much of a free hand in carrying them out, will also disallow public commitments with inadequate restraints on their greater power. Insofar as public obligations work like private ones, there is no reason to think that individuals in public roles are released from traditional moral requirements on the treatment of others, or that in public life, the end justifies the means.

IV

Let me now say what such an account leaves out. The moral impersonality of public action may be exaggerated and abused, but there is something in it, which a general theory of obligation cannot explain. Such a theory fails to explain why the *content* of public obligations differs systematically from that of private ones. The impersonality suitable for public action has two aspects: it implies both a heightened concern for results and a stricter requirement of impartiality. It warrants methods usually excluded for private individuals, and sometimes it licenses ruthlessness. This can be explained only by a direct application of moral theory to those public institutions that create the roles to which public obligations are tied.[3] To account for the difference between public and private life we must return to a point mentioned earlier: that public morality may be underivable from private not because they come from different sources, but because each of them contains elements derived independently from a common source.[4]

Morality is complicated at every level. My basic claim is that its impersonal aspects are more prominent in the assessment of institutions than in the assessment of individual actions, and that as a result, the design of institutions may include roles whose occupants must determine what to do by principles different from those that govern private individuals. This will be morally justified, however, by ultimate considerations that underlie individual morality as well. I shall present the view only in outline, and mostly without defending the moral opinions it expresses. My main contention is that the degree to which ruthlessness is acceptable in public life – the ways in which public actors may have to get their hands dirty – depends on

---

[3] What I say will be put in terms of the largest and most powerful institutions, the state and its agencies. But there is a wide range of public institutions, including universities, political parties, charitable organizations, and revolutionary movements. Much of what I shall say about nation-states applies to these cases also in some degree. They too come under a kind of public morality.

[4] This retracts something I said at pp. 139–40 of 'Libertarianism without Foundations', *Yale Law Journal*, LXXXV (1975).

moral features of the institutions through which public action is carried out.

Two types of concern determine the content of morality: concern with what will happen and concern with what one is doing.[5] Insofar as principles of conduct are determined by the first concern, they will be outcome-centered or consequentialist, requiring that we promote the best overall results. Insofar as they are determined by the second, the influence of consequences will be limited by certain restrictions on the means to be used, and also by a loosening of the requirement that one always pursue the best results. The action-centered aspects of morality include bars against treating others in certain ways which violate their rights, as well as the space allotted to each person for a life of his own, without the perpetual need to contribute to the general good in everything he does. Such provisions are described as action-centered because, while they apply to everyone, what they require of each person depends on his particular standpoint rather than on the impersonal consequentialist standpoint that surveys the best overall state of affairs and prescribes for each person whatever he can do to contribute to it.

The interaction and conflict between these two aspects of morality are familiar in private life. They result in a certain balance that emphasizes restrictions against harming or interfering with others, rather than requirements to benefit them, except in cases of serious distress. For the most part it leaves us free to pursue our lives and form particular attachments to some people, so long as we do not harm others.

When we apply the same dual conception to public institutions and activities, the results are different. There are several reasons for this. Institutions are not persons and do not have private lives, nor do institutional roles usually absorb completely the lives of their occupants. Public institutions are designed to serve purposes larger than those of particular individuals or families. They tend to pursue the interests of masses of people (a limiting case would be that of a world government, but most actual institutions have a less than universal constituency). In addition, public acts are diffused over many actors and sub-institutions; there is a division of labor both in execution and in decision. All this results in a different balance between the

---

[5] I discuss this distinction in chapter 5.

morality of outcomes and the morality of actions. These two types of moral constraint are differently expressed in public life, and both of them take more impersonal forms.

Some of the same agent-centered restrictions on means will apply to public action as to private. But some of them will be weaker, permitting the public employment of coercive, manipulative, or obstructive methods that would not be allowable for individuals. There is some public analogue to the individual's right to lead his own life free of the constant demand to promote the best overall results, but it appears in the relations of states to one another rather than in their relations to their citizens: states can remain neutral in external disputes, and can legitimately favor their own populations – though not at any cost whatever to the rest of the world.

There is no comparable right of self-indulgence or favoritism for public officials or institutions vis-à-vis the individuals with whom they deal. Perhaps the most significant action-centered feature of public morality is a special requirement to treat people in the relevant population equally. Public policies and actions have to be much more impartial than private ones, since they usually employ a monopoly of certain kinds of power and since there is no reason in their case to leave room for the personal attachments and inclinations that shape individual lives.[6]

In respect to outcomes, public morality will differ from private in according them greater weight. This is a consequence of the weakening of certain action-centered constraints and permissions already described, which otherwise would have restrictive effects. The greater latitude about means in turn makes it legitimate to design institutions whose aim is to produce certain desirable results on a large scale, and to define roles in those institutions whose responsibility is mainly to further those results. Within the appropriate limits, public decisions will be justifiably more consequentialist than private ones. They will also have larger consequences to take into account.

---

[6] Would a giant with immense power be obliged to act primarily on impersonal grounds, if he were unique among millions of ordinary people whose lives he could affect? I doubt it. He would presumably have a personal life as well, which made some claims on him. The state is the closest thing we know to such a giant, and it is not similarly encumbered.

To say that consequentialist reasons will be prominent is not to say what kinds of consequences matter. This is a well-worked field, and I shall avoid discussing the place of equality, liberty, autonomy and individual rights, as well as overall level of happiness, in a consequentialist view of the good. The point to remember is that consequentialist values need not be utilitarian; a consequentialist assessment of social institutions can be strongly egalitarian, in addition to valuing welfare, liberty, and individuality in themselves. Moreover, giving the members of a society the opportunity to lead their own lives free of consequentialist demands is one of the goods to be counted in a consequentialist social reckoning. But I will not try to present a complete system of public values here, for I am concerned with the more abstract claim that consequentialist considerations, together with impartiality, play a special role in the moral assessment and justification of public institutions.

The effect of these two deviations of public from private morality on the assessment of public action will be complex. The reason is that the constraints of public morality are not imposed as a whole in the same way on all public actions or on all public offices. Because public agency is itself complex and divided, there is a corresponding ethical division of labor, or ethical specialization. Different aspects of public morality are in the hands of different officials. This can create the illusion that public morality is more consequentialist or less restrictive than it is, because the general conditions may be wrongly identified with the boundaries of a particular role. But in fact those boundaries usually presuppose a larger institutional structure without which they would be illegitimate. (The most conspicuous example is the legitimacy conferred on legislative decisions by the limitation of constitutional protections enforced by the courts.)

By this rather complex route, the balance of outcome-oriented and action-oriented morality will justify the design of public institutions whose officials can do what would be unsuitable in private life. Some of the deviations will be conspicuously consequentialist: others will express the impersonality of public morality in other ways. Action-centered constraints will not be absent: there will still be restrictions on means. But those restrictions may be weaker in relation to the results than they are for individuals.

I have simply adapted a point made by Rawls in 'Two Concepts of Rules'.[7] He argued that utilitarianism could justify practices that exclude utilitarian reasoning in some circumstances. I am arguing that a more complex morality than utilitarianism will likewise have different implications for human conduct when applied to its assessment directly and when applied indirectly via the assessment of institutions through which action occurs. The details of this morality cannot be explained here, but many of its features depend on an idea of moral universality different from that which underlies utilitarianism. Utilitarian assessment decides, basically, whether something is acceptable from a general point of view that combines those of *all* individuals. The method of combination is basically majoritarian. The alternative is to ask whether something is acceptable from a schematic point of view that represents in essentials the standpoint of each individual. The method of combination here is a form of unanimity, since acceptability from the schematic point of view represents acceptability to each person. Both of these moral conceptions can claim to count everyone equally, yet they are very different. My own opinion is that morality should be based on acceptability to each rather than on acceptability to all. The problem is to define the two points of view that express these opposed moral conceptions.[8]

It could also be said that the separate application of these basic constraints to social institutions and to individual conduct yields a moral division of labor between the individual and society, in which individual and social ideals are inseparably linked. The impersonal benevolence of public morality is intended to provide a background against which individualism in private morality is acceptable. It is a pressing and difficult question whether private individualism and public benevolence are socially compatible, or whether the tension between them makes this an unstable moral conception and an unstable social ideal.

V

Because they are specialized, not all public institutions are

[7] *Philosophical Review*, LXIV (1955), 3–32.
[8] One attempt is made by Rawls in *A Theory of Justice* (Cambridge, Mass.: Harvard University Press, 1971), ch. III. See also chapter 8 below.

equally sensitive to overall consequences. An important exception is the judiciary, at least in a society where the courts are designed to protect individual rights against both public and private encroachment. Neither the institution itself nor the roles it defines – judge, juror, prosecutor – are dominated by a concern with overall results. They act on narrower grounds. To some extent this narrowing of grounds is itself justified by consequentialist reasoning about the overall effects of such an institution. However the courts also embody the state's action-centered moral constraints – impersonal but not consequentialist. Very importantly, they are supposed to enforce its impartiality in serious dealings with individual citizens. And by setting limits to the means that can be employed by other public institutions, they leave those institutions free to concentrate more fully on achieving results within those limits.

To illustrate the positive claim that these limits differ from those that operate in private life, let me consider two familiar examples of public action: taxation and conscription. Both are imposed by the legislature in our society, and it may be thought that they are therefore indirectly consented to by the population. I believe it is a desperate measure to impute consent to everyone who is drafted or pays income taxes, on the ground that he votes or accepts certain public services. Consent is not needed to justify such legislative action, because the legislature is an institution whose authority to make such decisions on consequentialist grounds is morally justified in other ways. Its periodic answerability to the electorate is one feature of the institution (another being the constitutional protection of rights) that contributes to its legitimacy – but not by implying each citizen's consent to its actions.[9] Particularly when those actions are coercive, the defense of consent is not credible.

Some would describe taxation as a form of theft and conscription as a form of slavery – in fact some would prefer to describe taxation as slavery too, or at least as forced labor.[10] Much might be said against these descriptions, but that is beside the point. For

---

[9] This conception of legitimacy is found in Thomas M. Scanlon, 'Nozick on Rights, Liberty, and Property', *Philosophy & Public Affairs*, VI, no. 1 (1976), 17–20.

[10] E.g. Robert Nozick, *Anarchy, State, and Utopia* (New York: Basic Books, 1974), pp. 169–74.

within proper limits, such practices when engaged in by governments are acceptable whatever they are called. If someone with an income of $2000 a year trains a gun on someone with an income of $100 000 a year and makes him hand over his wallet, that is robbery. If the federal government withholds a portion of the second person's salary (enforcing the laws against tax evasion with threats of imprisonment under armed guard) and gives some of it to the first person in the form of welfare payments, food stamps, or free health care, that is taxation. In the first case it is (in my opinion) an impermissible use of coercive means to achieve a worthwhile end. In the second case the means are legitimate, because they are impersonally imposed by an institution designed to promote certain results. Such general methods of distribution are preferable to theft as a form of private initiative and also to individual charity. This is true not only for reasons of fairness and efficiency, but also because both theft and charity are disturbances of the relations (or lack of them) between individuals and involve their individual wills in a way that an automatic, officially imposed system of taxation does not. The results achieved by taxation in an egalitarian welfare state would not be produced either by a right of individual expropriation or by a duty of charity. Taxation therefore provides a case in which public morality is derived not from private morality, but from impersonal consequentialist considerations applied directly to public institutions, and secondarily to action within those institutions. There is no way of analyzing a system of redistributive taxation into the sum of a large number of individual acts all of which satisfy the requirements of private morality.

In the case of conscription, the coercion is extreme, and so is what one is forced to do. You are told to try to kill people who are trying to kill you, the alternative being imprisonment. Quite apart from fighting, military service involves unusual restrictions of liberty. Even assuming agreement about when conscription is acceptable and what exemptions should be allowed, this is a kind of coercion that it would be unthinkable to impose privately. A cannot force B to help him fight a gang of hoodlums who are robbing them both, if B would rather give them his money. Again, the more impersonal viewpoint of public morality gives a different result.

But not everything is permitted. Restrictions on the treatment
of individuals continue to operate from a public point of view,
and they cannot be implemented entirely by the courts. One of
the hardest lines to draw in public policy is the one that defines
where the end stops justifying the means. If results were the only
basis for public morality then it would be possible to justify
anything, including torture and massacre, in the service of
sufficiently large interests. Whether the limits are drawn by
specific constitutional protections or not, the strongest constraints of individual morality will continue to limit what can be
publicly justified even by extremely powerful consequentialist
reasons.

VI

This completes my discussion of the continuities and discontinuities between public and private morality. I have argued that
some of the special features of public morality can be explained
in terms of a theory of obligation that also accounts for the steps
individuals can take to restrict the grounds on which they will
make certain choices. Public officials accept special obligations
to serve interests that their offices are designed to advance – and
to serve them in more or less well-defined ways. In doing so,
they correlatively reduce their right to consider other factors,
both their personal interests and more general ones not related to
the institution or their role in it.

I have also argued, however, that the special character of
public obligations – the weight they give both to results and to
impartiality – reflects the relative impersonality of public action:
its scale, its lack of individuality, its institutional structure. A
theory of obligation explains only part of the change that occurs
when an individual takes on a public role. It does not explain
either the prominence of consequentialism or the shift in
strength and character of action-centered reasons. I have tried to
explain these differences as the result of a direct application of
basic moral constraints to public institutions and therefore to the
public functions that individuals may undertake.

Both of these sources of public morality generate limits to
what a public official may do in the conduct of his office, even if
he is serving institutional interests. It is easy to forget about those
limits, for three reasons. First, restrictions against the use of

public power for private gain can seem like a moral cushion that insulates whatever else is done officially from moral reproach. Second, the fact that the holder of a public office takes on an obligation to a particular group may foster the idea that he is obliged not to consider anything except the interest of that group. Third, the impersonal morality of public institutions, and the moral specialization that inevitably arises given the complexity of public actions, lead naturally to the establishment of many roles whose terms of reference are primarily consequentialist. Lack of attention to the context that is necessary to make these roles legitimate can lead to a rejection of all limits on the means thought to be justified by ever greater ends. I have argued that these are all errors. It is important to remember that they are *moral* views: the opinion that in certain conditions a certain type of conduct is permissible has to be criticized and defended by moral argument.

Let me return finally to the individuals who occupy public roles. Even if public morality is not substantively derivable from private, it applies to individuals. If one of them takes on a public role, he accepts certain obligations, certain restrictions, and certain limitations on what he may do. As with any obligation, this step involves a risk that he will be required to act in ways incompatible with other obligations or principles that he accepts. Sometimes he will have to act anyway. But sometimes, if he can remember them, he will see that the limits imposed by public morality itself are being transgressed, and he is being asked to carry out a judicial murder or a war of unjust aggression. At this point there is no substitute for refusal and, if possible, resistance. Despite the impersonal character of public morality and its complex application to institutions in which responsibility is divided, it tells us not only how those institutions should be designed but also how people in them should act. Someone who has committed public wrongs in the exercise of his office can be just as guilty as a private criminal. Sometimes his responsibility is partly absorbed by the moral defects of the institution through which he acts; but the plausibility of that excuse is inversely proportional to the power and independence of the actor. Unfortunately this is not reflected in our treatment of former public servants who have often done far worse than take bribes.

7

The Policy of Preference

It is currently easier, or widely thought to be easier, to get certain jobs or to gain admission to certain educational institutions if one is black or a woman than if one is a white man. Whether or not this is true, many think it should be true, and many others think it should not. The issue is this: If a black person or a woman is admitted to a law school or medical school, or appointed to an academic or administrative post, in preference to a white man who is in other respects better qualified,[1] and if this is done in pursuit of a preferential policy or to fill a quota, is it unjust? Can the white man complain that he has been unjustly treated? It is important to investigate the justice of such practices, because if they are unjust, it is much more difficult to defend them on grounds of social utility. I shall argue that although preferential policies are not required by justice, they are not seriously unjust either – because the system from which they depart is already unjust for reasons having nothing to do with racial or sexual discrimination.

---

[1] By saying that the white man is 'in other respects better qualified' I mean that if, e.g., a black candidate with similar qualifications had been available for the position, he would have been selected in preference to the black candidate who was in fact selected; or, if the choice had been between two white male candidates of corresponding qualifications, this one would have been selected. Ditto for two white or two black women. (I realize that it may not always be easy to determine similarity of qualifications, and that in some cases similarity of credentials may give evidence of a difference in qualifications – because, e.g., one person had to overcome more severe obstacles to acquire those credentials.)

I

In the United States we have reached the present situation by the following steps. First, and not very long ago, it came to be widely accepted that deliberate barriers against the admission to desirable positions of blacks and women should be abolished. Their abolition is by no means complete, and certain educational institutions, for example, may be able to maintain limiting quotas on the admission of women for some time. But deliberate discrimination is widely condemned.

Secondly, it was recognized that even without explicit barriers there could be discrimination, either consciously or unconsciously motivated, and this gave support to self-conscious efforts at impartiality, careful consideration of candidates belonging to the class discriminated against, and attention to the proportions of blacks and women in desirable positions, as evidence that otherwise undetectable bias might be influencing the selections. (Another, related consideration was that criteria which were good predictors of performance for one group might turn out to be poor predictors of performance for another group, so that the continued employment of those criteria might introduce a concealed inequity.)

The third step came with the realization that a social system may continue to deny different races or sexes equal opportunity or equal access to desirable positions even after the discriminatory barriers to those positions have been lifted. Socially caused inequality in the capacity to use available opportunities or to compete for available positions may persist, because the society systematically provides to one group more than to another certain educational, social, or economic advantages. Such advantages improve one's competitive position in seeking access to jobs or places in professional schools. Where there has recently been widespread deliberate discrimination in many areas, it is not surprising if the formerly excluded group experiences relative difficulty in gaining access to newly opened positions, and it is plausible to explain the difficulty at least partly in terms of disadvantages produced by past discrimination. This leads to the adoption of compensatory measures, in the form of special training programs, or financial support, or day-care centers, or apprenticeships, or tutoring. Such measures are designed to qualify those whose reduced qualifications are due to racial or sexual discrimination, either because they have been its direct victims, or because they are deprived as a result of membership in a group or community many of whose other members have been discriminated against. The second of these types of influence covers a great deal, and the importance of the social contribution is not always easy to establish. Nevertheless its effects typically include the loss of such goods as self-esteem, self-confidence, motivation, and ambition – all of which contribute to competitive success and none of which is easily restored by special training programs. Even if social injustice has produced such effects, it may be difficult for society to eradicate them.

This type of justification for compensatory programs raises another question. If it depends on the claim that the disadvantages being compensated for are the product of social injustice, then it becomes important how great the contribution of social injustice actually is, and to what extent the situation is due to social causes not involving injustice, or to causes that are not social, but biological. If one believes that society's responsibility for compensatory measures extends only to those disadvantages caused by social injustice, one will assign political importance to the degree, if any, to which racial differences in average I.Q. are genetically influenced, or the innate contribution, if any, to the statistical differences in emotional or intellectual characteristics between men and women. Also, if one believes that among socially produced inequalities, there is a crucial distinction between those that were produced unjustly and those that are merely the incidental results of just social arrangements, then it will be very important to decide exactly where that line falls: whether, for example, certain intentions must be referred to in arguing that a disadvantage has been unjustly imposed and therefore merits compensation. But let me put those issues aside for the moment.

The fourth stage comes when it is acknowledged that some unjustly caused disadvantages that create difficulties of access to positions formally open to all cannot be overcome by special programs of preparatory or remedial training. One is then faced with two alternatives. One can permit the effects of social injustice to confer a disadvantage in access to desirable positions filled simply on the basis of qualifications relevant to performance. Or one can institute a system of preferential selection that will facilitate access for those whose qualifications are lower at least partly because of unjust discrimination in other situations and at other times (and possibly against other persons). This is a difficult choice, and ideally it would be far better to use a more direct method of rectification, than to balance inequality in one part of the social system by introducing a reverse inequality at a different point. If the society as a whole contains serious injustices with complex effects, there is no way for a single institution within that society to adjust its criteria for competitive admission or employment so that the effects of injustice are nullified as far as that institution is concerned. That gives appeal to the position that places should be filled solely by criteria relevant to performance, and if this tends to amplify or extend the effects of inequitable treatment elsewhere, the remedy must be found in a more direct attack on those differences in qualification, rather than in the introduction of irrelevant criteria of appointment or admission which will sacrifice efficiency, productivity, or effectiveness of the institution in its specific tasks.

At this fourth stage we therefore find a broad division of opinion. Some believe that nothing further can legitimately be done in the short run, once the *remediable* unjust inequalities of opportunity between individuals have been dealt with: the irremediable ones are unjust, but further steps to counterbalance them by reverse discrimination would also be unjust, because they must employ irrelevant criteria. On the other hand, some find it unacceptable in such circumstances to stay with the criteria usually related to successful performance, and believe that differential admission or hiring standards for worse-off groups are justified because they compensate in some approximate way for the inequalities of opportunity produced by past injustice.

But at this point there is also a temptation to resolve the dilemma and strengthen the argument for preferential standards by proceeding to a fifth stage. One may reflect that if the criteria relevant to the prediction of performance are not inviolable it may not matter whether one violates them to compensate for disadvantages caused by injustice or disadvantages caused in other ways. One does not have to settle the question of the degree to which racial or sexual discrepancies are socially produced, because the differentials in reward ordinarily correlated with differences in qualifications are not the result of natural justice. They simply arise in a competitive system when employers try to fill positions and perform tasks efficiently. Certain abilities may be relevant to filling a job from the point of view of efficiency, but they are not relevant from the point of view of justice, because they provide no indication that one deserves the rewards that go with the job. The qualities, experience, and attainments that make success in a certain position likely do not in themselves merit the rewards that happen to attach to occupancy of that position in a competitive economy.

Consequently it might be concluded that if women or black people are less qualified, for *whatever* reason, in the respects that lead to success in the professions that our society rewards most highly, then it would be just to compensate for this disadvantage, within the limits permitted by efficiency, by having suitably different standards for these groups, and thus bringing their access to desirable positions more into line with that of others. Preferential treatment would not, on this view, have to be tailored to deal only with the effects of past injustice.

But it is clear that this is not a stable position. For if, we abandon the condition that to qualify for compensation an inequity must be socially caused, then there is no reason to restrict the compensatory measures to well-defined racial or sexual groups. Compensatory selection procedures would have to be applied on an individual basis, within as well as between such groups – each person, regardless of race, sex, or qualifications, being granted equal access to the desirable positions, within limits set by efficiency. This might require randomization of law and medical school admissions, for example, from among all the candidates above some minimum standard enabling them to do the work. If we were to act on the principle that different abilities do not merit different rewards, it would result in much more equality than is demanded by proponents of preferential treatment.

There is no likelihood that such a radical course will be adopted in the United States, but the fact that it seems to follow

naturally from a certain view about how to deal with racial or
sexual injustice reveals something important. When we try to
deal with the inequality in advantages that results from a
disparity in qualifications (however produced) between races or
sexes, we are up against a feature of the system which at every
turn exacts costs and presents obstacles in response to attempts
to reduce the inequalities. We must face the possibility that the
primary injustice with which we have to contend lies in this
feature itself, and that some of the worst aspects of what we now
perceive as racial or sexual injustice are merely conspicuous
manifestations of the great social injustice of differential reward.

II

If differences in the capacities that any society rewards are
visibly correlated, for whatever reason, with other traits such as
race or religion or social origin, then a system of liberal equality
of opportunity will give the appearance of supporting racial or
religious or class injustice. Where there is no such correlation,
there can be the appearance of justice through equal opportunity.
But there is injustice in both cases, and it lies in the schedule of
rewards.

The liberal idea of equal treatment demands that people
receive equal opportunities if they are equally qualified by talent
or education to use those opportunities. In requiring the relativ-
ization of equal treatment to characteristics in which people are
very unequal, it guarantees that the social order will reflect and
probably magnify the initial distinctions produced by nature and
the past. Liberalism has therefore come under increasing attack
in recent years, on the ground that the familiar principle of equal
treatment, with its meritocratic conception of relevant differences, seems too weak to combat the inequalities dispensed by
nature and the ordinary workings of the social system.

This criticism of the view that people deserve the rewards that
accrue to them as a result of their natural talents is not based on
the idea that apart from social institutions no one can be said to
deserve anything.[2] For if no one deserves anything, then no

---

[2] Rawls appears to regard this as the basis of his own view. He believes it
makes sense to speak of positive desert only in the context of distributions
by a just system, and not as a pre-institutional conception that can be used
to measure the justice of the system. John Rawls, *A Theory of Justice*
(Cambridge, Mass: Harvard University Press, 1971), pp. 310–13.

inequalities are contrary to desert, and desert provides no argument for equality. But for many benefits and disadvantages, certain characteristics of the recipient *are* relevant to what he deserves. If people are equal in the relevant respects, that by itself constitutes a reason to distribute the benefit to them equally.[3]

The relevant features will vary with the benefit or disadvantage, and so will the weight of the resulting considerations of desert. Desert may sometimes, in fact, be a rather unimportant consideration in determining what ought to be done. But I do wish to claim, with reference to a central case, that differential abilities are not usually among the characteristics that determine whether people *deserve* economic and social benefits (though of course they determine whether people *get* such benefits). In fact, nearly all characteristics are irrelevant to what people deserve in this dimension, and most people therefore deserve to be treated equally.[4] Perhaps voluntary differences in effort or moral differences in conduct have some bearing on economic and social desert. But they are features in which most people do not differ enough to justify very wide differences in reward.[5] I shall not try to defend these claims here, or the legitimacy of the notion of desert itself. If these things make no sense, neither does the rest of the argument.

A decision that people are equally or unequally deserving in some respect is not the end of the story. First of all, desert can be overridden, for example by liberty or even by efficiency. In some cases the presumption of equality is rather weak, and not much is required to depart from it. This will be so if the interest

---

[3] Essentially this view is put forward by Bernard Williams in 'The Idea of Equality', in *Philosophy, Politics, and Society* (second series), ed. P. Laslett and W. G. Runciman (Oxford: Blackwell, 1964), pp. 110–131.

[4] This is distinct from a case in which nothing is relevant because there *is* no desert in the matter. In that case the fact that people differed in no relevant characteristics would not create a presumption that they be treated equally. It would leave the determination of their treatment entirely to other considerations.

[5] It is *not* my view that we cannot be said to deserve the *results* of anything which we do not deserve. It is true that a person does not deserve his intelligence, and I have maintained that he does not deserve the rewards that superior intelligence can provide. But neither does he deserve his bad moral character or his above-average willingness to work, yet he probably does deserve the punishments or rewards that flow from those qualities. For an illuminating discussion of these matters, see Robert Nozick, *Anarchy, State, and Utopia* (New York: Basic Books, 1974), ch. 7.

in question is minor or temporally circumscribed, and does not represent an important value in the subject's life.

Second, it may be that although an inequality is contrary to desert, no one can benefit from its removal: all that can be done is to worsen the position of those who benefit undeservedly from its presence. Even if one believes that desert is a very important factor in determining just distributions, one need not object to inequalities that are to no one's disadvantage. In other words, it is possible to accept something like Rawls' Difference Principle from the standpoint of an egalitarian view of desert.[6] (I say it is possible. It may not be required. Some may reject the Difference Principle because they regard equality of treatment as a more stringent requirement.)

Third (and most significantly for the present discussion), a determination of relative desert in the distribution of a particular advantage does not even settle the question of *desert* in every case, for there may be other advantages and disadvantages whose distribution is tied to that of the first, and the traits relevant to the determination of desert are not necessarily the same from one advantage to another.

This bears on the case under consideration. I have said that people with different talents do not thereby deserve different economic and social rewards. They may, however, deserve different opportunities to exercise and develop those talents.[7] Whenever the distribution of two different types of benefit is connected in this way, through social or economic mechanisms or through natural human reactions, it may be impossible to avoid a distribution contrary to the conditions of desert in respect of at least one of the benefits. There will be a dilemma in which injustice cannot be entirely avoided. It may then be necessary to assign justice in the distribution of one advantage priority over justice in the distribution of another that automatically goes with it.

In the case under discussion, there appears to be a conflict between justice in the distribution of educational and professional opportunities and justice in the distribution of economic

---

[6] Rawls, *Theory of Justice*, pp. 75–80.

[7] Either because differences of ability are relevant to degree of desert in these respects or because people are equally deserving of opportunities proportional to their talents. More likely the latter.

and social rewards. There is a presumption, based on something more than efficiency, in favor of giving equal opportunities to those equally likely to succeed. But if the presumption in favor of economic equality is considerably stronger, the justification for departing from it must be stronger too. So when 'educational' justice and economic justice come into conflict, it will sometimes be necessary to sacrifice the former to the latter.

III

In thinking about racial and sexual discrimination, the view that economic justice has priority may tempt some to favor admission quotas proportional to the representation of a given group in the population. Whatever explains the small number of women or blacks in the professions, it has the result that they have less of the financial and social benefits that accrue to members of the professions, and what accounts for those differences cannot justify them. So justice may seem to require that more women and blacks be admitted to the professions.

The trouble with this solution is that it does not locate the injustice accurately, but merely tries to correct the racially or sexually skewed economic distribution which is one of its more conspicuous symptoms. We are enabled to perceive the situation as unjust when we see it through its racial manifestations, because race is a subject by now associated in our minds with injustice. But little is gained by merely transferring the same system of differential rewards, suitably adjusted to achieve comparable proportions, to the class of blacks or the class of women. If it is unjust to reward people differentially for what certain qualities enable them to do, it is equally unjust whether the distinction is made between a white man and a black man or between two black men, or two white women, or two black women. There is no way of attacking the unjust reward schedules of a meritocratic system (if indeed they are unjust) by attacking their racial or sexual manifestations directly.

In most societies reward is a function of demand, and many of the human traits most in demand result largely from *gifts* or *talents*. The greatest injustice in our society, I believe, is neither racial nor sexual but intellectual. I do not mean that it is unjust that some people are more intelligent than others. Nor do I mean that society rewards people differentially simply on the basis of their intelligence: usually it does not. But it provides on the average much larger rewards for tasks that require superior intelligence than for those that do not. This is how things work out in a technologically advanced society with a market economy. It does not reflect a social judgment that smart people *deserve* the opportunity to make more money than dumb people. They may deserve richer educational opportunity, but they do not therefore deserve the material wealth that goes with it. The same could be said about society's differential reward of beauty, athletic ability, musicality, etc. But intelligence and its development by education provide a particularly significant and pervasive example.

A general reform of the current schedule of rewards, even if they are unjust, is beyond the power of individual educational or business institutions, working through their admissions or appointments policies. A competitive economy is bound to reward those with superior training and abilities: the refusal to do so will put any business enterprise in a poor competitive position. And those who succeed in medical school or law school will tend to earn more than those who do not – whatever criteria of admission the schools adopt. It is not the procedures of appointment or admission, based on criteria that predict success, that are unjust, but rather what happens as a result of success.

No completely just solution is available. If different factors determine what is deserved in the distribution of different benefits and disadvantages, and if the distribution of several distinct advantages is sometimes connected even though the relevant factors are not, then inevitably there will be injustice in some respect, and it may be impossible to substitute a principle of distribution that avoids it.

Justice may require that we try to reduce the automatic connections between material advantages, cultural opportunity, and institutional authority. But such changes can be brought about, if at all, only by large alterations in the social system, the system of taxation, and the salary structure. They will not be achieved by modifying the admissions or hiring policies of colleges and universities, or even banks, law firms, and businesses.

Compensatory measures in admission or appointment can be

defended on grounds of justice only to the extent that they compensate for specific disadvantages that have themselves been unjustly caused, by factors distinct from the general meritocratic character of the system of distribution. Such contributions are difficult to verify or estimate; they probably vary among individuals in the oppressed group. And even where a justification for preferential treatment exists, it may not be strong enough to create an obligation, since it is doubtful that one element of a pluralistic society is obliged to adopt discriminatory measures to counteract injustice due to another element, or even to the society as a whole.

IV

These considerations suggest that an argument on grounds of justice for the imposition of racial or sexual quotas would be difficult to construct without rather precise assumptions about the source of unequal qualifications between members of different groups. The more speculative the assumptions, the weaker the argument.

But the issue is different if we return to the question posed at the beginning of this essay. The question was not whether preferential treatment is *required* by justice, but whether it is *compatible* with justice. To that question we can give a different answer. If the reflections about differential reward to which we have been led are correct, then preferential treatment need not be seriously unjust, and it may be warranted not by justice but by considerations of social utility. I say not *seriously* unjust, to acknowledge that a departure from the standards relevant to distribution of intellectual opportunities *per se* is itself a kind of injustice. But its seriousness is lessened because the factors relevant to the distribution of intellectual opportunity are irrelevant to the distribution of the material benefits that go with it.

Where the allocation of one benefit on relevant grounds carries with it the allocation of other, more significant benefits to which those grounds are irrelevant, the departure from those grounds need not be a serious offense against justice. This may be so for two reasons. First, the presumption of equal treatment of relevantly equal persons in respect of the first benefit may not be very strong to begin with. Second, the fairness of abiding by that presumption may be overshadowed by the unfairness of the other distribution correlated with it. Consequently, it may be acceptable to depart from the 'relevant' grounds for undramatic reasons of social utility, or to serve legitimate institutional aims, which would not justify more flagrant and undiluted examples of unfairness. Naturally a deviation from the usual method will appear unjust to those who are accustomed to regarding ability to succeed as the correct criterion, but this appearance may be an illusion. That depends on how much injustice is involved in the usual method, and whether the reasons for departing from it are good enough, even though they do not correct the injustice.

The problem, of course, is to say what a good reason is. I do not want to produce an argument that will justify ordinary racial or sexual discrimination designed to preserve internal harmony in a business, for instance. Even someone who thought that the system of differential economic rewards for different abilities was unjust would presumably regard it as an *additional* injustice if standard racial, religious, or sexual discrimination were a factor in the assignment of individuals to highly rewarded positions.

I can offer only a partial account of what makes systematic racial or sexual discrimination so exceptionally unjust. It has no social advantages, and it attaches a sense of reduced worth to a feature with which people are born.[8] A psychological consequence of the systematic attachment of social disadvantages to an inborn feature is that both the possessors of the feature and others begin to regard it as an essential and important characteristic, one that reduces the esteem in which its possessor can be held.[9] Concomitantly, those without the characteristic gain free esteem by comparison, and the arrangement thus sacrifices the most basic personal interests of some for the interests of others,

[8] For a detailed and penetrating treatment of this and a number of other matters discussed here, see Owen M. Fiss, 'A Theory of Fair Employment Laws', *University of Chicago Law Review*, xxxviii (Winter, 1971), 235–314.

[9] This effect would not be produced by an idiosyncratic discriminatory practice limited to a few eccentrics. If some people decided they would have nothing to do with anyone left-handed, everyone else, including the left-handed, would regard it as a silly objection to an inessential feature. But if everyone shunned the left-handed, left-handedness would become a strong component of their self-image, and those discriminated against would feel they were being despised for their essence. What people regard as their essence is not independent of what they get admired and despised for.

with those sacrificed being on the bottom. (Because similar things can be said about the social and economic disadvantages attaching to low intelligence, that, too, is a major injustice.)

Reverse discrimination need not have these consequences, and it can have social advantages. Suppose, for example, that a substantial increase in the number of black doctors is desirable because the health needs of the black community are unlikely to be met otherwise. And suppose that, at the present average level of premedical qualifications among black applicants, it would require a huge expansion of total medical school enrollment to supply the desirable absolute number of black doctors without adopting differential admission standards. Such an expansion may be unacceptable either because of its cost or because it would produce a total supply of doctors, black and white, much greater than the society requires. This is a strong argument for preferential admissions, not on grounds of justice but on grounds of social utility. (In addition, there is the salutary effect on the aspirations and expectations of other blacks, from the visibility of exemplars in formerly inaccessible positions.)

The argument in the other direction, from the point of view of qualified white applicants who are turned away, is not nearly as strong as the argument against standard racial discrimination. The self-esteem of whites as a group is not endangered by such a practice, since the situation arises only because of their general social dominance, and the aim of the practice is only to benefit blacks, not to exclude whites. Moreover, although the interests of some are being sacrificed to the interests of others, it is the better placed who are being sacrificed and the worst placed who are being helped.[10] The policy is designed to favor a group whose social position is exceptionally depressed, with destructive consequences both for the self-esteem of members of the group and for the health and cohesion of the society.[11]

So, if a preferential admission or appointment policy is adopted to mitigate a grave social evil, and it favors a group in a particularly unfortunate social position, and if for these reasons it

[10] This is a preferable direction of sacrifice if one accepts Rawls' egalitarian assumptions about distributive justice. Rawls' *Theory of Justice*, pp. 100–3.

[11] It is therefore not, as some have feared, the first step toward an imposition of minimal or maximal quotas for all racial, religious, and ethnic subgroups of the society.

diverges from a meritocratic system that is not itself required by justice, then the preferential practice is probably not unjust.[12]

It is not without costs, however. Not only does it inevitably produce resentment in the better qualified who are passed over because of the policy, but it also allows those who would in any case have failed to gain a desired position on the basis of their qualifications to feel that they may have lost out to someone less qualified because of the preferential policy. Similarly, such a practice cannot do much for the self-esteem of those who know they have benefited from it, and it may threaten the self-esteem of those in the favored group who would in fact have gained their positions even in the absence of the discriminatory policy, but who cannot be sure that they are not among its beneficiaries. This has led some institutions to lie about their policies, or to hide them behind clouds of obscurantist rhetoric about the discriminatory character of standard admissions criteria. Such concealment is possible and even justified up to a point, but the costs cannot be entirely evaded, and preferential policies will be tolerable only so long as they contribute to the eradication of great social evils.

V

When racial and sexual injustice have been reduced, we shall still be left with the great injustice of the smart and the dumb, who are so differently rewarded for comparable effort. This would be an injustice even if the system of differential economic and social rewards had no systematic sexual or racial reflection. And if the social esteem and economic advantages attaching to different occupations and educational achievements were much more uniform, there would be little cause for concern about racial, ethnic, or sexual patterns in education or work. At present we have no way of divorcing professional status from social esteem and economic reward, at least not without a gigantic increase in total social control, on the Chinese model. Perhaps someone will discover a way to reduce the socially produced inequalities

---

[12] Adam Morton has suggested an interesting alternative, which I shall not try to develop: namely, that the practice is justified not by social utility, but because it will contribute to a more just situation in the future. The practice considered in itself may be unjust, but it is warranted by its greater contribution to justice over the long term, through eradication of a self-perpetuating pattern.

(especially the economic ones) between the intelligent and the unintelligent, the talented and the untalented, or even the beautiful and the ugly, without limiting the availability of opportunities, products and services, and without resort to increased coercion or decreased liberty in the choice of work or style of life. But in the absence of such a utopian solution, the familiar task of balancing liberty against equality will remain with us.

8

Equality

I

It is difficult to argue for the intrinsic social value of equality without begging the question. Equality can be defended up to a point in terms of other values like utility and liberty. But some of the most difficult questions are posed when it conflicts with these.

Contemporary political debate recognizes four types of equality: political, legal, social, and economic. The first three cannot be defined in formal terms. Political equality is not guaranteed by granting each adult one vote and the right to hold public office. Legal equality is not guaranteed by granting everyone the right to a jury trial, the right to bring suit for injuries, and the right to counsel. Social equality is not produced by the abolition of titles and official barriers to class mobility. Great substantive inequalities in political power, legal protection, social esteem and self-respect are compatible with these formal conditions. It is a commonplace that real equality of every kind is sensitive to economic factors. While formal institutions may guarantee a minimum social status to everyone, big differences in wealth and income will produce big distinctions above that – distinctions that may be inherited as well.

So the question of economic equality cannot be detached from the others, and this complicates the issue, because the value of the other types of equality may be of a very different kind. To put it somewhat paradoxically, their value may not be strictly egalitarian. It may depend on certain rights, like the right to fair treatment by the law, that must be impartially protected, and that cannot be protected without a measure of substantive equality. Rights are in an extended sense egalitarian, because everyone is supposed to have them; but this is not a matter of distributive justice. The equal protection of individual rights is usually thought to be a value independent of utility and of equality in the distribution of advantages. Later I shall comment on the relation among these values, but for now let us assume their distinctness. This means that the defense of economic equality on the ground that it is needed to protect political, legal, and social equality may not be a defense of equality *per se* — equality in the possession of benefits in general. Yet the latter is a further moral idea of great importance. Its validity would provide an independent reason to favor economic equality as a good in its own right. If, *per impossibile*, large economic inequalities did not threaten political, legal, and social equality, they would be much less objectionable. But there might still be something wrong with them.

In addition to the arguments that depend on its relation to other types of equality, there is at least one nonegalitarian, instrumental argument for economic equality itself, on grounds of utility. The principle of diminishing marginal utility states that for many goods, a particular further increment has less value to someone who already possesses a significant amount of the good than to someone who has less.[1] So if the total quantity of such a good and the number of recipients remains constant, an equal distribution of it will always have greater total utility than a less equal one.

This must be balanced against certain costs. First, attempts to reduce inequality may also reduce the total quantity of goods available, by affecting incentives to work and invest. For example, a progressive income tax and diminishing marginal utility make it more expensive to purchase the labor of those whose services are most in demand. Beyond a certain point, the pursuit of equality may sacrifice overall utility, or even the welfare of everyone in the society.

Second, the promotion of equality may require objectionable means. To achieve even moderate equality it is necessary to restrict economic liberty, including the freedom to make bequests. Greater equality may be attainable only by more

---

[1] This is obviously not true of things in which interest varies greatly, like recordings of bird songs, or horror comic books.

general coercive techniques, including ultimately the assignment
of work by public administration instead of private contracts.
Some of these costs may be unacceptable not only on utilitarian
grounds but because they violate individual rights. Opponents
of the goal of equality may argue that if an unequal distribution
of benefits results from the free interactions and agreements of
persons who do not violate each other's rights, then the results
are not objectionable, provided they do not include extreme
hardship for the worst off.

II

So there is much to be said about the instrumental value and
disvalue of equality; the question of its intrinsic value does not
arise in isolation. Yet the answer to that question determines
what instrumental costs are acceptable. If equality is in itself
good, then producing it may be worth a certain amount of
inefficiency and loss of liberty.

There are two types of argument for the intrinsic value of
equality, communitarian and individualistic. According to the
communitarian argument, equality is good for a society taken as
a whole. It is a condition of the right kind of relations among its
members, and of the formation in them of healthy fraternal
attitudes, desires, and sympathies. This view analyzes the value
of equality in terms of a social and individual ideal. The
individualistic view, on the other hand, defends equality as a
correct *distributive* principle – the correct way to meet the
conflicting needs and interests of distinct people, whatever those
interests may be, more or less. It does not assume the desirability
of any particular kinds of desires, or any particular kinds of
interpersonal relations. Rather it favors equality in the distribution of human goods, whatever these may be – whether or not
they necessarily include goods of community and fraternity.

Though the communitarian argument is very influential, I am
going to explore only the individualistic one, because that is the
type of argument that I think is more likely to succeed. It would
provide a moral basis for the kind of liberal egalitarianism that
seems to me plausible. I do not have such an argument. This
essay is a discussion of the form such an argument would have to
take, what its starting points should be, and what it must
overcome.

A preference for equality is at best one component in a theory of social choice, or choice involving numbers of people. Its defense does not require the rejection of other values with which it may come into conflict. However, it is excluded by theories of social choice which make certain other values dominant. Egalitarianism may once have been opposed to aristocratic theories, but now it is opposed in theoretical debate by the adherents of two nonaristocratic values: utility and individual rights. I am going to examine the dispute in order to see how equality might be shown to have a value that can resist these to some extent, without replacing them.

Though I am interested in the most general foundation for such a principle, I shall begin by discussing a more specialized egalitarian view, the position of John Rawls.[2] It applies specifically to the design of the basic social institutions, rather than to distributive choices, and perhaps it cannot be extended to other cases. But it is the most developed liberal egalitarian view in the field, and much debate about equality focuses on it. So I will initially pose the opposition between equality, utility, and rights in terms of his position. Later I shall explain how my own egalitarian view differs from his.

Rawls' theory assigns more importance to equal protection of political and personal liberties than to equality in the distribution of other benefits. Nevertheless it is strongly egalitarian in this respect also. His principle of distribution for general goods, once equality in the basic liberties is secure, is that inequalities are justified only if they benefit the worst-off group in the society (by yielding higher productivity and employment, for example).

This so-called Difference Principle is used not to determine allocation directly, but only for the assessment of economic and social institutions, which in turn influence the allocation of goods. While it is counted a good thing for anyone to be made better off, the value of improving the situation of those who are worse off takes priority over the value of improving the situation of those who are better off. This is largely independent of the relative quantities of improvement involved, and also of the relative numbers of persons. So given a choice between making a thousand poor people somewhat better off and making

[2] John Rawls, *A Theory of Justice* (Cambridge, Mass.: Harvard University Press, 1971).

two thousand middle class people considerably better off, the first choice would be preferred. It should be added that people's welfare for these purposes is assessed in terms of overall life prospects, not just prosperity at the moment.

This is a very strong egalitarian principle, though it is not the most radical we can imagine. It is constructed by adding to the general value of improvement a condition of priority to the worst off. A more egalitarian position would hold that some inequalities are bad even if they benefit the worst off, so that a situation in which *everyone* is worse off may be preferable if the inequalities are reduced enough. So long as the argument remains individualistic such a position could seem attractive only for reasons stemming from the connection between economic and social equality.[3]

Later I shall discuss Rawls' arguments for the view, and offer some additional ones, but first let me say something about the two positions to which it is naturally opposed, and against which it has to be defended. They are positions that do not accord intrinsic value to equality but admit other values whose pursuit or protection may require the acceptance of considerable inequality. Those values, as I have said, are utility and individual rights.

From a utilitarian point of view, it does not make sense to forego greater benefits for the sake of lesser, or benefits to more people for the sake of fewer, just because the benefits to the worst off will be greater. It is better to have more of what is good and less of what is bad, no matter how they are distributed.

According to a theory of individual rights, it is wrong to interfere with people's liberty to keep or bequeath what they can earn merely in order to prevent the development of inequalities in distribution. It may be acceptable to limit individual liberty to prevent grave evils, but inequality is not one of those. Inequalities are not wrong if they do not result from wrongs of one person against another. They must be accepted if the only way

---

[3] The argument would be that improvements in the well-being of the lowest class as a result of material productivity spurred by wage differentials are only apparent: damage to their self-respect outweighs the material gains. And even inequalities that genuinely benefit the worst off may destroy nondistributive values like community or fraternity. See Christopher Ake, 'Justice as Equality', *Philosophy & Public Affairs*, v, no. 1 (Fall, 1975), 69–89, esp. 76–7.

to prevent them is to abridge individual rights to the kind of free action that violates no one else's rights.

Both types of theory point out the costs of pursuing distributive equality, and deny that it has independent value that outweighs these costs. More specifically, the pursuit of equality is held to require the illegitimate sacrifice of the rights or interests of some individuals to the less important interests of others. These two theories are also radically opposed to one another. Together with egalitarianism they form a trio of fundamentally different views about how to settle conflicts among the interests of different people.

III

What is the nature of the dispute between them? The units about which the problem arises are individual persons, individual human lives. Each of them has a claim to consideration. In some sense the distinctness of these claims is at the heart of the issue. The question is whether (a) the worst off have a prior claim, or (b) the enforcement of that claim would ignore the greater claim of others not among the worst off, who would benefit significantly more if a less egalitarian policy were adopted instead, or (c) it would infringe the claims of other persons to liberty and the protection of their rights.

Now this looks like a dispute about the value of equality. But it can also be viewed as a dispute about *how* people should be treated equally, not about whether they should be. The three views share an assumption of moral equality between persons, but differ in their interpretations of it. They agree that the moral claims of all persons are, at a sufficiently abstract level, the same, but disagree over what these are.[4]

The defender of rights locates them in the freedom to do certain things without direct interference by others. The utilitarian locates them in the requirement that each person's

---

[4] This way of looking at the problem was suggested to me by a proposal of Rawls (personal communication, January 31, 1976):
'Suppose we distinguish between the equal treatment of persons and their (equal) right to be treated as equals. (Here persons are *moral* persons.) The *latter* is more basic: Suppose the Original Position represents the latter *re* moral persons when they agree on principles and suppose they *would* agree on *some* form of equal treatment. What more is needed?'

interests be fully counted as a component in the calculation of
utility used to decide which states of affairs are best and which
acts or policies are right. The egalitarian finds them in an equal
claim to actual or possible advantages. The issue remains acute
even though most social theories do not fall squarely into one of
these categories, but give primacy to one interpretation of moral
equality and secondary status to the others.

All three interpretations of moral equality attempt to give
equal weight, in essential respects, to each person's point of
view. This might even be described as the mark of an enligh-
tened ethic, though some theories that do not share it still qualify
as ethical. If the opposition of views about distributive equality
can be regarded as a disagreement about the proper interpretation of this basic requirement of moral equality, that provides a
common reference against which the opposing positions may be
measured. It should be possible to compare the quality of their
justifications, instead of simply registering their mutual incompatibility.

What it means to give equal weight to each person's point of
view depends on what is morally essential to that point of view,
what it is in each of us that must be given equal weight. It also
depends on how the weights are combined. And these two
aspects of the answer are interdependent. Let us consider each of
the positions from this point of view.

IV

The moral equality of utilitarianism is a kind of majority rule:
each person's interests count once, but some may be outweighed
by others. It is not really a majority of *persons* that determines the
result, but a majority of interests suitably weighted for intensity.
Persons are equal in the sense that each of them is given a 'vote'
weighted in proportion to the magnitude of his interests.
Although this means that the interests of a minority can
sometimes outweigh the interests of a majority, the basic idea is
majoritarian because each individual is accorded the same (vari-
able) weight and the outcome is determined by the largest total.

In the simplest version, all of a person's interests or preferences are counted, and given a relative weight depending on
their weight for him. But various modifications have been
suggested. One doubt voiced about utilitarianism is that it

counts positively the satisfaction of evil desires (sadistic or bigoted ones, for example). Mill employed a distinction between higher and lower pleasures, and gave priority to the former. (Could there be a corresponding distinction for pains?) Recently, Thomas Scanlon has argued that any distributive principle, utilitarian or egalitarian, must use some objective standard of interest, need, or urgency distinct from mere subjective preference to avoid unacceptable consequences. Even if the aim is to maximize the total of some quantity of benefit over all persons, it is necessary to pick a single measure of that quantity that applies fairly to everyone, and pure preference is not a good measure. 'The fact that someone would be willing to forego a decent diet in order to build a monument to his god does not mean that his claim on others for aid in his project has the same strength as a claim for aid in obtaining enough to eat (even assuming that the sacrifices required of others would be the same).'[5]

Even if a standard of objectivity is introduced, the range of morally relevant interests can still be quite broad, and it will vary from person to person. The individual as moral claimant continues to be more or less the whole person. On the other hand, anyone's claims can in principle be completely outvoted by the claims of others. In the final outcome a given individual's claims may be met hardly at all, though they have been counted in the majoritarian calculation used to arrive at that outcome.

Utilitarianism takes a generous view of individual moral claims and combines them aggregatively. It applies the resulting values to the assessment of overall results or states of affairs, and derives the assessment of actions from this as a secondary result. One is to do what will tend to promote the results that appear best from a point of view that combines all individual interests. The moral equality of utilitarianism consists in letting each person's interests contribute in the same way to determining what in sum would be best overall.

V

Rights are very different, both in structure and in content. They are not majoritarian or in any other way aggregative, and they

<hr />

[5] T. M. Scanlon, 'Preference and Urgency', *Journal of Philosophy*, LXXII, no. 19 (November 6, 1975), 659–60.

do not provide an assessment of overall results. Instead, they determine the acceptability of actions directly. The moral equality of persons under this conception is their equal claim against each other not to be interfered with in specified ways. Each person must be treated equally in certain definite respects by each other person.

In a sense, these claims are not combined at all. They must be respected individually. What anyone may do is restricted to what will not violate the rights of anyone else. Since the designated aspect of each person's point of view sets this limit *by itself*, the condition is a kind of unanimity requirement.

Rights may be absolute, or it may be permissible to override them when a significant threshold is reached in the level of harm that can be prevented by doing so. But however they are defined, they must be respected in every case where they apply. They give every person a limited veto over how others may treat him.

This kind of unanimity condition is possible only for rights that limit what one person may do to another. There cannot in this sense be rights to *have* certain things – a right to medical care, or to a decent standard of living, or even a right to life. The language of rights is sometimes used in this way, to indicate the special importance of certain human goods. But I believe that the true moral basis of such claims is the priority of more urgent over less urgent individual needs, and this is essentially an egalitarian principle. To preserve distinctions I shall use the term 'right' only for a claim that gives its possessor a kind of veto power, so that if everyone has the right, that places a condition of unanimous acceptability, in this respect, on action. There can be no literal right to life in that sense, because there are situations in which any possible course of action will lead to the death of someone or other; and if everyone had a right to stay alive, nothing would be permissible in those situations.[6]

Rights of the kind I am considering escape this problem because they are agent-centered. A right not to be killed, for example, is not a right that everyone do what is required to

---

[6] There may be circumstances in which nothing is permissible – true moral dilemmas in which every possible course of action is wrong. But these arise only from the clash of distinct moral principles and not from the application of one principle. See chapter 5, above.

insure that you are not killed. It is merely a right not to be killed, and it is correlated with other people's duty not to *kill* you.

Such an ethic does not enjoin that violations of rights be minimized. That would be to count them merely as particularly grave evils in the assessment of outcomes. Instead, rights limit action directly: each person is forbidden to violate directly the rights of others even if he could reduce the overall number of violations of rights indirectly by violating a few himself. It is hard to account for such agent-centered restrictions. One thing to say about them by way of interpretation is that they represent a higher degree of moral inviolability than principles requiring us to do whatever will minimize the violation of rights. For if that were the principle, then violation of the right would not always be wrong. The moral claim of a right not to be murdered even to prevent several other murders is stronger than the claim which merely counts murder as a great evil, for the former prohibits murders that the latter would permit. That is true even though the latter might enable one to prevent more murders than the former. But this does not go very far toward explaining agent-centered rights. A serious account would have to consider not only the protected interests but the relation between the agent and the person he is constrained not to treat in certain ways, even to achieve very desirable ends. The concern with what one is doing to whom, as opposed to the concern with what happens, is an important primary source of ethics that is poorly understood.

Having noted that rights yield an assessment in the first instance of actions rather than of outcomes, we can see that they also define individual moral claims more narrowly than does utilitarianism, and combine them differently. The utilitarian constructs an impersonal point of view in which those of all individuals are combined to give judgments of utility, which in turn are to guide everyone's actions. For a defender of rights, the respects in which each person is inviolable present a direct and *independent* limit to what any other person may do to him. There is no single combination of viewpoints which yields a common goal for everyone, but each of us must limit our actions to a range that is not unacceptable to anyone else in certain respects. Typically, the range of what may be done because it violates no rights is rather large.

For this reason the morality of rights tends to be a limited, even a minimal morality. It leaves a great deal of human life ungoverned by moral restrictions or requirements. That is why, if unsupplemented, it leads naturally to political theories of limited government, and, in the extreme, to the libertarian theory of the minimal state. The justification of broad government action to promote all aspects of the general welfare requires a much richer set of moral requirements.[7]

This type of limited morality also has the consequence that the numbers of people on either side of an issue do not count. In a perfectly unanimous morality the only number that counts is one. If moral acceptability is acceptability in a certain respect from each person's point of view, then even if in other respects one course of action is clearly more acceptable to most but not all of the people involved, no further moral requirement follows.[8]

The moral equality of rights, then, consists in assigning to each person the same domain of interests with respect to which he may not be directly interfered with by anyone else.

VI

Oddly enough, egalitarianism is based on a more obscure conception of moral equality than either of the less egalitarian theories. It employs a much richer version of each person's point of view than does a theory of rights. In that respect it is closer to utilitarianism. It also resembles utilitarianism formally, in being

---

[7] The issue over the *extent* of morality is one of the deepest in ethical theory. Many have felt it an objection to utilitarianism that it makes ethics swallow up everything, leaving only one optimal choice, or a small set of equally optimal alternatives, permissible for any person at any time. Those who offer this objection differ over the size and shape of the range of choices that should be left to individual inclination after the ethical boundaries have been drawn.

[8] John Taurek has recently defended essentially this position in his paper, 'Should the Numbers Count?', *Philosophy & Public Affairs*, vi, no. 4 (Summer, 1977), 293–316. He holds that given a choice between saving one life and saving five others, one is not required to save the five: one may save either the one or the five. I believe that he holds this because there is at least one point of view from which saving the five is not the better choice. Taurek does believe that some moral requirements derive from special rights and obligations, but in cases like this, where there are fundamental conflicts of interest, it is impossible to define a condition of universal acceptability, and the choice is therefore not governed by any moral requirement.

applied first to the assessment of outcomes rather than of actions. But it does not combine all points of view by a majoritarian method. Instead, it establishes an order of priority among needs and gives preference to the most urgent, regardless of numbers. In that respect it is closer to rights theory.

What conception of moral equality is at work here, i.e. what equal moral claim is being granted to everyone and how are these claims combined? Each individual's claim has a complex form: it includes more or less all his needs and interests, but in an order of relative urgency or importance. This determines both which of them are to be satisfied first and whether they are to be satisfied before or after the interests of others. Something close to unanimity is being invoked. An arrangement must be acceptable first from the point of view of everyone's most basic claims, then from the point of view of everyone's next most basic claims, etc. By contrast with a rights theory, the individual claims are not limited to specific restrictions on how one may be treated. They concern whatever may happen to a person, and in appropriate order of priority they include much more than protection from the most basic misfortunes. This means that the order of priority will not settle all conflicts, since there can be conflicts of interest even at the most basic level, and therefore unanimity cannot be achieved. Instead, one must be content to get as close to it as possible.

One problem in the development of this idea is the definition of the order of priority: whether a single, objective standard of urgency should be used in construing the claims of each person, or whether his interests should be ranked at his own estimation of their relative importance. In addition to the question of objectivity, there is a question of scale. Because moral equality is equality between persons, the individual interests to be ranked cannot be momentary preferences, desires, and experiences. They must be aspects of the individual's life taken as a whole: health, nourishment, freedom, work, education, self-respect, affection, pleasure. The determination of egalitarian social policy requires some choice among them, and the results will be very different depending on whether material advantages or individual liberty and self-realization are given priority.

But let me leave these questions aside. The essential feature of an egalitarian priority system is that it counts improvements to the welfare of the worse off as more urgent than improvements to the welfare of the better off. These other questions must be answered to decide who is worse off and who is better off, and how much, but what makes a system egalitarian is the priority it gives to the claims of those whose overall life prospects put them at the bottom, irrespective of numbers or of overall utility. Each individual with a more urgent claim has priority, in the simplest version of such a view, over each individual with a less urgent claim. The moral equality of egalitarianism consists in taking into account the interests of each person, subject to the same system of priorities of urgency, in determining what would be best overall.

VII

It is obvious that the three conceptions of moral equality with which we are dealing are extremely different. They define each person's equal moral claim differently, and they derive practical conclusions from sets of such claims in different ways. They seem to be radically opposed to one another, and it is very difficult to see how one might decide among them.

My own view is that we do not have to. A plausible social morality will show the influence of them all. This will certainly not be conceded by utilitarians or believers in the dominance of rights. But to defend liberal egalitarianism it is not necessary to show that moral equality *cannot* be interpreted in the ways that yield rights or utilitarianism. One has only to show that an egalitarian interpretation is also acceptable. The result then depends on how these disparate values combine.

Though my own view is somewhat different from that of Rawls, I shall begin by considering his arguments, in order to explain why another account seems to me necessary.[9] He gives two kinds of argument for his position. One is intuitive and belongs to the domain of ordinary moral reasoning. The other is theoretical and depends on the construction by which Rawls works out his version of the social contract and which he calls the Original Position. I shall begin with two prominent examples of the first kind of argument and then go on to a brief consideration of the theoretical construction.

[9] Some of my comments are developed in 'Rawls on Justice', *Philosophical Review*, LXXXIII (1973), 220–33.

One point Rawls makes repeatedly is that the natural and social contingencies that influence welfare — talent, early environment, class background — are not themselves deserved. So differences in benefit that derive from them are morally arbitrary.[10] They can be justified only if the alternative would leave the least fortunate even worse off. In that case everyone benefits from the inequalities, so the extra benefit to some is justified as a means to this. A less egalitarian principle of distribution, whether it is based on rights or on utility, allows social and natural contingencies to produce inequalities justified neither because everyone benefits nor because those who get more deserve more.

The other point is directed specifically against utilitarianism. Rawls maintains that utilitarianism applies to problems of social choice — problems in which the interests of many individuals are involved — a method of decision appropriate for one individual.[11] A single person may accept certain disadvantages in exchange for greater benefits. But no such compensation is possible when one person suffers the disadvantages and another gets the benefits.

So far as I can see, neither of these arguments is decisive. The first assumes that inequalities need justification, that there is a presumption against permitting them. Only that would imply that undeserved inequalities are morally arbitrary in an invidious sense, unless otherwise justified. If they were arbitrary only in the sense that there were no reasons for or against them, they would require no justification, and the aim of avoiding them could provide no reason to infringe on anyone's rights. In any case the utilitarian has a justification to offer for the inequalities that his system permits: that the sum of advantages is greater than it would be without the inequality. But even if an inequality were acceptable only if it benefited everyone, that would not have to imply anything as strong as the Difference Principle. More than one deviation from equality may benefit everyone to some extent, and it would require a specific egalitarian assumption to prefer the one that was most favorable to the worst off.

The second argument relies on a diagnosis of utilitarianism

---

[10] Rawls, *Theory of Justice*, pp. 74, 104.
[11] Rawls, *Theory of Justice*, pp. 27, 187.

that has recently been challenged by Derek Parfit.[12] But even if the diagnosis is correct, it does not supply an argument for equality, for it does not say why this method of summation is not acceptable for the experiences of many individuals. It certainly cannot be justified simply by extension from the individual case, but it has enough *prima facie* appeal to require displacement by some better alternative. It merely says that more of what is good is better than less, and less of what is bad is better than more. Someone might accept this conclusion without having reached it by extending the principle of individual choice to the social case. There is no particular reason to think that the principle will be either the same or different in the two cases.

In Utilitarianism intrapersonal compensation has no special significance. It acquires significance only against the background of a refusal *in general* to accept the unrestricted summation of goods and evils – a background to which it provides the exception. This background must be independently justified. By itself, the possibility of intrapersonal compensation neither supports nor undermines egalitarian theories. It implies only that *if* an egalitarian theory is accepted, it should apply only across lives rather than within them. It is a reason for taking individual human lives, rather than individual experiences, as the units over which any distributive principle should operate. But it could serve this function for anti-egalitarian as well as for egalitarian views. This is the reverse of Rawls' argument: no special distributive principle should be applied *within* human lives because that would be to extend to the individual the principle of choice appropriate for society. Provided that condition is met, intrapersonal compensation is neutral among distributive principles.

Next let me consider briefly Rawls' contractarian argument. Though he stresses that his theory is about the morality of social institutions, its general ideas about equality can I think be applied more widely. The Original Position, his version of the

---

[12] 'Later Selves and Moral Principles', in *Philosophy & Personal Relations*, ed. A. Montefiore (London: Routledge & Kegan Paul, 1973). Parfit suggests that utilitarianism could express the dissolution of temporally extended individuals into experiential sequences rather than the conflation of separate individuals into a mass person.

social contract, is a constructed unanimity condition which attributes to each person a schematic point of view that abstracts from the differences between people, but allows for the main categories of human interest. The individual is expected to choose principles for the assessment of social institutions on the assumption that he may be anyone, but without assuming that he has an equal chance of being anyone, or that his chance of being in a certain situation is proportional to the number of people in that situation.

The resulting choice brings out the priorities that are generally shared, and combines interests ranked by these priorities without regard to the numbers of people involved. The principles unanimously chosen on the basis of such priorities grant to each person the same claim to have his most urgent needs satisfied prior to the less urgent needs of anyone else. Priority is given to individuals who, taking their lives as a whole, have more urgent needs, rather than to the needs that more individuals have.

There has been much controversy over whether the rational choice under the conditions of uncertainty and ignorance that prevail in the Original Position would be what Rawls says it is, or even whether any choice could be rational under those conditions. But there is another question that is prior. Why does what it would be rational to agree to under those conditions determine what is right?

Let us focus this question more specifically on the features of the Original Position that are responsible for the egalitarian result. There are two of them. One is that the choice must be unanimous, and therefore everyone must be deprived of all information about his conception of the good or his position in society. The other is that the parties are not allowed to choose as if they had an equal chance of being anyone in the society, because in the absence of any information about probabilities it is not, according to Rawls, rational to assign some arbitrarily, using the Principle of Insufficient Reason. The Original Position is constructed by subtracting information without adding artificial substitutes. This results directly in the maximin strategy of choice, which leads to principles that favor the worst off in general and impose even more stringent equality in the basic liberties.

Suppose Rawls is right about what it would be rational to

choose under those conditions. We must then ask why a unanimous choice under conditions of ignorance, without an assumption that one has an equal chance of being anyone in the society, correctly expresses the constraints of morality. Other constructions also have a claim to counting all persons as moral equals. What makes these conditions of unanimity under ignorance the right ones? They insure that numbers do not count[13] and urgency does, but that is the issue. A more fundamental type of argument is needed to settle it.

VIII

The main question is whether a kind of unanimity should enter into the combination of different points of view when evaluative judgments are being made about outcomes. This is an issue between egalitarian and utilitarian theories, both of which concern themselves with outcomes. Rights theories are opposed to both, because although they use a kind of unanimity condition, it is a condition on the acceptability of actions rather than of outcomes. In defending an interpretation of moral equality in terms of unanimity applied in the assessment of outcomes, I am therefore denying that either utilitarianism or rights theories, or both, represent the whole truth about ethics.

As I have said, acceptance of egalitarian values need not imply total exclusion of the others. Egalitarians may allow utility independent weight, and liberal egalitarians standardly acknowledge the importance of certain rights, which limit the means that may be used in pursuing equality and other ends.[14] I believe that rights exist and that this agent-centered aspect of morality is very important. The recognition of individual rights is a way of accepting a requirement of unanimous acceptability when weighing the claims of others in respect to what one may do. But a theory based exclusively on rights leaves out too much

---

[13] Since the Difference Principle is applied not to individuals but to social classes, conflicts of interest within the worst off or any other groups are absorbed in a set of average expectations. This means that the numbers count in a sense *within* a social class, in determining which policy benefits it most on average. But numbers do not count in determining priority among classes in the urgency of their claims. That is why the problems of this conception of social justice are similar to those of a more individually tailored egalitarianism.

[14] Such a view is defended by Ronald Dworkin in *Taking Rights Seriously* (Cambridge, Mass.: Harvard University Press, 1977).

that is morally relevant, even if the interests it includes are among the most basic. A moral view that gives no weight to the value of overall outcomes cannot be correct.[15]

So let me return to the issue of unanimity in the assessment of outcomes. The essence of such a criterion is to try in a moral assessment to include each person's point of view separately, so as to achieve a result which is in a significant sense acceptable to each person involved or affected. Where there is conflict of interests, no result can be completely acceptable to everyone. But it is possible to assess each result from each point of view to try to find the one that is least unacceptable to the person to whom it is most unacceptable. This means that any other alternative will be more unacceptable to someone than this alternative is to anyone. The preferred alternative is in that sense the least unacceptable, considered from each person's point of view separately. A radically egalitarian policy of giving absolute priority to the worst off, regardless of numbers, would result from always choosing the least unacceptable alternative, in this sense.

This ideal of individual acceptability is in fundamental opposition to the aggregative ideal, which constructs a special moral point of view by combining those of individuals into a single conglomerate viewpoint distinct from all of them. That is done in utilitarianism by adding them up. Both the separate and the conglomerate methods count everyone fully and equally. The difference between them is that the second moves beyond individual points of view to something more comprehensive than any of them, though based on them. The first stays closer to the points of view of the individuals considered.

It is this ideal of acceptability to each individual that underlies the appeal of equality. We can see how it operates even in a case involving small numbers. Suppose I have two children, one of which is normal and quite happy, and the other of which suffers from a painful handicap. Call them respectively the first child and the second child. I am about to change jobs. Suppose I must decide between moving to an expensive city where the second child can receive special medical treatment and schooling, but

[15] I have said more about this in 'Libertarianism without Foundations', *Yale Law Journal*, LXXXV, (1975), a review of Robert Nozick, *Anarchy, State, and Utopia* (New York: Basic Books, 1974).

where the family's standard of living will be lower and the neighborhood will be unpleasant and dangerous for the first child – or else moving to a pleasant semi-rural suburb where the first child, who has a special interest in sports and nature, can have a free and agreeable life. This is a difficult choice on any view. To make it a test for the value of equality, I want to suppose that the case has the following feature: the gain to the first child of moving to the suburb is substantially greater than the gain to the second child of moving to the city. After all, the second child will also suffer from the family's reduced standard of living and the disagreeable environment. And the educational and therapeutic benefits will not make him happy but only less miserable. For the first child, on the other hand, the choice is between a happy life and a disagreeable one. Let me add as a feature of the case that there is no way to compensate either child significantly for its loss if the choice favoring the other child is made. The family's resources are stretched, and neither child has anything else to give up that could be converted into something of significant value to the other.

If one chose to move to the city, it would be an egalitarian decision. It is more urgent to benefit the second child, even though the benefit we can give him is less than the benefit we can give the first child. This urgency is not necessarily decisive. It may be outweighed by other considerations, for equality is not the only value. But it is a factor, and it depends on the worse off position of the second child. An improvement in his situation is more important than an equal or somewhat greater improvement in the situation of the first child.

Suppose a third child is added to the situation, another happy, healthy one, and I am faced with the same choice in allocation of indivisible goods. The greater urgency of benefiting the second child remains. I believe that this factor is essentially unchanged by the addition of the third child. It remains just as much more urgent to benefit the second child in this case as it was when there were only two children.[16]

---

[16] Note that these thoughts do not *depend* on any idea of personal identity over time, though they can *employ* such an idea. All that is needed to evoke them is a distinction between persons at a time. The impulse to distributive equality arises so long as we can distinguish between two experiences being had by two persons and their being had by one person. The criteria of personal identity over time merely determine the size of

The main point about a measure of urgency is that it is done by pairwise comparison of the situations of individuals. The simplest method would be to count *any* improvement in the situation of someone worse off as more urgent than any improvement in the situation of someone better off; but this is not especially plausible. It is more reasonable to accord greater urgency to large improvements somewhat higher in the scale than to very small improvements lower down. Such a modified principle could still be described as selecting the alternative that was least unacceptable from each point of view. This method can be extended to problems of social choice involving large numbers of people. So long as numbers do not count it remains a type of unanimity criterion, defined by a suitable measure of urgency. The problem of justifying equality then becomes the problem of justifying the pursuit of results that are acceptable to each person involved.

Before turning to a discussion of this problem, let me say why I think that even if it were solved, it would not provide the foundation for a correct egalitarian theory. It seems to me that no plausible theory can avoid the relevance of numbers completely. There may be some disparities of urgency so great that the priorities persist whatever numbers are involved. But if the choice is between preventing severe hardship for some who are very poor and deprived, and preventing less severe but still substantial hardship for those who are better off but still struggling for subsistence, then it is very difficult for me to believe that the numbers do not count, and that priority of urgency goes to the worse off however many more there are of the better off. It might be suggested that this is a case where equality is outweighed by utility. But if egalitarian urgency is itself sensitive to numbers in this way, it does not seem that any form of unanimity criterion could explain the foundation of the view. Nor does any alternative foundation suggest itself.

IX

For a view of the more uncompromising type, similar in structure to that of Rawls, we need an explanation of why

---

the units over which a distributive principle operates. That, briefly, is what I think is wrong with Parfit's account of the relation between distributive justice and personal identity.

individual pairwise comparison to find the individually least
unacceptable alternative is a good way to adjudicate among
competing interests. What would it take to justify this method of
combining individual claims? I think the only way to answer this
question is to ask another: what is the source of morality? How
do the interests of others secure a hold on us in moral reasoning,
and does this imply a way in which they must be considered in
combination?

I have a view about the source of other-regarding moral
reasons that suggests an answer to this question. The view is not
very different from the one I defended in *The Possibility of
Altruism*,[17] and I will only sketch it here. I believe that the general
form of moral reasoning is to put yourself in other people's
shoes. This leads to acceptance of an impersonal concern for
them corresponding to the impersonal concern for yourself that
is needed to avoid a radical incongruity between your attitudes
from the personal and impersonal standpoints, i.e. from inside
and outside your life. Some considerable disparity remains,
because the personal concerns remain in relation to yourself and
your life: they are not to be replaced or absorbed by the
impersonal ones that correspond to them.[18] (One is also typically
concerned in a personal way for the interests of certain others to
whom one is close.) But we derive moral reasons by forming in
addition a parallel impersonal concern corresponding to the
interests of all other individuals. It will be as strong or as weak,
as comprehensive or as restricted, as the impersonal concern we
are constrained by the pressures of congruency to feel about
ourselves. In a sense, the requirement is that you love your
neighbor as yourself: but only as much as you love yourself
when you look at yourself from outside, with fair detachment.

The process applies separately to each individual and yields a
set of concerns corresponding to the individual lives. There may
be disparities between a person's objective interests and his own
subjectively perceived interests or wishes, but apart from this,
his claims enter the impersonal domain of reasons unchanged, as
those of an individual. They do not come detached from him
and go into a big hopper with all the others. The impersonal

---

[17] Oxford: Clarendon Press, 1970.
[18] In this respect my present view differs from the one in *The Possibility of
Altruism*.

concern of ethics is an impersonal concern for oneself and all others as individuals. It derives from the necessary generalization of an impersonal concern for one's own life and interests, and the generalization preserves the individualistic form of the original.

For this reason the impersonal concern that results is fragmented: it includes a separate concern for each person, and it is realized by looking at the world from each person's point of view separately and individually, rather than by looking at the world from a single comprehensive point of view. Imaginatively one must split into all the people in the world, rather than turn oneself into a conglomeration of them.

This, it seems to me, makes pairwise comparison the natural way to deal with conflicting claims. There may be cases where the policy chosen as a result will seek to maximize satisfaction rather than equalizing it, but this will only be where all individuals have an equal chance of benefiting, or at least not a conspicuously unequal chance.[19] At the most basic level, the way to choose from many separate viewpoints simultaneously is to maintain them intact and give priority to the most urgent individual claims.

As I have said, equality is only one value and this is only one method of choice. We can understand a radically egalitarian system just as we can understand a radical system of rights, but I assume neither is correct. Utility is a legitimate value, and the majoritarian or conglomerate viewpoint on which it depends is an allowable way of considering the conflicting interests of numbers of different people at once. Still, the explanation of egalitarian values in terms of separate assessment from each point of view is a step toward understanding; and if it does not imply that these values are absolute, that is not necessarily a drawback.

---

[19] I leave aside the question when the equality of chances can be counted as real enough to supersede the inequality of actual outcomes. Perhaps that applies only to certain kinds of outcomes, and certain ways of determining chances.

9

The Fragmentation of Value

I want to discuss some problems created by a disparity between the fragmentation of value and the singleness of decision. These problems emerge in the form of practical conflicts, and they usually have moral components.

By a practical conflict I do not mean merely a difficult decision. Decisions may be difficult for a number of reasons: because the considerations on different sides are very evenly balanced; because the facts are uncertain; because the probability of different outcomes of the possible courses of action is unknown. A difficult choice between chemotherapy and surgery, when it is uncertain which will be more effective, is not an example of what I mean by practical conflict, because it does not involve conflict between values which are incomparable for reasons apart from uncertainty about the facts. There can be cases where, even if one is fairly sure about the outcomes of alternative courses of action, or about their probability distributions, and even though one knows how to distinguish the pros and cons, one is nevertheless unable to bring them together in a single evaluative judgment, even to the extent of finding them evenly balanced. An even balance requires comparable quantities.

The strongest cases of conflict are genuine dilemmas, where there is decisive support for two or more incompatible courses of action or inaction. In that case a decision will still be necessary, but it will seem necessarily arbitrary. When two choices are very evenly balanced, it does not matter which choice one makes, and arbitrariness is no problem. But when each seems right for reasons that appear decisive and sufficient, arbitrariness means the lack of reasons where reasons are needed, since either choice will mean acting against some reasons without being able to claim that they are *outweighed*.

There are five fundamental types of value that give rise to basic conflict. Conflicts can arise within as well as between them, but the latter are especially difficult. (I have not included self-interest in the group; it can conflict with any of the others.)

First, there are specific obligations to other people or institutions: obligations to patients, to one's family, to the hospital or university at which one works, to one's community or one's country. Such obligations have to be incurred, either by a deliberate undertaking or by some special relation to the person or institution in question. Their existence depends in either case on the subject's relation to others, although the relation does not have to be voluntary. (Even though young children are not at liberty to choose their parents or guardians, parental care creates some obligation of reciprocal future concern.)

The next category is that of constraints on action deriving from general rights that everyone has, either to do certain things or not to be treated in certain ways. Rights to liberty of certain kinds, or to freedom from assault or coercion, do not depend on specific obligations that others have incurred not to interfere, assault, or coerce. Rather, they are completely general, and restrict what others may do to their possessor, whoever those others may be. Thus a doctor has both specific obligations to his patients and general duties to treat anyone in certain ways.

The third category is that which is technically called utility. This is the consideration that takes into account the effects of what one does on everyone's welfare – whether or not the components of that welfare are connected to special obligations or general rights. Utility includes all aspects of benefit and harm to all people (or all sentient beings), not just those to whom the agent has a special relation, or has undertaken a special commitment. The general benefits of medical research and education obviously come under this heading.

The fourth category is that of perfectionist ends or values. By this I mean the intrinsic value of certain achievements or creations, apart from their value *to* individuals who experience or use them. Examples are provided by the intrinsic value of scientific discovery, of artistic creation, of space exploration, perhaps. These pursuits do of course serve the interests of the individuals directly involved in them, and of certain spectators. But typically the pursuit of such ends is not justified solely in terms of those interests. They are thought to have an intrinsic value, so that it is important to achieve fundamental advances, for example, in mathematics or astronomy even if very few people come to understand them and they have no practical effects. The mere existence of such understanding, somewhere in the species, is regarded by many as worth substantial sacrifices. Naturally opinions differ as to what has this kind of worth. Not everyone will agree that reaching the moon or Mars has the intrinsic value necessary to justify its current cost, or that the performance of obscure or difficult orchestral works has any value apart from its worth to individuals who enjoy them. But many things people do cannot be justified or understood without taking into account such perfectionist values.

The final category is that of commitment to one's own projects or undertakings, which is a value in addition to whatever reasons may have led to them in the first place. If you have set out to climb Everest, or translate Aristotle's *Metaphysics*, or master the *Well-Tempered Clavier*, or synthesize an amino acid, then the further pursuit of that project, once begun, acquires remarkable importance.[1] It is partly a matter of justifying earlier investment of time and energy, and not allowing it to have been in vain. It is partly a desire to be the sort of person who finishes what he begins. But whatever the reason, our projects make autonomous claims on us, once undertaken, which they need not have made in advance. Someone who has determined to master the *Well-Tempered Clavier* may say 'I can't go to the movies, I have to practice'; but it would be strange for him to say that he had to master the *Well-Tempered Clavier*.

These commitments should not be confused with self-interest, for self-interest aims at the integrated fulfillment over time of *all* one's interests and desires (or at least those desires one does not wish to eliminate). Special commitments may, in their pursuit, be inimical to self-interest thus defined. They need not have been undertaken for self-interested reasons, and their pursuit certainly

[1] See Gilbert Harman, 'Practical Reasoning', *Review of Metaphysics*, XXIX (1976), 432–63.

need not be controlled by self-interest.

Obligations, rights, utility, perfectionist ends, and private commitments – these values enter into our decisions constantly, and conflicts among them, and within them, arise in medical research, in politics, in personal life, or wherever the grounds of action are not artificially restricted. What would it mean to give a system of priorities among them? A simpler moral conception might permit a solution in terms of a short list of clear prohibitions and injunctions, with the balance of decision left to personal preference or discretion, but that will not work with so mixed a collection. One might try to order them. For example: never infringe general rights, and undertake only those special obligations that cannot lead to the infringement of anyone's rights; maximize utility within the range of action left free by the constraints of rights and obligations; where utility would be equally served by various policies, determine the choice by reference to perfectionist ends; and finally, where this leaves anything unsettled, decide on grounds of personal commitment or even simple preference. Such a method of decision is absurd, not because of the particular order chosen but because of its absoluteness. The ordering I have given is not arbitrary, for it reflects a degree of relative stringency in these types of values. But it is absurd to hold that obligations can never outweigh rights, or that utility, however large, can never outweigh obligation.

However, if we take the idea of outweighing seriously, and try to think of an alternative to ordering as a method of rationalizing decision in conditions of conflict, the thing to look for seems to be a single scale on which all these apparently disparate considerations can be measured, added, and balanced. Utilitarianism is the best example of such a theory, and interesting attempts have been made to explain the apparent priority of rights and obligations over utility in utilitarian terms. The same might be tried for perfectionist goals and personal commitments. My reason for thinking that such explanations are unsuccessful, or at best partially successful, is not just that they imply specific moral conclusions that I find intuitively unacceptable (for it is always conceivable that a new refinement of the theory may iron out many of those wrinkles). Rather, my reason for doubt is theoretical: I do not believe that the source of value

is unitary – displaying apparent multiplicity only in its application to the world. I believe that value has fundamentally
different kinds of sources, and that they are reflected in the
classification of values into types. Not all values represent the
pursuit of some single good in a variety of settings.

Think for example of the contrast between perfectionist and
utilitarian values. They are *formally* different, for the latter takes
into account the number of people whose interests are affected,
and the former does not. Perfectionist values have to do with the
mere level of achievement and not with the spread either of
achievement or of gratification. There is also a formal contrast
between rights or obligations and any ends, whether utilitarian
or perfectionist, that are defined in terms of the outcome of
actions – in terms of how things are as a result. The claims
represented by individual obligations begin with relations between individuals, and although the maintenance of those relations in a satisfactory form must be part of any utilitarian
conception of a good state of affairs, that is not the basic motive
behind claims of obligation. It may be a good thing that people
keep their promises or look after their children, but the reason a
person has to keep his own promises is very different from the
reason he has to want other people unconnected with him to
keep their promises – just because it would be a good thing,
impersonally considered. A person does not feel bound to keep
his promises or look after his children because it would be a
good thing, impersonally considered. There certainly are things
we do for such reasons, but in the motive behind obligations a
more personal outlook is essential. It is your *own* relation to the
other person or the institution or community that moves you,
not a detached concern for what would be best overall.

Reasons of this kind may be described as agent-centered or
subjective (though the term 'subjective' here should not be
misunderstood – it does not mean that the general principles of
obligation are matters of subjective preference which may vary
from person to person). The reasons in each case apply primarily
to the individual involved, as reasons for *him* to want to fulfil his
obligations – even though it is also a good thing, impersonally
considered, for him to do so.

General rights are less personal in their claims, since a right to
be free from interference or assault, for example, does not derive

from the possessor's relation to anyone in particular: everyone is obliged to respect it. Nevertheless, they are agent-centered in the sense that the reasons for action they provide apply primarily to individuals whose actions are in danger of infringing such rights. Rights mainly provide people with reasons not to do certain things to other people – not to treat them or interfere with them in certain ways. Again, it is objectively a good thing that people's rights not be violated, and this provides disinterested parties with some reason for seeing that X's rights are not violated by Y. But this is a secondary motive, not so powerful as the reason one has not to violate anyone's rights directly. (That is why it is reasonable for defenders of civil liberties to object to police and judicial practices that violate the rights of criminal suspects, even when the aim of those policies is to prevent greater violations by criminals of the rights of their victims.) In that sense the claims deriving from general rights are agent-centered: less so than those deriving from special obligations, but still definitely agent-centered in a sense in which the claims of utility or perfectionist ends are not. Those latter claims are impersonal or outcome-centered; they have to do with what happens, not, in the first instance, with what one does. It is the contribution of what one does to what happens or what is achieved that matters.

This great division between personal and impersonal, or between agent-centered and outcome-centered, or subjective and objective reasons, is so basic that it renders implausible any reductive unification of ethics – let alone of practical reasoning in general. The formal differences among these types of reasons correspond to deep differences in their sources. We appreciate the force of impersonal reasons when we detach from our personal situation and our special relations to others. Utilitarian considerations arise in this way when our detachment takes the form of adopting a general point of view that comprehends everyone's view of the world within it. Naturally the results will not always be clear. But such an outlook is obviously very different from that which appears in a person's concern for his special obligations to his family, friends, or colleagues. There he is thinking very much of his particular situation in the world. The two motives come from two different points of view, both important, but fundamentally irreducible to a common basis.

I have said nothing about the still more agent-centered motive of commitment to one's own projects, but since that involves one's own life and not necessarily any relations with others, the same points obviously apply. It is a source of reasons that cannot be assimilated either to utility, or perfectionism, or rights, or obligations (except that they might be described as obligations to oneself).

My general point is that the formal differences among types of reason reflect differences of a fundamental nature in their sources, and that this rules out a certain kind of solution to conflicts among these types. Human beings are subject to moral and other motivational claims of very different kinds. This is because they are complex creatures who can view the world from many perspectives – individual, relational, impersonal, ideal, etc. – and each perspective presents a different set of claims. Conflict can exist within one of these sets, and it may be hard to resolve. But when conflict occurs between them, the problem is still more difficult. Conflicts between personal and impersonal claims are ubiquitous. They cannot, in my view, be resolved by subsuming either of the points of view under the other, or both under a third. Nor can we simply abandon any of them. There is no reason why we should. The capacity to view the world simultaneously from the point of view of one's relations to others, from the point of view of one's life extended through time, from the point of view of everyone at once, and finally from the detached viewpoint often described as the view *sub specie aeternitatis* is one of the marks of humanity. This complex capacity is an obstacle to simplification.

Does this mean, then, that basic practical conflicts have no solution? The unavailability of a single, reductive method or a clear set of priorities for settling them does not remove the necessity for making decisions in such cases. When faced with conflicting and incommensurable claims we still have to do something – even if it is only to do nothing. And the fact that action must be unitary seems to imply that unless justification is also unitary, nothing can be either right or wrong and all decisions under conflict are arbitrary.

I believe this is wrong, but the alternative is hard to explain. Briefly, I contend that there can be good judgment without total justification, either explicit or implicit. The fact that one cannot say why a certain decision is the correct one, given a particular balance of conflicting reasons, does not mean that the claim to correctness is meaningless. Provided one has taken the process of practical justification as far as it will go in the course of arriving at the conflict, one may be able to proceed without further justification, but without irrationality either. What makes this possible is *judgment* – essentially the faculty Aristotle described as practical wisdom, which reveals itself over time in individual decisions rather than in the enunciation of general principles. It will not always yield a solution: there are true practical dilemmas that have no solution, and there are also conflicts so complex that judgment cannot operate confidently. But in many cases it can be relied on to take up the slack that remains beyond the limits of explicit rational argument.

This view has sometimes been regarded as defeatist and empty since it was expressed by Aristotle. In reply, let me say two things. First, the position does not imply that we should abandon the search for more and better reasons and more critical insight in the domain of practical decision. It is just that our capacity to resolve conflicts in particular cases may extend beyond our capacity to enunciate general principles that explain those resolutions. Perhaps we are working with general principles unconsciously, and can discover them by codifying our decisions and particular intuitions. But this is not necessary either for the operation or for the development of judgment. Second, the search for general principles in ethics, or other aspects of practical reasoning, is more likely to be successful if systematic theories restrict themselves to one aspect of the subject – one component of rational motivation – than if they try to be comprehensive.

To look for a single general theory of how to decide the right thing to do is like looking for a single theory of how to decide what to believe. Such progress as we have made in the systematic justification and criticism of beliefs has not come mostly from general principles of reasoning but from the understanding of particular areas, marked out by the different sciences, by history, by mathematics. These vary in exactness, and large areas of belief are left out of the scope of any theory. These must be governed by common sense and ordinary, prescientific reasoning. Such reasoning must also be used where the results of various more systematic methods bear on the matter at hand, but no one of them determines a conclusion. In civil engineering problems, for example, the solution depends both on physical factors capable of precise calculation and behavioral or psychological factors that are not. Obviously one should use exact principles and methods to deal with those aspects of a problem for which they are available, but sometimes there are other aspects as well, and one must resist the temptation either to ignore them or to treat them by exact methods to which they are not susceptible.

We are familiar with this fragmentation of understanding and method when it comes to belief, but we tend to resist it in the case of decision. Yet it is as irrational to despair of systematic ethics because one cannot find a completely general account of what should be done as it would be to give up scientific research because there is no general method of arriving at true beliefs. I am not saying that ethics is a science, only that the relation between ethical theory and practical decisions is analogous to the relation between scientific theory and beliefs about particular things or events in the world.

In both areas, some problems are much purer than others, that is, their solutions are more completely determined by factors that admit of precise understanding. Sometimes the only significant factor in a practical decision is personal obligation, or general utility, and then one's reasoning can be confined to that (however precisely it may be understood). Sometimes a process of decision is artificially insulated against the influence of more than one type of factor. This is not always a good thing, but sometimes it is. The example I have in mind is the judicial process, which carefully excludes, or tries to exclude, considerations of utility and personal commitment, and limits itself to claims of right. Since the systematic recognition of such claims is very important (and also tends over the long run not to conflict unacceptably with other values), it is worth isolating these factors for special treatment. As a result, legal argument has been one of the areas of real progress in the understanding of a special aspect of practical reason. Systematic theory and the search for general principles and methods may succeed elsewhere if we accept a fragmentary approach. Utilitarian theory, for example, has a great deal to contribute if it is not required to account for everything. Utility is an extremely important factor in decisions, particularly in public policy, and philosophical work on its definition, the coordination problems arising in the design of institutions to promote utility, its connections with preference, with equality, and with efficiency, can have an impact on such decisions.

This and other areas can be the scene of progress even if none of them aspires to the status of a general and complete theory of right and wrong. There will never be such a theory, in my view, since the role of judgment in resolving conflicts and applying disparate claims and considerations to real life is indispensable. Two dangers can be avoided if this idea of noncomprehensive systematization is kept in mind. One is the danger of romantic defeatism, which abandons rational theory because it inevitably leaves many problems unsolved. The other is the danger of exclusionary overrationalization, which bars as irrelevant or empty all considerations that cannot be brought within the scope of a general system admitting explicit defensible conclusions. This yields skewed results by counting only measurable or otherwise precisely describable factors, even when others are in fact relevant. The alternative is to recognize that the legitimate grounds of decision are extremely various and understood to different degrees. This has both theoretical and practical implications.

On the theoretical side, I have said that progress in particular areas of ethics and value theory need not wait for the discovery of a general foundation (even if there is such a thing). This is recognized by many philosophers and has recently been urged by John Rawls, who claims not only that the pursuit of substantive moral theory, for example the theory of justice, can proceed independently of views about the foundation of ethics, but that until substantive theory is further developed, the search for foundations may be premature.[2]

This seems too strong, but it is certainly true of any field that one need not make progress at the most fundamental level to make progress at all. Chemistry went through great develop-

---

[2] John Rawls, *A Theory of Justice* (Cambridge: Harvard University Press, 1971), pp. 51–60. See also 'The Independence of Moral Theory', *Proceedings and Addresses of the American Philosophical Association* (1974–5) pp. 5–22.

ments during the century before its basis in atomic physics came to be understood. Mendelian genetics was developed long before any understanding of the molecular basis of heredity. At present, progress in psychology must be pursued to a great extent independently of any idea about its basis in the operation of the brain. It may be that all psychological phenomena are ultimately explainable in terms of the theory of the central nervous system, but our present understanding of that system is too meager to permit us even to look for a way to close the gap.

The corresponding theoretical division in ethics need not be so extreme. We can continue to work on the foundations while exploring the superstructure, and the two pursuits should reinforce each other. I myself do not believe that all value rests on a single foundation or can be combined into a unified system, because different types of values represent the development and articulation of different points of view, all of which combine to produce decisions. Ethics is unlike physics, which represents one point of view, that which apprehends the spatiotemporal properties of the universe described in mathematical terms. Even in this case, where it is reasonable to seek a unified theory of all physical phenomena, it is also possible to understand a great deal about more particular aspects of the physical universe – gravitation, mechanics, electromagnetic fields, radiation, nuclear forces – without having such a theory.

But ethics is more like understanding or knowledge in general than it is like physics. Just as our understanding of the world involves various points of view – among which the austere viewpoint of physics is the most powerfully developed and one of the most important – so values come from a number of viewpoints, some more personal than others, which cannot be reduced to a common denominator any more than history, psychology, philology, and economics can be reduced to physics. Just as the types of understanding available to us are distinct, even though they must all coexist and cooperate in our minds, so the types of value that move us are disparate, even though they must cooperate as well as they can in determining what we do.

With regard to practical implications, it seems to me that the fragmentation of effort and of results that is theoretically to be expected in the domain of value has implications for the strategy to be used in applying these results to practical decisions, especially questions of public policy. The lack of a general theory of value should not be an obstacle to the employment of those areas of understanding that do exist; and we know more than is generally appreciated. The lack of a general theory leads too easily to a false dichotomy: either fall back entirely on the unsystematic intuitive judgment of whoever has to make a decision, or else cook up a unified but artificial system like cost-benefit analysis,[3] which will grind out decisions on any problem presented to it. (Such systems may be useful if their claims and scope of operation are less ambitious.) What is needed instead is a mixed strategy, combining systematic results where these are applicable with less systematic judgment to fill in the gaps.

However, this requires the development of an approach to decisions that will use available ethical understanding where it is relevant. Such an approach is now being sought by different groups working in applied ethics, with what success we shall not know for some time. I want to suggest that the fragmentation of value provides a rationale for a particular way of looking at the task, and an indication of what needs to be done.

What we need most is a method of breaking up or analyzing practical problems to say what evaluative principles apply, and how. This is not a method of decision. Perhaps in special cases it would yield a decision, but more usually it would simply indicate the points at which different kinds of ethical considerations needed to be introduced to supply the basis for a responsible and intelligent decision. This component approach to problems is familiar enough in connection with other disciplines. It is expected that important policy decisions may depend on economic factors, political factors, ecological factors, medical safety, scientific progress, technological advantages, military security, and other concerns. Advice on all these matters can be obtained by responsible officials if there is anyone available whose job it is to think about them. In some cases well-established disciplines are involved. Their practitioners may vary widely in understanding of the subject, and on many issues they will disagree with one another. But even to be exposed to

---

[3] See Lawrence Tribe, 'Policy Science: Analysis or Ideology?', *Philosophy & Public Affairs*, II, no. 1 (Fall, 1972), 66–110.

these controversies (about inflation or nuclear power safety or recombinant DNA risk) is better than hearing nothing at all. Moreover it is important that within most serious disciplines there is agreement about what is controversial and what is not. Anyone with an important decision to make, whether he is a legislator or a cabinet officer or a department official, can get advice on different aspects of the problem from people who have thought much more than he has about each of those aspects, and know what others have said about it. The division of disciplines and a consensus about what dimensions of a problem have to be considered are very useful in bringing together the problems and such expertise as there is.

We need a comparable consensus about what important ethical and evaluative questions have to be considered if a policy decision is to be made responsibly. This is not the same thing as a consensus in ethics. It means only that there are certain aspects of any problem that most people who work in ethics and value theory would agree should be considered, and can be professionally considered in such a way that whoever is going to make the decision will be exposed to the relevant ideas currently available. Sometimes the best ideas will not be very good, or they will include diametrically opposed views; but this is true everywhere, not just in ethics.

It might be suggested that the best approach would be to emulate the legal system by setting up an advocacy procedure before a kind of court whose job would be to render decisions on ethically loaded policy questions. (The recent proposal of a science court shows the attractions of the legal model: its non-democratic character has great intellectual appeal.) But I think the actual situation is too fluid for anything like that. Values are relevant to policy in too many ways, and in combination with too many other kinds of knowledge and opinion, to be treatable in this manner. Although some legal decisions are very difficult, courts are designed to decide clear, narrowly defined questions to which a relatively limited set of arguments and reasons is relevant. (Think of the function of a judge in striking material from the record or refusing to admit certain data or testimony in evidence: such restrictions do not in general apply to legislative or administrative deliberations.) Most practical issues are much messier than this, and their ethical dimensions are much more complex. One needs a method of insuring that where relevant understanding exists, it is made available, and where there is an aspect of the problem that no one understands very well, this is understood too.

I have not devised such a method, but clearly it would have to provide that factors considered should include, among others, the following: economic, political, and personal liberty, equality, equity, privacy, procedural fairness, intellectual and aesthetic development, community, general utility, desert, avoidance of arbitrariness, acceptance of risk, the interests of future generations, the weight to be given to interests of other states or countries. There is much to be said about each of these. The method would have to be more organized to be useful, but a general position on the ways in which ethics is relevant to policy could probably be agreed on by a wide range of ethical theorists, from relativists to utilitarians to Kantians. Radical disagreement about the basis of ethics is compatible with substantial agreement about what the important factors are in real life. If this consensus, which I believe already exists among ethical theorists, were to gain wider acceptance among the public and those who make policy, then the extensive but fragmented understanding that we possess in this area could be put to better use than it is now. It would then be more difficult simply to ignore certain questions, and even if the ethical considerations, once offered, were disregarded or rejected, the reasons or absence of reasons for such rejection would become part of the basis for any decision made. There is a modicum of power even in being able to state a *prima facie* case.

This conception of the role of moral theory also implies an answer to the question of its relation to politics, and other methods of decision. Ethics is not being recommended as a decision procedure, but as an essential resource for making decisions, just as physics, economics, and demography are. In fundamental constitutional decisions of the Supreme Court, one branch of ethics plays a central role in a process that takes precedence over the usual methods of political and administrative decision. But for most of the questions that need deciding, ethical considerations are multiple, complex, often cloudy, and mixed up with many others. They need to be considered in a systematic way, but in most cases a reasonable decision can be reached only by sound judgment, informed as well as possible by the best arguments that any relevant disciplines have to offer.

10

Ethics without Biology

The usefulness of a biological approach to ethics depends on what ethics is. If it is just a certain type of behavioral pattern or habit, accompanied by some emotional responses, then biological theories can be expected to teach us a great deal about it. But if it is a theoretical inquiry that can be approached by rational methods, and that has internal standards of justification and criticism, the attempt to understand it from outside by means of biology will be much less valuable. This is true for the same reason that the search for a biological explanation of mathematical or physical theories, or biological theories for that matter, would be relatively futile. First, we have no general biological understanding of human thought. Second, it is not a fixed set of behavioral and intellectual habits but a process of development that advances by constant reexamination of the total body of results to date. A being who is engaged in such an open-ended process of discovery cannot at the same time understand it fully from outside: otherwise he would have a decision procedure rather than a critical method. In most interesting subjects we do not want a decision procedure because we want to pursue a deeper level of understanding than that represented by our current questions and the methods we have for answering them.

No one, to my knowledge, has suggested a biological theory of mathematics, yet the biological approach to ethics has aroused a great deal of interest. There is a reason for this. Ethics exists on both the behavioral and the theoretical level. Its appearance in some form in every culture and subculture as a pattern of conduct and judgments about conduct is more conspicuous than its theoretical treatment by philosophers, political and legal theorists, utopian anarchists, and evangelical reformers. Not only is ethical theory and the attempt at ethical discovery less socially conspicuous than common behavioral morality, but the amount of disagreement about ethics at both levels produces doubt that it is a field for rational discovery at all. Perhaps there is nothing to be discovered about it by such methods, and it can be understood *only* as a social and psychological peculiarity of human life. In that case biology will provide a good foundation, though psychology and sociology will be important as well.

In this essay I want to explain the reality of ethics as a theoretical subject. Its progress is slow and uncertain, but it is important both in itself and in relation to the non-theoretical forms that ethics takes, because the two levels influence each other. The ethical commonplaces of any period include ideas that may have been radical discoveries in a previous age. This is true of modern conceptions of liberty, equality, and democracy, and we are in the midst of ethical debates which will probably result two hundred years hence in a disseminated moral sensibility that people of our time would find very unfamiliar. Although the rate of progress is much slower, the form of these developments is somewhat analogous to the gradual assimilation of revolutionary scientific discoveries into the common worldview.

As in science, also, by the time one advance has been widely assimilated it is being superseded by the next, and further developments use accepted current understanding as the basis for extension and revision. In ethics the two levels interact in both directions, and the division between them is not sharp. Acute questions of social policy produce widespread attempts to theorize about the basic principles of ethics.

A common idea of progress is found in all these fields, although it is not very well understood in any of them. It is assumed that we begin, as a species, with certain primitive intuitions and responses that may have biological sources. But in addition we have a critical capacity that has allowed us, starting a long time ago, to assess, systematize, extend, and in some cases reject these pre-reflective responses. Instead of estimating size and weight by touch and vision, we develop devices of measurement. Instead of guessing about numerical quantities we develop mathematical reasoning. Instead of sticking to an idea of the physical world that comes directly from our senses, we have progressively asked questions and developed methods of answering them that yield a picture of physical reality farther and farther removed from appearance. We could not have done any of these things if we had not, as a species, had some pre-reflective, intuitive beliefs about numbers and the world. Progress beyond this has required both the efforts of creative individuals and the communal activities of criticism, justification, acceptance, and rejection. The motivating idea has been that there is always more to be discovered, that our current intuitions or understanding, even if commendable for their date, are only a stage in an indefinite developmental process.

In applying this idea to ethics we must allow for the big difference that ethics is meant to govern action, not just belief. In trying to solve ethical problems we are trying to find out how to live and how to arrange our social institutions – we are not just trying to develop a more accurate picture of the world and the people in it. Therefore ethics is connected with motivation. It begins not with pre-reflective ideas about what the world is like, but with pre-reflective ideas about what to do, how to live, and how to treat other people. It progresses by the subjection of these impulses to examination, codification, questioning, criticism, and so on. As in other areas, this is partly an individual process and partly a social one. And the progress of earlier ages is included as part of the socialization of members of later ones, some of whom may make advances in turn.

The development in this case is not just intellectual but motivational, and it cannot be pursued exclusively by small groups of experts, as some scientific or technical subjects can. Because the questions are about how men should live and how societies should be arranged, the answers must be accepted and internalized by many people to take effect, even if only as steps in a continuing process. Though they need not be internalized equally by everyone, this requirement makes ethics a more democratic subject than any science, and severely limits its rate of progress. The community of debate is not a set of experts, except in special institutional cases like the judicial system.

Still, the premise of this view of ethics as a subject for rational development is that motives, like beliefs, can be criticized, justified, and improved – in other words that there is such a thing as practical reason. This means that we can reason not only, as Hume thought, about the most effective methods of achieving what we want, but also about what we should want, both for ourselves and for others.

It is of the utmost importance that such an investigation, such reasoning, is internal to the subject. It does not proceed by the application to this subject of methods developed in relation to other subjects, or of a general method of problem-solving and question-answering. While there are some extremely general conditions of rationality, they will not get you very far in any specific area of inquiry. Whether it is molecular biology, algebra, or distributive justice, one has to develop questions, concepts, arguments, and principles by thinking about that field and allowing reason and intuition to respond to its specific character. It happens again and again that the methods of one subject are taken as a model of intellectual respectability or objective rationality, and are then applied to a quite different subject for which they were not developed and for which they are unsuited. The results are shallow questions, nonexplanatory theories, and the anathematization of important questions as meaningless. Fields that lack a well-developed method of their own, like the social sciences, psychology, and ethics, are particularly vulnerable to such intellectual displacement.

The point is that ethics is a subject. It is pursued by methods that are continually being developed in response to the problems that arise within it. Obviously the creatures who engage in this activity are organisms about whom we can learn a great deal from biology. Moreover their capacity to perform the reflective and critical tasks involved is presumably somehow a function of their organic structure. But it would be as foolish to seek a biological evolutionary explanation of ethics as it would be to seek such an explanation of the development of physics. The development of physics is an intellectual process. Presumably the human intellectual capacity that has permitted this extremely rapid process to occur was in some way an effect, perhaps only a side-effect, of a process of biological evolution that took a very long time. But the latter can provide no explanation of physical theories that is not trivial. What human beings have discovered in themselves is a capacity to subject their pre-reflective or innate responses to criticism and revision, and to create new forms of understanding. It is the exercise of that rational capacity that explains the theories.

Ethics, though more primitive, is similar. It is the result of a human capacity to subject innate or conditioned pre-reflective motivational and behavioral patterns to criticism and revision, and to create new forms of conduct. The capacity to do this presumably has some biological foundation, even if it is only a side-effect of other developments. But the history of the exercise of this capacity and its continual reapplication in criticism and revision of its own products is not part of biology. Biology may tell us about perceptual and motivational starting points, but in its present state it has little bearing on the thinking process by which these starting points are transcended.

There may be biological obstacles to the achievement of certain kinds of moral progress. Without question there are psychological and social obstacles, and some of them may have biological causes. That does not make them insurmountable. They must be recognized and dealt with by any moral theory that is not utopian. But this recognition does not amount to acceptance of a biological foundation for ethics. It is no more than an acknowledgment that morality, like any other process of cultural development, must reckon with its starting points and with the nature of the materials it is attempting to transform.

11

Brain Bisection and the Unity of Consciousness

I

There has been considerable optimism recently, among philosophers and neuroscientists, concerning the prospect for major discoveries about the neurophysiological basis of mind. The support for this optimism has been extremely abstract and general. I wish to present some grounds for pessimism. That type of self-understanding may encounter limits which have not been generally foreseen: the personal, mentalist idea of human beings may resist the sort of coordination with an understanding of humans as physical systems, that would be necessary to yield anything describable as an understanding of the physical basis of mind. I shall not consider what alternatives will be open to us if we should encounter such limits. I shall try to present grounds for believing that the limits may exist – grounds derived from extensive data now available about the interaction between the two halves of the cerebral cortex, and about what happens when they are disconnected. The feature of the mentalist conception of persons which may be recalcitrant to integration with these data is not a trivial or peripheral one, that might easily be abandoned. It is the idea of a *single* person, a single subject of experience and action, that is in difficulties. The difficulties may be surmountable in ways I have not foreseen. On the other hand, this may be only the first of many dead ends that will emerge as we seek a physiological understanding of the mind.

To seek the physical basis or realization of features of the phenomenal world is in many areas a profitable first line of inquiry, and it is the line encouraged, for the case of mental phenomena, by those who look forward to some variety of empirical reduction of mind to brain, through an identity theory, a functionalist theory, or some other device. When physical reductionism is attempted for a phenomenal feature of the external world, the results are sometimes very successful, and can be pushed to deeper and deeper levels. If, on the other hand, they are not entirely successful, and certain features of the phenomenal picture remain unexplained by a physical reduction, then we can set those features aside as *purely* phenomenal, and postpone our understanding of them to the time when our knowledge of the physical basis of mind and perception will have advanced sufficiently to supply it. (An example of this might be the moon illusion, or other sensory illusions which have no discoverable basis in the objects perceived.)

However, if we encounter the same kind of difficulty in exploring the physical basis of the phenomena of the mind itself, we cannot adopt the same line of retreat. That is, if a phenomenal feature of mind is left unaccounted for by the physical theory, we cannot postpone the understanding of it to the time when we study the mind itself – for that is exactly what we are supposed to be doing. To defer to an understanding of the basis of mind which lies beyond the study of the physical realization of certain aspects of it is to admit the irreducibility of the mental to the physical. A clearcut version of this admission would be some kind of dualism. But if one is reluctant to take such a route, then it is not clear what one should do about central features of the mentalistic idea of persons which resist assimilation to an understanding of human beings as physical systems. It may be true of some of these features that we can neither find an objective basis for them, nor give them up. It may be impossible for us to abandon certain ways of conceiving and representing ourselves, no matter how little support they get from scientific research. This, I suspect, is true of the idea of the unity of a person: an idea whose validity may be called into question with the help of recent discoveries about the functional duality of the cerebral cortex. It will be useful to present those results here in outline.

II

The higher connections between the two cerebral hemispheres have been severed in men, monkeys, and cats, and the results have led some investigators to speak of the creation of two separate centers of consciousness in a single body. The facts are as follows.[1] By and large, the left cerebral hemisphere is associated with the right side of the body and the right hemisphere with the left side. Tactual stimuli from one side are transmitted to the opposite hemisphere – with the exception of the head and neck, which are connected to both sides. In addition, the left half of each retina, i.e. that which scans the right half of the visual field, sends impulses to the left hemisphere, and impulses from the left half of the visual field are transmitted by the right half of each retina to the right hemisphere. Auditory impulses from each ear are to some degree transmitted to both hemispheres. Smells, on the other hand, are transmitted ipsilaterally: the left nostril transmits to the left hemisphere and the right nostril to the right. Finally, the left hemisphere usually controls the production of speech.

Both hemispheres are linked to the spinal column and peripheral nerves through a common brain stem, but they also communicate directly with one another, by a large transverse band of nerve fibres called the corpus callosum, plus some smaller pathways. These direct cerebral commissures play an essential role in the ordinary integration of function between the hemispheres of normal persons. It is one of the striking features of the subject that this fact remained unknown, at least in the English-speaking world, until the late 1950s, even though a number of patients had had their cerebral commissures surgi-

---

[1] The literature on split brains is sizeable. An excellent recent survey is Michael S. Gazzaniga, *The Bisected Brain* (New York: Appleton-Century-Crofts, 1970). Its nine-page list of references is not intended to be a complete bibliography of the subject, however. Gazzaniga has also written a brief popular exposition: 'The Split Brain in Man', *Scientific American*, CCXVII (1967), 24–9. The best general treatment for philosophical purposes is to be found in several papers by R. W. Sperry, the leading investigator in the field: 'The Great Cerebral Commissure', *Scientific American*, CCX (1964), 42; 'Brain Bisection and Mechanisms of Consciousness', in *Brain and Conscious Experience*, ed. J. C. Eccles, (Berlin: Springer-Verlag, 1966); 'Mental Unity Following Surgical Disconnections of the Cerebral Hemispheres', *The Harvey Lectures*, series LXII (New York: Academic Press, 1968), pp. 293–323; 'Hemisphere Deconnection and Unity in Conscious Awareness', *American Psychologist*, XXIII (1968), 723–33. Several interesting papers are to be found in *Functions of the Corpus Callosum: Ciba Foundation Study Group No. 20*, ed G. Ettlinger (London: J. and A. Churchill, 1965).

cally severed in operations for the treatment of epilepsy a decade earlier. No significant behavioral or mental effects on these patients could be observed, and it was conjectured that the corpus callosum had no function whatever, except perhaps to keep the hemispheres from sagging.

Then R. E. Myers and R. W. Sperry introduced a technique

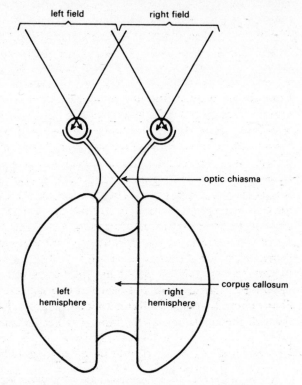

left field   right field

optic chiasma

left   right
hemisphere   hemisphere

corpus callosum

Fig. 1   A very schematic top view of the eyes and cerebral cortex.

for dealing with the two hemispheres separately.[2] They sectioned the optic chiasma of cats, so that each eye sent direct

[2] R. E. Myers and R. W. Sperry, 'Interocular Transfer of a Visual Form Discrimination Habit in Cats after Section of the Optic Chiasm and Corpus Callosum', *Anatomical Record*, cxv (1953), 351–2; R. E. Myers, 'Interocular Transfer of Pattern Discrimination in Cats Following Section of Crossed Optic Fibers', *Journal of Comparative and Physiological Psychology*, xlviii (1955), 470–3.

information (information about the opposite half of the visual field) only to one side of the brain. It was then possible to train the cats in simple tasks using one eye, and to see what happened when one made them use the other eye instead. In cats whose callosum was intact, there was very good transfer of learning. But in some cats, they severed the corpus callosum as well as the optic chiasma; and in these cases nothing was transmitted from one side to the other. In fact the two severed sides could be taught conflicting discriminations simultaneously, by giving the two eyes opposite stimuli during a single course of reinforcement. Nevertheless this capacity for independent function did not result in serious defects of behavior. Unless inputs to the two hemispheres were artificially segregated, the animal seemed normal (though if a split-brain monkey gets hold of a peanut with both hands, the result is sometimes a tug of war.)

Instead of summarizing all the data, I shall concentrate on the human cases, a reconsideration of which was prompted by the findings with cats and monkeys.[3] In the brain-splitting operation for epilepsy, the optic chiasma is left intact, so one cannot get at the two hemispheres separately just through the two eyes. The solution to the problem of controlling visual input is to flash signals on a screen, on one or other side of the midpoint of the patient's gaze, long enough to be perceived but not long enough to permit an eye movement which would bring the signal to the opposite half visual field and hence to the opposite side of the brain. This is known as tachistoscopic stimulation. Tactile inputs through the hands are for the most part very efficiently segregated, and so are smells through the two nostrils. Some success has even been achieved recently in segregating auditory input,

---

[3] The first publication of these results was M. S. Gazzaniga, J. E. Bogen, and R. W. Sperry, 'Some Functional Effects of Sectioning the Cerebral Commissures in Man', *Proceedings of the National Academy of Sciences*, XLVIII (1962), pt 2, 1765–9. Interestingly, the same year saw publication of a paper proposing the interpretation of a case of human brain *damage* along similar lines, suggested by the earlier findings with animals. Cf. N. Geschwind and E. Kaplan, 'A Human Cerebral Deconnection Syndrome', *Neurology*, XII (1962), 675. Also of interest is Geschwind's long two-part survey of the field, which takes up some philosophical questions explicitly: 'Disconnexion Syndromes in Animals and Man', *Brain* LXXXVIII (1965) 247–94, 585–644. Parts of it are reprinted, with other material, in *Boston Studies in the Philosophy of Science*, vol. IV (1969). See also his paper 'The Organization of Language and the Brain', *Science*, CLXX (1970), 940.

since each ear seems to signal more powerfully to the contralateral than to the ipsilateral hemisphere. As for output, the clearest distinction is provided by speech, which is exclusively the product of the left hemisphere.[4] Writing is a less clear case: it can occasionally be produced in rudimentary form by the right hemisphere, using the left hand. In general, motor control is contralateral, i.e. by the opposite hemisphere, but a certain amount of ipsilateral control sometimes occurs, particularly on the part of the left hemisphere.

The results are as follows. What is flashed to the right half of the visual field, or felt unseen by the right hand, can be reported verbally. What is flashed to the left half field or felt by the left hand cannot be reported, though if the word 'hat' is flashed on the left, the left hand will retrieve a hat from a group of concealed objects if the person is told to pick out what he has seen. At the same time he will insist verbally that he saw nothing. Or, if two different words are flashed to the two half fields (e.g. 'pencil' and 'toothbrush') and the individual is told to retrieve the corresponding object from beneath a screen, with both hands, then the hands will search the collection of objects independently, the right hand picking up the pencil and discarding it while the left hand searches for it, and the left hand similarly rejecting the toothbrush which the right hand lights upon with satisfaction.

If a concealed object is placed in the left hand and the person is asked to guess what it is, wrong guesses will elicit an annoyed frown, since the right hemisphere, which receives the tactile information, also hears the answers. If the speaking hemisphere should guess correctly, the result is a smile. A smell fed to the right nostril (which stimulates the right hemisphere) will elicit a verbal denial that the subject smells anything, but if asked to point with the left hand at a corresponding object he will succeed in picking out, for example, a clove of garlic, protesting all the while that he smells absolutely nothing, so how can he possibly point to what he smells. If the smell is an unpleasant one like that

---

[4] There are individual exceptions to this, as there are to most generalizations about cerebral function: left-handed people tend to have bilateral linguistic control, and it is common in early childhood. All the subjects of these experiments, however, were right-handed, and displayed left cerebral dominance.

of rotten eggs, these denials will be accompanied by wrinklings of the nose and mouth, and guttural exclamations of disgust.[5]

One particularly poignant example of conflict between the hemispheres is as follows. A pipe is placed out of sight in the patient's left hand, and he is then asked to write with his left hand what he was holding. Very laboriously and heavily, the left hand writes the letters P and I. Then suddenly the writing speeds up and becomes lighter, the I is converted to an E, and the word is completed as PENCIL. Evidently the left hemisphere has made a guess based on the appearance of the first two letters, and has interfered, with ipsilatral control. But then the right hemisphere takes over control of the hand again, heavily crosses out the letters ENCIL, and draws a crude picture of pipe.[6]

There are many more data. The split brain patient cannot tell whether shapes flashed to the two half visual fields or held out of sight in the two hands are the same or different – even if he is asked to indicate the answer by nodding or shaking his head (responses available to both hemispheres). The subject cannot distinguish a continuous from a discontinuous line flashed across both halves of the visual field, if the break comes in the middle. Nor can he tell whether two lines meet at an angle, if the joint is in the middle. Nor can he tell whether two spots in opposite half-fields are the same or different in color – though he can do all these things if the images to be compared fall within a single half field. On the whole the right hemisphere does better at spatial relations tests, but is almost incapable of calculation. It appears susceptible to emotion, however. For example, if a photograph of a naked woman is flashed to the left half field of a male patient, he will grin broadly and perhaps blush, without being able to say what has pleased him, though he may say 'Wow, that's quite a machine you've got there'.

All this is combined with what appears to be complete

[5] H. W. Gordon and R. W. Sperry, 'Lateralization of Olfactory Perception in the Surgically Separated Hemispheres in Man', *Neuropsychologia*, VII (1969), 111–20. One patient, however, was able to say in these circumstances that he smelled something unpleasant, without being able to describe it further.

[6] Reported in Jerre Levy, 'Information Processing and Higher Psychological Functions in the Disconnected Hemispheres of Human Commissurotomy Patients' (unpublished doctoral dissertation, California Institute of Technology, 1969).

normalcy in ordinary activities, when no segregation of input to the two hemispheres has been artificially created. Both sides fall asleep and wake up at the same time. The patients can play the piano, button their shirts, swim, and perform well in other activities requiring bilateral coordination. Moreover they do not report any sensation of division or reduction of the visual field. The most notable deviation in ordinary behavior was in a patient whose left hand appeared to be somewhat hostile to the patient's wife. But by and large the hemispheres cooperate admirably, and it requires subtle experimental techniques to get them to operate separately. If one is not careful, they will give each other peripheral cues, transmitting information by audible, visible, or otherwise sensorily perceptible signals which compensate for the lack of a direct commissural link. (One form of communication is particularly difficult to prevent, because it is so direct: both hemispheres can move the neck and facial muscles, and both can feel them move; so a response produced in the face or head by the right hemisphere can be detected by the left, and there is some evidence that they send signals to one another via this medium.)[7]

III

What one naturally wants to know about these patients is how many minds they have. This immediately raises questions about the sense in which an ordinary person can be said to have one mind, and what the conditions are under which diverse experiences and activities can be ascribed to the same mind. We must have some idea what an ordinary person is one of in order to understand what we want to know whether there is *one or two* of, when we try to describe these extraordinary patients.

However, instead of beginning with an analysis of the unity of the mind, I am going to proceed by attempting to apply the

[7] Moreover, the condition of radical disconnection may not be stable: there may be a tendency toward the formation of new interhemispheric pathways through the brain stem, with the lapse of time. This is supported partly by observation of commissurotomy patients, but more importantly by cases of agenesis of the callosum. People who have grown up without one have learned to manage without it; their performance on the tests is much closer to normal than that of recently operated patients. (Cf. L. J. Saul and R. W. Sperry, 'Absence of Commissurotomy Symptoms and Agenesis of the Corpus Callosum', *Neurology*, XVIII (1968).) This fact is very important, but for the present I shall put it aside to concentrate on the immediate results of disconnection.

ordinary, unanalyzed conception directly in the interpretation of these data, asking whether the patients have one mind, or two, or some more exotic configuration. My conclusion will be that the ordinary conception of a single, countable mind cannot be applied to them at all, and that there is no number of such minds that they possess, though they certainly engage in mental activity. A clearer understanding of the idea of an individual mind should emerge in the course of this discussion but the difficulties which stand in the way of its application to the split-brain cases will provide ground for more general doubts. The concept may not be applicable to ordinary human beings either, for it embodies too simple a conception of the way in which human beings function.

Nevertheless I shall employ the notion of an individual mind in discussing the cases initially, for I wish to consider systematically how they might be understood in terms of countable minds, and to argue that they cannot be. After having done this, I shall turn to ordinary people like you and me.

There appear to be five interpretations of the experimental data which utilize the concept of an individual mind.

(1) The patients have one fairly normal mind associated with the left hemisphere, and the responses emanating from the nonverbal right hemisphere are the responses of an automaton, and are not produced by conscious mental processes.

(2) The patients have only one mind, associated with the left hemisphere, but there also occur (associated with the right hemisphere) isolated conscious mental phenomena, not integrated into a mind at all, though they can perhaps be ascribed to the organism.

(3) The patients have two minds, one which can talk and one which cannot.

(4) They have one mind, whose contents derive from both hemispheres and are rather peculiar and dissociated.

(5) They have one normal mind most of the time, while the hemispheres are functioning in parallel, but two minds are elicited by the experimental situations which yield the interesting results. (Perhaps the single mind splits in two and reconvenes after the experiment is over.)

I shall argue that each of these interpretations is unacceptable for one reason or another.

IV

Let me first discuss hypotheses (1) and (2), which have in common the refusal to ascribe the activities of the right hemisphere to a mind, and then go on to treat hypotheses (3), (4), and (5), all of which associate a mind with the activities of the right hemisphere, though they differ on what mind it is.

The only support for hypothesis (1), which refuses to ascribe consciousness to the activities of the right hemisphere at all, is the fact that the subject consistently denies awareness of the activities of that hemisphere. But to take this as proof that the activities of the right hemisphere are unconscious is to beg the question, since the capacity to give testimony is the exclusive ability of the left hemisphere, and of course the left hemisphere is not conscious of what is going on in the right. If on the other hand we consider the manifestations of the right hemisphere itself, there seems no reason in principle to regard verbalizability as a *necessary* condition of consciousness. There may be other grounds for the ascription of conscious mental states that are sufficient even without verbalization. And in fact, what the right hemisphere can do on its own is too elaborate, too intentionally directed and too psychologically intelligible to be regarded merely as a collection of unconscious automatic responses.

The right hemisphere is not very intelligent and it cannot talk; but it is able to respond to complex visual and auditory stimuli, including language, and it can control the performance of discriminatory and manipulative tasks requiring close attention – such as the spelling out of simple words with plastic letters. It can integrate auditory, visual, and tactile stimuli in order to follow the experimenter's instructions, and it can take certain aptitude tests. There is no doubt that if a person were deprived of his left hemisphere entirely, so that the only capacities remaining to him were those of the right, we should not on that account say that he had been converted into an automaton. Though speechless, he would remain conscious and active, with a diminished visual field and partial paralysis on the right side from which he would eventually recover to some extent. In view of this, it would seem arbitrary to deny that the activities of the right hemisphere are conscious, just because they occur side by side with those of the left hemisphere, about whose consciousness there is no question.

I do not wish to claim that the line between conscious and unconscious mental activity is a sharp one. It is even possible that the distinction is partly relative, in the sense that a given item of mental activity may be assignable to consciousness or not, depending on what other mental activities of the same person are going on at the same time, and whether it is connected with them in a suitable way. Even if this is true, however, the activities of the right hemisphere in split-brain patients do not fall into the category of events whose inclusion in consciousness depends on what else is going on in the patient's mind. Their determinants include a full range of psychological factors, and they demand alertness. It is clear that attention, even concentration is demanded for the tasks of the concealed left hand and tachistoscopically stimulated left visual field. The subjects do not take their experimental tests in a dreamy fashion: they are obviously in contact with reality. The left hemisphere occasionally complains about being asked to perform tasks which the right hemisphere can perform, because it does not know what is going on when the right hemisphere controls the response. But the right hemisphere displays enough awareness of what it is doing to justify the attribution of conscious control in the absence of verbal testimony. If the patients did not deny any awareness of those activities, no doubts about their consciousness would arise at all.

The considerations that make the first hypothesis untenable also serve to refute hypothesis (2), which suggests that the activities of the right hemisphere are conscious without belonging to a mind at all. There may be problems about the intelligibility of this proposal, but we need not consider them here, because it is rendered implausible by the high degree of organization and intermodal coherence of the right hemisphere's mental activities. They are not free-floating, and they are not organized in a fragmentary way. The right hemisphere follows instructions, integrates tactile, auditory and visual stimuli, and does most of the things a good mind should do. The data present us not merely with slivers of purposive behavior, but with a system capable of learning, reacting emotionally, following instructions, and carrying out tasks which require the integration of diverse psychological determinants. It seems clear that the right hemisphere's activities are not unconscious, and that they belong to something having a characteristically mental structure: a subject of experience and action.

V

Let me now turn to the three hypotheses according to which the conscious mental activities of the right hemisphere are ascribed to a mind. They have to be considered together, because the fundamental difficulty about each of them lies in the impossibility of deciding among them. The question, then, is whether the patients have two minds, one mind, or a mind that occasionally splits in two.

There is much to recommend the view that they have two minds, i.e. that the activities of the right hemisphere belong to a mind of their own.[8] Each side of the brain seems to produce its own perceptions, beliefs, and actions, which are connected with one another in the usual way, but not to those of the opposite side. The two halves of the cortex share a common body, which they control through a common midbrain and spinal cord. But their higher functions are independent not only physically but psychologically. Functions of the right hemisphere are inaccessible not only to speech but to any direct combination with corresponding functions of the left hemisphere – i.e. with functions of a type that the right hemisphere finds easy on its home ground, like shape or color discrimination.

One piece of testimony by the patients' left hemispheres may appear to argue against two minds. They report no diminution of the visual field, and little absence of sensation on the left side. Sperry dismisses this evidence on the ground that it is comparable to the testimony of victims of scotoma (partial destruction of the retina), that they notice no gaps in their visual field – although these gaps can be discovered by others observ-

---

[8] It is Sperry's view. He puts it as follows:
Instead of the normally unified single stream of consciousness, these patients behave in many ways as if they have two independent streams of conscious awareness, one in each hemisphere, each of which is cut off from and out of contact with the mental experiences of the other. In other words, each hemisphere seems to have its own separate and private sensations; its own perceptions; its own concepts; and its own impulses to act, with related volitional, cognitive, and learning experiences. Following the surgery, each hemisphere also has thereafter its own separate chain of memories that are rendered inaccessible to the recall process of the others (*American Psychologist*, XXIII, 724.)

ing their perceptual deficiences. But we need not assume that an elaborate confabulatory mechanism is at work in the left hemisphere to account for such testimony. It is perfectly possible that although there are two minds, the mind associated with each hemisphere receives, through the common brain stem, a certain amount of crude ipsilateral stimulation, so that the speaking mind has a rudimentary and undifferentiated appendage to the left side of its visual field, and vice versa for the right hemisphere.[9]

The real difficulties for the two-minds hypothesis coincide with the reasons for thinking we are dealing with one mind – namely the highly integrated character of the patients' relations to the world in ordinary circumstances. When they are not in the experimental situation, their startling behavioral dissociation disappears, and they function normally. There is little doubt that information from the two sides of their brains can be pooled to yield integrated behavioral control. And although this is not accomplished by the usual methods, it is not clear that this settles the question against assigning the integrative functions to a single mind. After all, if the patient is permitted to touch things with both hands and smell them with both nostrils, he arrives at a unified idea of what is going on around him and what he is doing, without revealing any left–right inconsistencies in his behavior or attitudes. It seems strange to suggest that we are not in a position to ascribe all those experiences to the same person, just because of some peculiarities about how the integration is achieved. The people who *know* these patients find it natural to relate to them as single individuals.

Nevertheless, if we ascribe the integration to a single mind, we must also ascribe the experimentally evoked dissociation to that mind, and that is not easy. The experimental situation reveals a variety of dissociation or conflict that is unusual not only because of the simplicity of its anatomical basis, but because such a wide *range* of functions is split into two noncommunicating branches. It is not as though two conflicting volitional centers shared a common perceptual and reasoning apparatus. The split is much deeper than that. The one-mind hypothesis

---

[9] There is some direct evidence for such primitive ipsilateral inputs, both visual and tactile; cf. Gazzaniga, *The Bisected Brain*, ch. 3.

must therefore assert that the contents of the individual's single consciousness are produced by two independent control systems in the two hemispheres, each having a fairly complete mental structure. If this dual control were accomplished during experimental situations by temporal alternation, it would be intelligible, though mysterious. But that is not the hypothesis, and the hypothesis as it stands does not supply us with understanding. For in these patients there appear to be things happening *simultaneously* which cannot fit into a single mind: simultaneous attention to two incompatible tasks, for example, without interaction between the purposes of the left and right hands.

This makes it difficult to conceive what it is like to *be* one of these people. Lack of interaction at the level of a preconscious control system would be comprehensible. But lack of interaction in the domain of visual experience and conscious intention threatens assumptions about the unity of consciousness which are basic to our understanding of another individual as a person. These assumptions are associated with our conception of ourselves, which to a considerable extent constrains our understanding of others. And it is just these assumptions, I believe, that make it impossible to arrive at an interpretation of the cases under discussion in terms of a countable number of minds.

Roughly, we assume that a single mind has sufficiently immediate access to its conscious states so that, for elements of experience or other mental events occurring simultaneously or in close temporal proximity, the mind which is their subject can also experience the simpler *relations* between them if it attends to the matter. Thus, we assume that when a single person has two visual impressions, he can usually also experience the sameness or difference of their coloration, shape, size, the relation of their position and movement within his visual field, and so forth. The same can be said of cross-modal connections. The experiences of a single person are thought to take place in an *experientially* connected domain, so that the relations among experiences can be substantially captured in experiences of those relations.[10]

---

[10] The two can of course diverge, and this fact underlies the classic philosophical problem of inverted spectra, which is only distantly related to the subject of this paper. A type of relation can hold between elements in the experience of a single person that cannot hold between elements of the experience of distinct persons: looking similar in color, for example. Insofar as our concept of similarity of experience in the case of a single

Split-brain patients fail dramatically to conform to these assumptions in experimental situations, and they fail over the simplest matters. Moreover the dissociation holds between two classes of conscious states each characterized by significant *internal* coherence: normal assumptions about the unity of consciousness hold intrahemispherically, although the requisite comparisons cannot be made across the interhemispheric gap.

These considerations lead us back to the hypothesis that the patients have two minds each. It at least has the advantage of enabling us to understand what it is like to *be* these individuals, so long as we do not try to imagine what it is like to be both of them at the same time. Yet the way to a comfortable acceptance of this conclusion is blocked by the compelling behavioral integration which the patients display in ordinary life, in comparison to which the dissociated symptoms evoked by the experimental situation seem peripheral and atypical. We are faced with diametrically conflicting bodies of evidence, in a case which does not admit of arbitrary decision. There is a powerful inclination to feel that there must be *some* whole number of minds in those heads, but the data prevent us from deciding how many.

This dilemma makes hypothesis (5) initially attractive, especially since the data which yield the conflict are to some extent gathered at different times. But the suggestion that a second mind is brought into existence only during experimental situations loses plausibility on reflection. First, it is entirely *ad hoc*: it proposes to explain one change in terms of another without suggesting any explanation of the second. There is nothing about the experimental situation that might be expected to produce a fundamental internal change in the patient. In fact it produces no anatomical changes and merely elicits a noteworthy set of symptoms. So unusual an event as a mind's popping in and out of existence would have to be explained by something more than its explanatory convenience.

But secondly, the behavioral evidence would not even be explained by this hypothesis, simply because the patients' integrated responses and their dissociated responses are not clearly

---

person is dependent on his experience of similarity, the concept is not applicable between persons.

separated in time. During the time of the experiments the patient
is functioning largely as if he were a single individual: in his
posture, in following instructions about where to focus his eyes,
in the whole range of trivial behavioral control involved in
situating himself in relation to the experimenter and the experimental apparatus. The two halves of his brain cooperate completely except in regard to those very special inputs that reach
them separately and differently. For these reasons hypothesis (5)
does not seem to be a real option; if two minds are operating in
the experimental situation, they must be operating largely in
harmony although partly at odds. And if there are two minds
then, why can there not be two minds operating essentially in
parallel the rest of the time?

Nevertheless the psychological integration displayed by the
patients in ordinary life is so complete that I do not believe it is
possible to accept that conclusion, nor any conclusion involving
the ascription to them of a whole number of minds. These cases
fall midway between ordinary persons with intact brains (between whose cerebral hemispheres there is also cooperation,
though it works largely via the corpus callosum), and pairs of
individuals engaged in a performance requiring exact behavioral
coordination, like using a two-handed saw, or playing a duet. In
the latter type of case we have two minds which communicate
by subtle peripheral cues; in the former we have a single mind.
Nothing taken from either of those cases can compel us to
assimilate the split-brain patient to one or the other of them. If
we decided that they definitely had two minds, then it would be
problematical why we did not conclude on anatomical grounds
that everyone has two minds, but that we do not notice it except
in these odd cases because most pairs of minds in a single body
run in perfect parallel due to the direct communication between
the hemispheres which provide their anatomical bases. The two
minds each of us has running in harness would be much the
same except that one could talk and the other could not. But it is
clear that this line of argument will get us nowhere. For if the
idea of a single mind applies to anyone it applies to ordinary
individuals with intact brains, and if it does not apply to them it
ought to be scrapped, in which case there is no point in asking
whether those with split brains have one mind or two.[11]

[11] In case anyone is inclined to embrace the conclusion that we all have two

VI

If I am right, and there is no whole number of individual minds that these patients can be said to have, then the attribution of conscious, significant mental activity does not require the existence of a single mental subject. This is extremely puzzling in itself, for it runs counter to our need to construe the mental states we ascribe to others on the model of our own. Something in the ordinary conception of a person, or in the ordinary conception of experience, leads to the demand for an account of these cases which the same conception makes it impossible to provide. This may seem a problem not worth worrying about very much. It is not so surprising that, having begun with a phenomenon which is radically different from anything else previously known, we should come to the conclusion that it cannot be adequately described in ordinary terms. However, I believe that consideration of these very unusual cases should cause us to be skeptical about the concept of a single subject of consciousness as it applies to ourselves.

The fundamental problem in trying to understand these cases in mentalistic terms is that we take ourselves as paradigms of psychological unity, and are then unable to project ourselves into their mental lives, either once or twice. But in thus using ourselves as the touchstone of whether another organism can be said to house an individual subject of experience or not, we are subtly ignoring the possibility that our own unity may be nothing absolute, but merely another case of integration, more or less effective, in the control system of a complex organism. This system speaks in the first person singular through our mouths, and that makes it understandable that we should think of its unity as in some sense numerically absolute, rather than relative and a function of the integration of its contents.

But this is quite genuinely an illusion. The illusion consists in

---

minds, let me suggest that the trouble will not end there. For the mental operations of a single hemisphere, such as vision, hearing, speech, writing, verbal comprehension, etc., can to a great extent be separated from one another by suitable cortical deconnections; why then should we regard *each* hemisphere as inhabited by several cooperating minds with specialized capacities? Where is one to stop? If the decision on the number of minds associated with a brain is largely arbitrary, the original point of the question has disappeared.

projecting inward to the center of the mind the very subject whose unity we are trying to explain: the individual person with all his complexities. The ultimate account of the unity of what we call a single mind consists of an enumeration of the types of functional integration that typify it. We know that these can be eroded in different ways, and to different degrees. The belief that even in their complete version they can be explained by the presence of a numerically single subject is an illusion. Either this subject contains the mental life, in which case it is complex and its unity must be accounted for in terms of the unified operation of its components and functions, or else it is an extensionless point, in which case it explains nothing.

An intact brain contains two cerebral hemispheres each of which possesses perceptual, memory, and control systems adequate to run the body without the assistance of the other. They cooperate in directing it with the aid of a constant two-way internal communication system. Memories, perceptions, desires, and so forth therefore have duplicate physical bases on both sides of the brain, not just on account of similarities of initial input, but because of subsequent exchange. The cooperation of the undetached hemispheres in controlling the body is more efficient and direct than the cooperation of a pair of detached hemispheres, but it is cooperation nonetheless. Even if we analyze the idea of unity in terms of functional integration, therefore, the unity of our own consciousness may be less clear than we had supposed. The natural conception of a single person controlled by a mind possessing a single visual field, individual faculties for each of the other senses, unitary systems of memory, desire, belief, and so forth, may come into conflict with the physiological facts when it is applied to ourselves.

The concept of a person might possibly survive an application to cases which require us to speak of two or more persons in one body, but it seems strongly committed to some form of whole number countability. Since even this seems open to doubt, it is possible that the ordinary, simple idea of a single person will come to seem quaint some day, when the complexities of the human control system become clearer and we become less certain that there is anything very important that we are *one* of. But it is also possible that we shall be unable to abandon the idea no matter what we discover.

12

What is it like to be a bat?

Consciousness is what makes the mind–body problem really intractable. Perhaps that is why current discussions of the problem give it little attention or get it obviously wrong. The recent wave of reductionist euphoria has produced several analyses of mental phenomena and mental concepts designed to explain the possibility of some variety of materialism, psychophysical identification, or reduction.[1] But the problems dealt with are those common to this type of reduction and other types, and what makes the mind–body problem unique, and unlike the water–H_2O problem or the Turing machine–IBM machine problem or the lightning–electrical discharge problem or the gene–DNA problem or the oak tree–hydrocarbon problem, is ignored.

[1] Examples are J. J. C. Smart, *Philosophy and Scientific Realism* (London: Routledge & Kegan Paul, 1963); David K. Lewis, 'An Argument for the Identity Theory', *Journal of Philosophy*, LXIII (1966), reprinted with addenda in David M. Rosenthal, *Materialism & the Mind–Body Problem*, (Engelwood Cliffs, N.J.: Prentice-Hall, 1971); Hilary Putnam, 'Psychological Predicates', in *Art, Mind, & Religion*, ed. W. H. Capitan and D. D. Merrill (Pittsburgh: University of Pittsburgh Press, 1967), reprinted in *Materialism*, ed. Rosenthal, as 'The Nature of Mental States'; D. M. Armstrong, *A Materialist Theory of the Mind* (London: Routledge & Kegan Paul, 1968); D. C. Dennett, *Content and Consciousness* (London: Routledge & Kegan Paul, 1969). I have expressed earlier doubts in 'Armstrong on the Mind', *Philosophical Review*, LXXIX (1970), 394–403; a review of Dennett, *Journal of Philosophy*, LXIX (1972); and chapter 11 above. See also Saul Kripke, 'Naming and Necessity', in *Semantics of Natural Language*, ed. D. Davidson and G. Harman (Dordrecht: Reidel, 1972), esp. pp. 334–42; and M. T. Thornton, 'Ostensive Terms and Materialism', *The Monist*, LVI (1972), 193–214.

Every reductionist has his favorite analogy from modern science. It is most unlikely that any of these unrelated examples of successful reduction will shed light on the relation of mind to brain. But philosophers share the general human weakness for explanations of what is incomprehensible in terms suited for what is familiar and well understood, though entirely different. This has led to the acceptance of implausible accounts of the mental largely because they would permit familiar kinds of reduction. I shall try to explain why the usual examples do not help us to understand the relation between mind and body—why, indeed, we have at present no conception of what an explanation of the physical nature of a mental phenomenon would be. Without consciousness the mind–body problem would be much less interesting. With consciousness it seems hopeless. The most important and characteristic feature of conscious mental phenomena is very poorly understood. Most reductionist theories do not even try to explain it. And careful examination will show that no currently available concept of reduction is applicable to it. Perhaps a new theoretical form can be devised for the purpose, but such a solution, if it exists, lies in the distant intellectual future.

Conscious experience is a widespread phenomenon. It occurs at many levels of animal life, though we cannot be sure of its presence in the simpler organisms, and it is very difficult to say in general what provides evidence of it. (Some extremists have been prepared to deny it even of mammals other than man.) No doubt it occurs in countless forms totally unimaginable to us, on other planets in other solar systems throughout the universe. But no matter how the form may vary, the fact that an organism has conscious experience *at all* means, basically, that there is something it is like to *be* that organism. There may be further implications about the form of the experience; there may even (though I doubt it) e implications about the behavior of the organism. But fundamentally an organism has conscious mental states if and only if there is something that it is like to *be* that organism – something it is like *for* the organism.

We may call this the subjective character of experience. It is not captured by any of the familiar, recently devised reductive analyses of the mental, for all of them are logically compatible with its absence. It is not analyzable in terms of any explanatory system of functional states, or intentional states, since these could be ascribed to robots or automata that behaved like people though they experienced nothing.[2] It is not analyzable in terms of the causal role of experiences in relation to typical human behavior – for similar reasons.[3] I do not deny that conscious mental states and events cause behavior, nor that they may be given functional characterizations. I deny only that this kind of thing exhausts their analysis. Any reductionist program has to be based on an analysis of what is to be reduced. If the analysis leaves something out, the problem will be falsely posed. It is useless to base the defense of materialism on any analysis of mental phenomena that fails to deal explicitly with their subjective character. For there is no reason to suppose that a reduction which seems plausible when no attempt is made to account for consciousness can be extended to include consciousness. Without some idea, therefore, of what the subjective character of experience is, we cannot know what is required of physicalist theory.

While an account of the physical basis of mind must explain many things, this appears to be the most difficult. It is impossible to exclude the phenomenological features of experience from a reduction in the same way that one excludes the phenomenal features of an ordinary substance from a physical or chemical reduction of it – namely, by explaining them as effects on the minds of human observers.[4] If physicalism is to be defended, the phenomenological features must themselves be given a physical account. But when we examine their subjective character it seems that such a result is impossible. The reason is that every subjective phenomenon is essentially connected with a single point of view, and it seems inevitable that an objective, physical theory will abandon that point of view.

---

[2] Perhaps there could not actually be such robots. Perhaps anything complex enough to behave like a person would have experiences. But that, if true, is a fact which cannot be discovered merely by analyzing the concept of experience.

[3] It is not equivalent to that about which we are incorrigible, both because we are not incorrigible about experience and because experience is present in animals lacking language and thought, who have no beliefs at all about their experiences.

[4] Cf. Richard Rorty, 'Mind–Body Identity, Privacy, and Categories', *Review of Metaphysics*, xix (1965), esp. 37–8.

Let me first try to state the issue somewhat more fully than by referring to the relation between the subjective and the objective, or between the *pour soi* and the *en soi*. This is far from easy. Facts about what it is like to be an X are very peculiar, so peculiar that some may be inclined to doubt their reality, or the significance of claims about them. To illustrate the connexion between subjectivity and a point of view, and to make evident the importance of subjective features, it will help to explore the matter in relation to an example that brings out clearly the divergence between the two types of conception, subjective and objective.

I assume we all believe that bats have experience. After all, they are mammals, and there is no more doubt that they have experience than that mice or pigeons or whales have experience. I have chosen bats instead of wasps or flounders because if one travels too far down the phylogenetic tree, people gradually shed their faith that there is experience there at all. Bats, although more closely related to us than those other species, nevertheless present a range of activity and a sensory apparatus so different from ours that the problem I want to pose is exceptionally vivid (though it certainly could be raised with other species). Even without the benefit of philosophical reflection, anyone who has spent some time in an enclosed space with an excited bat knows what it is to encounter a fundamentally *alien* form of life.

I have said that the essence of the belief that bats have experience is that there is something that it is like to be a bat. Now we know that most bats (the microchiroptera, to be precise) perceive the external world primarily by sonar, or echolocation, detecting the reflections, from objects within range, of their own rapid, subtly modulated, high-frequency shrieks. Their brains are designed to correlate the outgoing impulses with the subsequent echoes, and the information thus acquired enables bats to make precise discriminations of distance, size, shape, motion, and texture comparable to those we make by vision. But bat sonar, though clearly a form of perception, is not similar in its operation to any sense that we possess, and there is no reason to suppose that it is subjectively like anything we can experience or imagine. This appears to create difficulties for the notion of what it is like to be a bat. We must consider whether any method will permit us to extrapolate to the inner life of the bat from our own case,[5] and if not, what alternative methods there may be for understanding the notion.

Our own experience provides the basic material for our imagination, whose range is therefore limited. It will not help to try to imagine that one has webbing on one's arms, which enables one to fly around at dusk and dawn catching insects in one's mouth; that one has very poor vision, and perceives the surrounding world by a system of reflected high-frequency sound signals; and that one spends the day hanging upside down by one's feet in an attic. Insofar as I can imagine this (which is not very far), it tells me only what it would be like for *me* to behave as a bat behaves. But that is not the question. I want to know what it is like for a *bat* to be a bat. Yet if I try to imagine this, I am restricted to the resources of my own mind, and those resources are inadequate to the task. I cannot perform it either by imagining additions to my present experience, or by imagining segments gradually subtracted from it, or by imagining some combination of additions, subtractions, and modifications.

To the extent that I could look and behave like a wasp or a bat without changing my fundamental structure, my experiences would not be anything like the experiences of those animals. On the other hand, it is doubtful that any meaning can be attached to the supposition that I should possess the internal neuro-physiological constitution of a bat. Even if I could by gradual degrees be transformed into a bat, nothing in my present constitution enables me to imagine what the experiences of such a future stage of myself thus metamorphosed would be like. The best evidence would come from the experiences of bats, if we only knew what they were like.

So if extrapolation from our own case is involved in the idea of what it is like to be a bat, the extrapolation must be incomplet-able. We cannot form more than a schematic conception of what it *is* like. For example, we may ascribe general *types* of experience on the basis of the animal's structure and behavior. Thus we describe bat sonar as a form of three-dimensional forward perception; we believe that bats feel some versions of pain, fear, hunger, and lust, and that they have other, more familiar types

---

[5] By 'our own case' I do not mean just 'my own case', but rather the mentalistic ideas that we apply unproblematically to ourselves and other human beings.

of perception besides sonar. But we believe that these experiences also have in each case a specific subjective character, which it is beyond our ability to conceive. And if there is conscious life elsewhere in the universe, it is likely that some of it will not be describable even in the most general experiential terms available to us.[6] (The problem is not confined to exotic cases, however, for it exists between one person and another. The subjective character of the experience of a person deaf and blind from birth is not accessible to me, for example, nor presumably is mine to him. This does not prevent us each from believing that the other's experience has such a subjective character.)

If anyone is inclined to deny that we can believe in the existence of facts like this whose exact nature we cannot possibly conceive, he should reflect that in contemplating the bats we are in much the same position that intelligent bats or Martians[7] would occupy if they tried to form a conception of what it was like to be us. The structure of their own minds might make it impossible for them to succeed, but we know they would be wrong to conclude that there is not anything precise that it is like to be us: that only certain general types of mental state could be ascribed to us (perhaps perception and appetite would be concepts common to us both; perhaps not). We know they would be wrong to draw such a skeptical conclusion because we know what it is like to be us. And we know that while it includes an enormous amount of variation and complexity, and while we do not possess the vocabulary to describe it adequately, its subjective character is highly specific, and in some respects describable in terms that can be understood only by creatures like us. The fact that we cannot expect ever to accommodate in our language a detailed description of Martian or bat phenomenology should not lead us to dismiss as meaningless the claim that bats and Martians have experiences fully comparable in richness of detail to our own. It would be fine if someone were to develop concepts and a theory that enabled us to think about those things; but such an understanding may be permanently denied to us by the limits of our nature. And to deny the

---

[6] Therefore the analogical form of the English expression 'what it is *like*' is misleading. It does not mean 'what (in our experience) it *resembles*', but rather 'how it is for the subject himself'.

[7] Any intelligent extraterrestrial beings totally different from us.

reality or logical significance of what we can never describe or understand is the crudest form of cognitive dissonance.

This brings us to the edge of a topic that requires much more discussion than I can give it here: namely, the relation between facts on the one hand and conceptual schemes or systems of representation on the other. My realism about the subjective domain in all its forms implies a belief in the existence of facts beyond the reach of human concepts. Certainly it is possible for a human being to believe that there are facts which humans never *will* possess the requisite concepts to represent or comprehend. Indeed, it would be foolish to doubt this, given the finiteness of humanity's expectations. After all, there would have been transfinite numbers even if everyone had been wiped out by the Black Death before Cantor discovered them. But one might also believe that there are facts which *could* not ever be represented or comprehended by human beings, even if the species lasted for ever – simply because our structure does not permit us to operate with concepts of the requisite type. This impossibility might even be observed by other beings, but it is not clear that the existence of such beings, or the possibility of their existence, is a precondition of the significance of the hypothesis that there are humanly inaccessible facts. (After all, the nature of beings with access to humanly inaccessible facts is presumably itself a humanly inaccessible fact.) Reflection on what it is like to be a bat seems to lead us, therefore, to the conclusion that there are facts that do not consist in the truth of propositions expressible in a human language. We can be compelled to recognize the existence of such facts without being able to state or comprehend them.

I shall not pursue this subject, however. Its bearing on the topic before us (namely, the mind–body problem) is that it enables us to make a general observation about the subjective character of experience. Whatever may be the status of facts about what it is like to be a human being, or a bat, or a Martian, these appear to be facts that embody a particular point of view.

I am not adverting here to the alleged privacy of experience to its possessor. The point of view in question is not one accessible only to a single individual. Rather it is a *type*. It is often possible to take up a point of view other than one's own, so the comprehension of such facts is not limited to one's own case.

There is a sense in which phenomenological facts are perfectly objective: one person can know or say of another what the quality of the other's experience is. They are subjective, however, in the sense that even this objective ascription of experience is possible only for someone sufficiently similar to the object of ascription to be able to adopt his point of view – to understand the ascription in the first person as well as in the third, so to speak. The more different from oneself the other experiencer is, the less success one can expect with this enterprise. In our own case we occupy the relevant point of view, but we will have as much difficulty understanding our own experience properly if we approach it from another point of view as we would if we tried to understand the experience of another species without taking up *its* point of view.[8]

This bears directly on the mind–body problem. For if the facts of experience – facts about what it is like *for* the experiencing organism – are accessible only from one point of view, then it is a mystery how the true character of experiences could be revealed in the physical operation of that organism. The latter is a domain of objective facts *par excellence* – the kind that can be observed and understood from many points of view and by individuals with differing perceptual systems. There are no comparable imaginative obstacles to the acquisition of knowledge about bat neurophysiology by human scientists, and intelligent bats or Martians might learn more about the human brain than we ever will.

This is not by itself an argument against reduction. A Martian

---

8 It may be easier than I suppose to transcend inter-species barriers with the aid of the imagination. For example, blind people are able to detect objects near them by a form of sonar, using vocal clicks or taps of a cane. Perhaps if one knew what that was like, one could by extension imagine roughly what it was like to possess the much more refined sonar of a bat. The distance between oneself and other persons and other species can fall anywhere on a continuum. Even for other persons the understanding of what it is like to be them is only partial, and when one moves to species very different from oneself, a lesser degree of partial understanding may still be available. The imagination is remarkably flexible. My point, however, is not that we cannot *know* what it is like to be a bat. I am not raising that epistemological problem. My point is rather that even to form a *conception* of what it is like to be a bat (and *a fortiori* to know what it is like to be a bat) one must take up the bat's point of view. If one can take it up roughly, or partially, then one's conception will also be rough or partial. Or so it seems in our present state of understanding.

scientist with no understanding of visual perception could understand the rainbow, or lightning, or clouds as physical phenomena, though he would never be able to understand the human concepts of rainbow, lightning, or cloud, or the place these things occupy in our phenomenal world. The objective nature of the things picked out by these concepts could be apprehended by him because, although the concepts themselves are connected with a particular point of view and a particular visual phenomenology, the things apprehended from that point of view are not: they are observable from the point of view but external to it; hence they can be comprehended from other points of view also, either by the same organisms or by others. Lightning has an objective character that is not exhausted by its visual appearance, and this can be investigated by a Martian without vision. To be precise, it has a *more* objective character than is revealed in its visual appearance. In speaking of the move from subjective to objective characterization, I wish to remain noncommittal about the existence of an end point, the completely objective intrinsic nature of the thing, which one might or might not be able to reach. It may be more accurate to think of objectivity as a direction in which the understanding can travel. And in understanding a phenomenon like lightning, it is legitimate to go as far away as one can from a strictly human viewpoint.[9]

In the case of experience, on the other hand, the connexion with a particular point of view seems much closer. It is difficult to understand what could be meant by the *objective* character of an experience, apart from the particular point of view from which its subject apprehends it. After all, what would be left of what it was like to be a bat if one removed the viewpoint of the bat? But if experience does not have, in addition to its subjective character, an objective nature that can be apprehended from many different points of view, then how can it be supposed that a Martian investigating my brain might be observing physical

---

[9] The problem I am going to raise can therefore be posed even if the distinction between more subjective and more objective descriptions or viewpoints can itself be made only within a larger human point of view. I do not accept this kind of conceptual relativism, but it need not be refuted to make the point that psychophysical reduction cannot be accommodated by the subjective-to-objective model familiar from other cases.

processes which were my mental processes (as he might observe physical processes which were bolts of lightning), only from a different point of view? How, for that matter, could a human physiologist observe them from another point of view?[10]

We appear to be faced with a general difficulty about psychophysical reduction. In other areas the process of reduction is a move in the direction of greater objectivity, toward a more accurate view of the real nature of things. This is accomplished by reducing our dependence on individual or species-specific points of view toward the object of investigation. We describe it not in terms of the impressions it makes on our senses, but in terms of its more general effects and of properties detectable by means other than the human senses. The less it depends on a specifically human viewpoint, the more objective is our description. It is possible to follow this path because although the concepts and ideas we employ in thinking about the external world are initially applied from a point of view that involves our perceptual apparatus, they are used by us to refer to things beyond themselves – toward which we *have* the phenomenal point of view. Therefore we can abandon it in favor of another, and still be thinking about the same things.

Experience itself, however, does not seem to fit the pattern. The idea of moving from appearance to reality seems to make no sense here. What is the analogue in this case to pursuing a more objective understanding of the same phenomena by abandoning the initial subjective viewpoint toward them in favour of another that is more objective but concerns the same thing? Certainly it *appears* unlikely that we will get closer to the real nature of human experience by leaving behind the particularity of our human point of view and striving for a description in terms accessible to beings that could not imagine what it was like to be us. If the subjective character of experience is fully comprehensible only from one point of view, then any shift to greater objectivity – that is, less attachment to a specific viewpoint – does not take us nearer to the real nature of the phenomenon: it takes us farther away from it.

[10] The problem is not just that when I look at the *Mona Lisa*, my visual experience has a certain quality, no trace of which is to be found by someone looking into my brain. For even if he did observe there a tiny image of the *Mona Lisa*, he would have no reason to identify it with the experience.

In a sense, the seeds of this objection to the reducibility of experience are already detectable in successful cases of reduction; for in discovering sound to be, in reality, a wave phenomenon in air or other media, we leave behind one viewpoint to take up another, and the auditory, human or animal viewpoint that we leave behind remains unreduced. Members of radically different species may both understand the same physical events in objective terms, and this does not require that they understand the phenomenal forms in which those events appear to the senses of members of the other species. Thus it is a condition of their referring to a common reality that their more particular viewpoints are not part of the common reality that they both apprehend. The reduction can succeed only if the species-specific viewpoint is omitted from what is to be reduced.

But while we are right to leave this point of view aside in seeking a fuller understanding of the external world, we cannot ignore it permanently, since it is the essence of the internal world, and not merely a point of view on it. Most of the neobehaviorism of recent philosophical psychology results from the effort to substitute an objective concept of mind for the real thing, in order to have nothing left over which cannot be reduced. If we acknowledge that a physical theory of mind must account for the subjective character of experience, we must admit that no presently available conception gives us a clue how this could be done. The problem is unique. If mental processes are indeed physical processes, then there is something it is like, intrinsically,[11] to undergo certain physical processes. What it is for such a thing to be the case remains a mystery.

---

[11] The relation would therefore not be a contingent one, like that of a cause and its distinct effect. It would be necessarily true that a certain physical state felt a certain way. Saul Kripke in *Semantics of Natural Language*, (ed. Davidson and Harman) argues that causal behaviorist and related analyses of the mental fail because they construe, e.g., 'pain' as a merely contingent name of pains. The subjective character of an experience ('its immediate phenomenological quality' Kripke calls it (p. 340)) is the essential property left out by such analyses, and the one in virtue of which it is, necessarily, the experience it is. My view is closely related to his. Like Kripke, I find the hypothesis that a certain brain state should *necessarily* have a certain subjective character incomprehensible without further explanation. No such explanation emerges from theories which view the mind–brain relation as contingent, but perhaps there are other alternatives, not yet discovered.

A theory that explained how the mind–brain relation was necessary

What moral should be drawn from these reflections, and what should be done next? It would be a mistake to conclude that physicalism must be false. Nothing is proved by the inadequacy of physicalist hypotheses that assume a faulty objective analysis of mind. It would be truer to say that physicalism is a position we cannot understand because we do not at present have any conception of how it might be true. Perhaps it will be thought unreasonable to require such a conception as a condition of understanding. After all, it might be said, the meaning of physicalism is clear enough: mental states are states of the body; mental events are physical events. We do not know *which* physical states and events they are, but that should not prevent us from understanding the hypothesis. What could be clearer than the words 'is' and 'are'?

But I believe it is precisely this apparent clarity of the word 'is' that is deceptive. Usually, when we are told that X is Y we know *how* it is supposed to be true, but that depends on a conceptual or theoretical background and is not conveyed by the 'is' alone. We know how both 'X' and 'Y' refer, and the kinds of

---

would still leave us with Kripke's problem of explaining why it nevertheless appears contingent. That difficulty seems to me surmountable, in the following way. We may imagine something by representing it to ourselves either perceptually, sympathetically, or symbolically. I shall not try to say how symbolic imagination works, but part of what happens in the other two cases is this. To imagine something perceptually, we put ourselves in a conscious state resembling the state we would be in if we perceived it. To imagine something sympathetically, we put ourselves in a conscious state resembling the thing itself. (This method can be used only to imagine mental events and states–our own or another's.) When we try to imagine a mental state occurring without its associated brain state, we first sympathetically imagine the occurrence of the mental state: that is, we put ourselves into a state that resembles it mentally. At the same time, we attempt perceptually to imagine the nonoccurrence of the associated physical state, by putting ourselves into another state unconnected with the first: one resembling that which we would be in if we perceived the nonoccurrence of the physical state. Where the imagination of physical features is perceptual and the imagination of mental features is sympathetic, it appears to us that we can imagine any experience occurring without its associated brain state, and vice versa. The relation between them will appear contingent even if it is necessary, because of the independence of the disparate types of imagination.

(Solipsism, incidentally, results if one misinterprets sympathetic imagination as if it worked like perceptual imagination: it then seems impossible to imagine any experience that is not one's own.)

things to which they refer, and we have a rough idea how the two referential paths might converge on a single thing, be it an object, a person, a process, an event or whatever. But when the two terms of the identification are very disparate it may not be so clear how it could be true. We may not have even a rough idea of how the two referential paths could converge, or what kind of things they might converge on, and a theoretical framework may have to be supplied to enable us to understand this. Without the framework, an air of mysticism surrounds the identification.

This explains the magical flavor of popular presentations of fundamental scientific discoveries, given out as propositions to which one must subscribe without really understanding them. For example, people are now told at an early age that all matter is really energy. But despite the fact that they know what 'is' means, most of them never form a conception of what makes this claim true, because they lack the theoretical background.

At the present time the status of physicalism is similar to that which the hypothesis that matter is energy would have had if uttered by a pre-Socratic philosopher. We do not have the beginnings of a conception of how it might be true. In order to understand the hypothesis that a mental event is a physical event, we require more than an understanding of the word 'is'. The idea of how a mental and a physical term might refer to the same thing is lacking, and the usual analogies with theoretical identification in other fields fail to supply it. They fail because if we construe the reference of mental terms to physical events on the usual model, we either get a reappearance of separate subjective events as the effects through which mental reference to physical events is secured, or else we get a false account of how mental terms refer (for example, a causal behaviorist one).

Strangely enough, we may have evidence for the truth of something we cannot really understand. Suppose a caterpillar is locked in a sterile safe by someone unfamiliar with insect metamorphosis, and weeks later the safe is reopened, revealing a butterfly. If the person knows that the safe has been shut the whole time, he has reason to believe that the butterfly is or was once the caterpillar, without having any idea in what sense this might be so. (One possibility is that the caterpillar contained a tiny winged parasite that devoured it and grew into the butterfly.)

It is conceivable that we are in such a position with regard to physicalism. Donald Davidson has argued that if mental events have physical causes and effects, they must have physical descriptions. He holds that we have reason to believe this even though we do not – and in fact *could* not – have a general psychophysical theory.[12] His argument applies to intentional mental events, but I think we also have some reason to believe that sensations are physical processes, without being in a position to understand how. Davidson's position is that certain physical events have irreducibly mental properties, and perhaps some view describable in this way is correct. But nothing of which we can now form a conception corresponds to it; nor have we any idea what a theory would be like that enabled us to conceive of it.[13]

Very little work has been done on the basic question (from which mention of the brain can be entirely omitted) whether any sense can be made of experiences' having an objective character at all. Does it make sense, in other words, to ask what my experiences are *really* like, as opposed to how they appear to me? We cannot genuinely understand the hypothesis that their nature is captured in a physical description unless we understand the more fundamental idea that they *have* an objective nature (or that objective processes can have a subjective nature).[14]

I should like to close with a speculative proposal. It may be possible to approach the gap between subjective and objective from another direction. Setting aside temporarily the relation between the mind and the brain, we can pursue a more objective understanding of the mental in its own right. At present we are completely unequipped to think about the subjective character of experience without relying on the imagination – without taking up the point of view of the experiential subject. This

---

[12] See 'Mental Events' in *Experience and Theory*, ed. Lawrence Foster and J. W. Swanson (Amherst: University of Massachusetts Press, 1970); though I do not understand the argument against psychophysical laws.

[13] Similar remarks apply to my paper 'Physicalism', *Philosophical Review*, LXXIV (1965), 339–56, reprinted with postscript in *Modern Materialism*, ed. John O'Connor (New York: Harcourt Brace Jovanovich, 1969).

[14] This question also lies at the heart of the problem of other minds, whose close connection with the mind–body problem is often overlooked. If one understood how subjective experience could have an objective nature, one would understand the existence of subjects other than oneself.

should be regarded as a challenge to form new concepts and devise a new method – an objective phenomenology not dependent on empathy or the imagination. Though presumably it would not capture everything, its goal would be to describe, at least in part, the subjective character of experiences in a form comprehensible to beings incapable of having those experiences.

We would have to develop such a phenomenology to describe the sonar experiences of bats; but it would also be possible to begin with humans. One might try, for example, to develop concepts that could be used to explain to a person blind from birth what it was like to see. One would reach a blank wall eventually, but it should be possible to devise a method of expressing in objective terms much more than we can at present, and with much greater precision. The loose intermodal analogies – for example, 'Red is like the sound of a trumpet' – – which crop up in discussions of this subject are of little use. That should be clear to anyone who has both heard a trumpet and seen red. But structural features of perception might be more accessible to objective description, even though something would be left out. And concepts alternative to those we learn in the first person may enable us to arrive at a kind of understanding even of our own experience which is denied us by the very ease of description and lack of distance that subjective concepts afford.

Apart from its own interest, a phenomenology that is in this sense objective may permit questions about the physical[15] basis of experience to assume a more intelligible form. Aspects of subjective experience that admitted this kind of objective description might be better candidates for objective explanations of a more familiar sort. But whether or not this guess is correct,

---

[15] I have not defined the term 'physical'. Obviously it does not apply just to what can be described by the concepts of contemporary physics, since we expect further developments. Some may think there is nothing to prevent mental phenomena from eventually being recognized as physical in their own right. But whatever else may be said of the physical, it has to be objective. So if our idea of the physical ever expands to include mental phenomena, it will have to assign them an objective character–whether or not this is done by analyzing them in terms of other phenomena already regarded as physical. It seems to me more likely, however, that mental–physical relations will eventually be expressed in a theory whose fundamental terms cannot be placed clearly in either category.

it seems unlikely that any physical theory of mind can be contemplated until more thought has been given to the general problem of subjective and objective. Otherwise we cannot even pose the mind–body problem without sidestepping it.

13

Panpsychism

By panpsychism I mean the view that the basic physical constituents of the universe have mental properties, whether or not they are parts of living organisms. It appears to follow from a few simple premises, each of which is more plausible than its denial, though not perhaps more plausible than the denial of panpsychism.

1. *Material composition*

Any living organism, including a human being, is a complex material system. It consists of a huge number of particles combined in a special way. Each of us is composed of matter that had a largely inanimate history before finding its way onto our plates or those of our parents. It was once probably part of the sun, but matter from another galaxy would do as well. If it were brought to earth, and grass were grown in it, and milk from a cow that ate the grass were drunk by a pregnant woman, then her child's brain would be partly composed of that matter. Anything whatever, if broken down far enough and rearranged, could be incorporated into a living organism. No constituents besides matter are needed.

2. *Nonreductionism*

Ordinary mental states like thought, feeling, emotion, sensation, or desire are not physical properties of the organism – behavioral, physiological, or otherwise – and they are not implied by physical properties alone.[1]

---

[1] Strictly speaking, the argument requires only that *some* mental states are not reducible.

3. *Realism*

Nevertheless they are properties of the organism, since there is no soul, and they are not properties of nothing at all.[2]

4. *Nonemergence*

There are no truly emergent properties of complex systems. All properties of a complex system that are not relations between it and something else derive from the properties of its constituents and their effects on each other when so combined. Emergence is an epistemological condition: it means that an observed feature of the system cannot be derived from the properties currently attributed to its constituents. But this is a reason to conclude that either the system has further constituents of which we are not yet aware, or the constituents of which we are aware have further properties that we have not yet discovered.

Panpsychism seems to follow from these four premises. If the mental properties of an organism are not implied by any physical properties but must derive from properties of the organism's constituents, then those constituents must have nonphysical properties from which the appearance of mental properties follows when the combination is of the right kind. Since any matter can compose an organism, all matter must have these properties. And since the same matter can be made into different types of organisms with different types of mental life (of which we have encountered only a tiny sample), it must have properties that imply the appearance of different mental phenomena when the matter is combined in different ways. This would amount to a kind of mental chemistry.

The conclusion has its attractions as a general explanation of how conscious life arises in the universe. But there are three problems about the argument that I want to discuss.

1. Why call these inferred properties of matter mental? What is meant by a physical property and why does that concept not apply to them?
2. What view of causality is involved in the denial of emergence?

---

[2] Some of them, like belief and perception, are relational properties, but all involve some nonrelational aspect.

3. Do the features of mental phenomena that argue against reduction also argue against Realism?[3]

To deal with the first question, we must consider what makes a newly discovered property or phenomenon physical. Since the class of known physical properties is constantly expanding, the physical cannot be defined in terms of the concepts of contemporary physics, but must be more general. New properties are counted as physical if they are discovered by explanatory inference from those already in the class. This repeated process starts from a base of familiar, observable spatio-temporal phenomena and proceeds to take in mass, force, kinetic energy, charge, valence, gravitational and electromagnetic fields, quantum states, anti-particles, strangeness, charm, and whatever physics will bring us next.[4]

What the argument claims is that a similar chain of explanatory inference beginning from familiar mental phenomena would lead to general properties of matter that would not be reached along the path of explanatory inference by which physics is extended. Let us put aside for the moment the uneasiness that one may well feel about the suggestion that mental phenomena should derive from any properties of matter at all.

The claim is that if such properties exist, they are not physical in the sense explained. No properties of the organism or its constituents discovered solely by physics will be the familiar mental properties with their conscious or preconscious aspects, nor will they be the more basic proto-mental properties that imply these; for it will never be legitimate to infer, as a theoretical explanation of physical phenomena alone, a property that includes or implies the consciousness of its subject. We do infer explicitly mental explanations of physical behavior, but these employ concepts understood independently and not introduced through physical theory. Theories constructed on the basis of physical observations and parallels alone will not include terms that imply the consciousness of the system.

---

[3] I shall capitalize this term when using it in the special sense of premise 3.

[4] This is roughly equivalent to Feigl's 'physical$_2$'. See H. Feigl, 'The "Mental" and the "Physical" ', *Minnesota Studies in the Philosophy of Science*, vol. II, ed. H. Feigl, M. Scriven, and G. Maxwell (Minneapolis: University of Minnesota Press, 1958).

It is this assumption about inference that underlies the position that the physical will never include the mental. If it is true, then in the event that any properties of matter are discoverable by explanatory inference from observable mental phenomena, they will have mental implications of a kind that physically inferred properties will never have. In that sense the ultimate properties inferred to explain mental processes would be mental and not physical.

However, this needs modification, for there is a third possibility. Perhaps there are not two chains of inference, but one chain leading from the mental and the physical to a common source. It is conceivable in the abstract that if mental phenomena derive from the properties of matter at all, those may be identical at some level with nonphysical properties from which physical phenomena also derive.

This merits a brief digression. Such reducibility to a common base would have the advantage of explaining how there could be necessary causal connexions in either direction, between mental and physical phenomena. It would also make less problematic the possibility that a single event like a bodily movement could have both a mental cause and a complete physical explanation. The mental cause, sufficiently analyzed, could be part of the physical cause, sufficiently analyzed. But if this were so, the common reducing properties would not be physical. They could not be reached by a chain of explanatory inference from physical phenomena alone, for physical data alone would provide no grounds for postulating explanatory theories that also had mentalistic consequences. The theories that physical data provide grounds for may take extraordinary leaps which permit the deduction of radical physical consequences (the convertibility of matter and energy, the deflection of light by gravity). But without any mentalistic evidence there is no reason to give mental content to the explanation of physical events. (Someone who infers from a drought that the rain god is angry is not basing his hypothesis on physical evidence alone. He is making a psychological interpretation of the drought, based on familiarity with human motivation. Any inference of this kind, reasonable or unreasonable, does not belong to physics.) Therefore even if there are common ultimate properties underlying both the mental and the physical, they do not lie on the path of physical discovery, the path of explanatory inference from observable physical phenomena alone, and so they are not physical properties.

If there were such properties, they would be discoverable only by explanatory inference from both mental and physical phenomena. This seems in fact somewhat less implausible than that there are two quite distinct chains of explanation leading back to two distinct sets of basic properties. If it were true, then it would be improper to describe the basic properties as mental for the same reason that they could not be described as physical. Strictly, only what is inferred to explain mental phenomena (including actions) should be called mental. This clearly admits concepts like repression and utility function, or perhaps universal grammar.[5] They appear at a level of psychological theory not far removed from familiar mental processes. But even if by some criterion the fundamental particles had properties that were not mental but neither mental nor physical, the conclusion of the argument would survive in a modified form. There would be properties of matter that were not physical from which the mental properties of organic systems were derived. This could still be called panpsychism.

The second question is about causality and emergence. What is the view of causal explanation from which it follows that true emergence is impossible? I have said that the properties of a complex system must *derive* from the properties of its constituents, plus the way they are combined. The argument assumes that uniform correlations cannot provide an adequate basis for the explanation of complex phenomena. It therefore rejects what is often called, inaccurately, a Humean analysis of causation. According to Hume, our idea of causal necessity is a kind of illusion, because all we ever observe are natural regularities and correlations, and never necessary connexions of cause and effect. Hume did not think that our idea of cause was that of an instance of a constant conjunction in nature.

---

[5] I have discussed the sense in which such concepts of psychological theory are mental in 'Linguistics and Epistemology', in *Language and Philosophy*, ed. Sidney Hook (New York: New York University Press, 1969), and in 'Freud's Anthropomorphism', in *Freud*, ed. Richard Wollheim (New York: Doubleday, 1974).

He was right, in my opinion, to say that if this were all there was, then causality would be an illusion. But I do not believe it is an illusion. True causes *do* necessitate their effects: they make them happen or make them the case. Uniform correlations are at best evidence of such underlying necessities. This seems to me clearly true in elementary cases: heat causing water to boil, rocks causing glass to break, magnets inducing electric current, the wind making waves. Given what heat is and what water is, it is literally impossible for water to be heated beyond a certain point at normal atmospheric pressure without boiling.

Causal necessity operates even at the most fundamental levels. An electron is a particle with a certain charge and a certain mass. Those properties imply that it will interact in a definite way with fields and with other objects. Some of the implications will be probabilistic, but that does not affect the point. And similar things are true of other subatomic particles. Ordinary physics and chemistry explain macroscopic phenomena, so far as they can be explained, as the necessary consequences of the properties of the particles (sometimes essential properties) and their interactions. They do not rely merely on contingent correlations.

This is particularly clear when we consider the relation between properties of complex systems and properties of their components *at the same time.* Consider the physical properties of a diamond. Some of them, like shape, size, weight, and crystal structure, are directly entailed by the physical properties and relations of its constituents and their effects on each other when they are so combined. Others, like color, glitter, and hardness, involve interaction between the diamond and other things, and must be explained in terms of the effects of the diamond's constituents on those other things.

The supposition that a diamond or an organism should have truly (not just epistemologically) emergent properties is that those properties appear at certain complex levels of organization but are not explainable in terms of any more fundamental properties, known or unknown, of the constituents of the system. If causal connexions were nothing but instances of contingent regularities, such a situation would be compatible with the existence of causal explanations of the emergent properties at a complex level. There would probably be many uniform psycho-physical correlations of the form; 'Whenever an organism is in *exactly* physical state P it is also in mental state M.' This may be true of my present total physical and mental states, for example. No doubt more general correlations also exist.

On a correlation view that should be enough for M to be causally explained by P. But it is not enough on a stronger view of causation. A stronger view requires that P somehow *necessitate* M; but at this complex level, no necessary connexions can be discovered. There is no sense in which my body's physical state *by itself* makes it the case that I am in mental state M. It is of course obvious that what is going on in my brain causes my mental state, just as it is obvious that when I touch a hot pan it causes pain. There *must* be some kind of necessity here. What we cannot understand is *how* the heat, or the brain process, necessitates the sensation. So long as we remain at the level of a purely physical conception of what goes on in the brain, this will continue to appear impossible. The conclusion is that unless we are prepared to accept the alternative that the appearance of mental properties in complex systems has no causal explanation at all, we must take the current epistemological emergence of the mental as a reason to believe that the constituents have properties of which we are not aware, and which do necessitate these results.

The demand for an account of how mental states necessarily appear in physical organisms cannot be satisfied by the discovery of uniform correlations between mental states and physical brain states, though that is how psycho-physical laws have traditionally been conceived. Instead, intrinsic properties of the components must be discovered from which the mental properties of the system follow necessarily. This may be unattainable, but if mental phenomena have a causal explanation such properties must exist, and they will not be physical.[6]

The third question, about Realism, is the most difficult. What is the reason to deny that mental properties can be entailed by physical ones? It is certainly conceivable that the physiological and behavioral characteristics of a living organism should follow necessarily from the physical properties of fundamental particles

---

[6] The inference to such properties is not trivial, like the statement that opium puts people to sleep because it has a dormative virtue. Although the causes are formulated so as to entail their effects, the reverse implication does not hold, as it does in the joke.

when they are combined in that way, though we can never expect to possess more than fragments of such an explanation. This is true also of functional states, so called, if they are defined in terms of their relations to one another, to stimuli, and to behavior. If the definition is general enough, the functional state could appear in a wide variety of physical systems, including organisms whose behavior took widely different forms. But its presence could still be entailed by the physical micro-properties of any organism in which it appeared.

A physical explanation of behavioral or functional states does not explain the mental because it does not explain its subjective features: what any conscious mental state is like for its possessor. Let me say briefly what I mean by this, though it is too large a topic for proper discussion here.[7] A feature of experience is subjective if it can in principle be fully understood only from one *type* of point of view: that of a being like the one having the experience, or at least like it in the relevant modality. The phenomenological qualities of our own experiences are subjective in this way. The physical events in our brains are not. Human physiologists may take a special interest in them; but they can, in principle, be understood just as well, or even better, by creatures totally unlike us in physical and mental structure. To understand them such creatures need not take up our point of view. Physical brain processes can be understood objectively, from the outside, because they are not subjective phenomena. And no description or analysis of the objective nervous system, however complete, will ever by itself imply anything which is not objective, i.e. which can be understood only from one kind of viewpoint, that of the being whose states are being described. One cannot derive a *pour soi* from an *en soi*.

Not all mental states are conscious, but all of them are capable of producing states that are. So any derivation of the mental properties of an organism from the properties of its components would have to show that subjective states necessarily arise from them. Of course if, as was suggested earlier, the explanation of behavior leads ultimately to properties that are neither mental nor physical, then a sufficiently basic explanation of the physical aspects of behavior might also explain subjective experience as a

----

[7] I try to give a fuller account of this idea in chapter 12 above.

necessary part of the process. But physical properties alone could not give this result; they explain not how things are from a particular subjective point of view but how they are objectively, in ways that can be apprehended from different points of view and do not belong to any.

This gap is logically unbridgeable. If a bodiless god wanted to create a conscious being, he could not expect to do it by combining together in organic form a lot of particles with none but physical properties.[8] Given an account of the phenomenology of a particular kind of perception, it may be possible to deduce how a particular objective state of affairs would appear from that point of view. But the subjective premise seems essential. And this is no less true when the objective state is a physical brain state, and the appearance is what it is like to be *in* that brain state, rather than what it is like to observe it.

That, in brief, is the argument against reductionism. Because of the way in which it relies on the subjectivity of the mental, I believe that it casts doubt on Realism, though I find this hard to explain.

For Realism as I have defined it to be true, physical organisms must have subjective properties. What seems unacceptable about this is that the organism does not have a point of view: the person or creature does. It seems absurd to try to discover the basis of the point of view of the person in an atomistic breakdown of the organism, because that object is not a possible subject for the point of view to which the person's experiences appear. And if it makes no sense to ascribe subjective states to the complex whole, there will be no basis for ascribing proto-mental states to its constituents; so *they* cannot be appealed to in explanation of what it means for an organism to have experiences. I simply record this feeling of impossibility because I have no more to say about it. When a mouse is frightened it does not seem to me that a small material object is frightened.

The trouble with this intuition is that it leads nowhere. What is the alternative? I assume that neither I nor the mouse has a soul, to bear these mental properties. And even if we did, it would not remove the problem, because insofar as it is possible

---

[8] Cf. Saul Kripke, 'Naming and Necessity', in *Semantics of Natural Language*, ed. D. Davidson and G. Harman (Dodrecht: Reidel, 1972), pp. 340–1.

to grasp the idea of a nonmaterial thing, there is just as much difficulty in understanding how *it* could have a point of view. But if the occurrence of a subjective experience is not the possession of a property by *something*, what is it? And what connexion does it have with the organism? Evidently in some way experiences depend on the material organism even if they are not states of it.

The only view I know of that may qualify as an alternative is found in the *Philosophical Investigations*. According to Wittgenstein as I understand him the person (or mouse) who is the subject of mental states is not to be identified with an organism or a soul or anything else. He holds that all kinds of familiar propositions about the mental states of individual living beings are true, but that there is almost nothing to be said about what property must be possessed by what thing if one of these ascriptions is to be true. All such specifications of truth conditions are trivial. What can be more fully described, however, are the kinds of circumstances, including evidential grounds, that make the ascription appropriate: criteria rather than truth conditions. For third-person ascriptions the grounds are behavior, stimuli, circumstances, and testimony (once the subject has learned the relevant mental vocabulary). For self-ascriptions no evidential grounds are needed.

Although facts about the body are among the criteria for ascribing mental states to others, and also for ascribing to them an understanding of the terms they use to ascribe mental states to themselves, the mental states are not states of the body. The view is not reductionist. Mental states are no less real than behavior, physical stimuli, and physiological processes. In fact their situation with respect to one another is symmetrical, because physical processes have mental (specifically observational) criteria just as mental processes have physical criteria. According to Wittgenstein, everything there is must be systematically connected with other things in a way that permits public agreement, or at least public disagreement, about whether it is there or not. Mental phenomena meet this condition through their connexion with behaviour and circumstances, but they are perfectly real in their own right. They cannot be analyzed as dispositions to behavior or properties of the organism, any more than physical phenomena can be analyzed as multiple possibilities of sensation or of observation. If asked to say what any of these kinds of thing really *is*, or what statements about them really *assert*, we can give no reply that is not trivial.

In some ways that is an attractive position. It does justice to the subjectivity of the mental, because of the central place it assigns to criterionless mental self-ascriptions. How things appear to someone must hang together with how they appear to others to appear to him; but these facts are inextricably connected with his point of view, as this can be publicly identified. There is clear support for the idea that mental states are subjective if they are ascribed to creatures who can ascribe them to themselves without observation, by other creatures who can ascribe similar states to *themselves* in the same way. And since it does not seem correct to describe these states of the individual as states of the organism, this idea provides an alternative to Realism.

My difficulty with the view is that it depends too heavily on our language. Essentially its account of mental phenomena is an account of how they are ascribed, particularly in the first person. But not all conscious beings are capable of language, and that leaves the difficult problem of how this view accommodates the subjectivity of *their* mental states.

We ascribe experience to animals on the basis of their behavior, structure, and circumstances, but we are not just ascribing to them behavior, structure, and circumstances. So what are we saying? The same kind of thing we say of people when we say they have experiences, of course. But here the special relation between first- and third-person ascription is not available as an indication of the subjectivity of the mental. We are left with concepts that are anchored in their application to humans, and that apply to other creatures by a natural extension from the behavioral and contextual criteria that operate in ordinary human cases.

This seems definitely unsatisfactory, because the experiences of other creatures are certainly independent of the reach of an analogy with the human case. They have their own reality and their own subjectivity. They are not, I assume, of indeterminate character in cases where the natural extension from human behavior and circumstances gives no determinate result. To take a very clear case, if things emerged from a spaceship which we could not be sure were machines or conscious beings, what we were wondering about would have an answer even if the things were so different from anything we were familiar with that we could never discover it. It would depend on whether there was something it was like to be them, not on whether behavioral similarities warranted our saying so.

This seems true quite apart from the question of what the subject of mental states is. They may not be states of the body, but they certainly exist in forms beyond the reach of our language. So they cannot be analyzed in terms of human criteria for their ascription. And since human experiences have the same kind of reality, must not the same be true of them? What they are is not fully captured by an account of the conditions under which first- and third-person ascriptions of experience are appropriate.

I will mention that this raises problems about whether the concept of experience, as I am applying it, meets basic conditions of publicity that it must meet to be well-defined at all. It is widely accepted that one cannot always define a type of similarity or a type of thing simply by pointing to an instance and saying 'the same as *this*'. And it may be doubted whether someone who wonders whether the things coming out of the spaceship have experience, without any idea of the possibility of determining whether they do or not, is really asking a well-defined question. I think that in this case the conditions of meaning are met, but I will not try to defend the claim here. Experience must have systematic connexions with behavior and circumstances in order for experiential qualities and experiential similarity to be real. But we need not know what these connexions are in order to ask whether experience is present in an alien thing.

I therefore seem to be drawn to a position more 'realistic' than Wittgenstein's. This may be because I am drawn to positions more realistic than Wittgenstein's about everything, not just the mental. I believe that the question about whether the things coming out of the spaceship are conscious must have an answer. Wittgenstein would presumably say that this assumption reflects a groundless confidence that a certain picture unambiguously determines its own application. That is the picture of something going on in their heads (or whatever they have in place of heads) that cannot be observed by dissection.

Whatever picture I may use to represent the idea, it does seem to me that I know what it means to ask whether there is something it is like to be them, and that the answer to that question is what determines whether they are conscious – not the possibility of extending mental ascriptions on evidence analogous to the human case. Conscious mental states are real states of something, whether they are mine or those of an alien creature. Perhaps Wittgenstein's view can accommodate this intuition, but I do not at the moment see how.

Where does this leave us? I have now expressed dissatisfaction with three alternative interpretations of mental states: that they are states of the body, that they are states of the soul, and that all we can say about their essence is to give criteria or conditions for their ascription. But what is left? If they are real states of something in the world, if they depend on what is going on in the creature's body, if they are intimately connected with stimuli and behavior, and if the creature does not consist of a body plus something else, what can experience be but states of the organism? If one accepts realism in a broad sense about mental states, it is very difficult to avoid Realism in the more specific sense that forms a premise of the argument for panpsychism.

This of course expresses that fatal step in the philosophy of mind, the argument by elimination. There is no reason to think that all possibilities have been thought of, so there is no reason to assume that a view is correct if all currently conceivable alternatives are even more unacceptable. Still, when a mouse or a fly or a man comes to exist because matter has been combined in certain ways, the resulting mental states seem to have to belong to the organism for want of a better home. Realism may be the weakest premise in the argument, but it is more plausible at the moment than its denial.

I therefore believe that panpsychism should be added to the current list of mutually incompatible and hopelessly unacceptable solutions to the mind–body problem. It can be avoided by denying any of the premises of the argument. Denial of the first results in dualism. This still leaves problems about the causal connexions between mind and body: either (a) those connexions are pure correlations and not necessary; or (b) the body will have properties that necessitate mental effects in the soul and effects of the soul on the body; or else (c) the soul will have properties that enable it to be acted on by the body and vice versa. If (b), then the body will have mental or at least non-physical properties. If (c), then the soul will have physical properties as well as mental ones.

Denial of the second premise is fairly common among contemporary philosophers, but the only motive I can see for accepting any of the resulting kinds of reductionism is a desire to make the mind–body problem go away. None of them has any intrinsic plausibility.

Denial of the third premise, Realism, is more attractive but awaits the development of a viable alternative, some way of admitting the reality of mental occurrences without ascribing them to either organisms or souls as subjects.

Denial of the fourth premise, nonemergence, involves accepting the existence of irreducible contingent laws connecting complex organic states with mental states. In a sense this would mean that mental states had no causal explanation: that they were not necessitated by anything. I do not believe the world is like that, but here, as with the other premises, one *can* take that escape route. It would be useful to develop all the alternatives more fully.

As for panpsychism, it is difficult to imagine how a chain of explanatory inference could ever get from the mental states of whole animals back to the proto-mental properties of dead matter. It is a kind of breakdown we cannot envision, perhaps it is unintelligible. Presumably the components out of which a point of view is constructed would not themselves have to have points of view. (How could a single self be composed of many selves?) Yet they would have to be recombinable to form different points of view, for not only can a single organism have different experiences, but its matter can be recombined to form other organisms with totally different forms of experience. The mental properties of all matter, therefore, would have to be not species-specific but universal, since they would underlie all possible forms of consciousness. In a sense, they would be less subjective than any of the specific forms.

Panpsychism in this sense does not entail panpsychism in the more familiar sense, according to which trees and flowers, and perhaps even rocks, lakes, and blood cells have consciousness of a kind. But we know so little about how consciousness arises from matter in our own case and that of the animals in which we can identify it that it would be dogmatic to assume that it does not exist in other complex systems, or even in systems the size of a galaxy, as the result of the same basic properties of matter that are responsible for us.[9]

[9] My ideas on this topic, especially on the concept of the physical and the role of necessity in causal explanation, have been strongly influenced by Rebecca Goldstein and William L. Stanton. Their own views are developed in Stanton's 'Anomalous Monism and The Mental Qua Mental' (Ph.D. dissertation, Princeton University, 1975) and Goldstein's 'Reduction, Realism, and Mind' (Ph.D. dissertation, Princeton University, 1976).

14

Subjective and Objective

There is a problem that emerges in several areas of philosophy whose connexion with one another is not obvious. I believe that it can be given a general form, and that some treatment of it is possible in abstraction from its particular instances – with results that can be applied to the instances eventually. This discussion is a preliminary sketch for what I hope will be a more thorough treatment.

The problem is one of opposition between subjective and objective points of view. There is a tendency to seek an objective account of everything before admitting its reality. But often what appears to a more subjective point of view cannot be accounted for in this way. So either the objective conception of the world is incomplete, or the subjective involves illusions that should be rejected.

Instead of trying to define these terms at the outset, I shall begin with some examples, drawn from ethics and metaphysics. The parallels between them should emerge as I proceed.

Consider first a problem about the meaning of life.[1] There is a way of considering human pursuits from within life, which allows justification of some activities in terms of others, but does not permit us to question the significance of the whole thing, unless we are asking, from within life, whether the allocation of energy or attention to different segments of it makes sense in virtue of their relative importance. This view comes under challenge from a position that regards life in detachment from

[1] See chapter 2 above.

specific or general human purposes. People, and oneself in particular, are perceived as having no significance, and absurd because they seem to accord their lives great importance in action, even though they can also appreciate a broader point of view from which they have no importance.

Each of the two points of view claims priority. The internal view asks, what is the importance for individual life of insignificance from an external point of view? Life is lived from inside, and issues of significance are significant only if they can be raised from inside. It therefore does not matter that from a point of view outside my life, my life does not matter.

The external view, on the other hand, comprehends within its scope of observation all the aims and commitments by reference to which internal significance is measured. It presents itself as the *right* way for the individual to look at the world and his place in it: the big picture. He develops this kind of detachment naturally, to counter the egocentric distortion of a purely internal view, and to correct the parochialism engendered by the contingencies of his overspecific nature and circumstances. But it is not merely corrective. It claims a position of dominance, as the only complete conception of how things really are. This dominance is not imposed from outside, but derives from the intrinsic appeal of impersonality to individual reflection. Life seems absurd because it seems absurd to *oneself*, taking up a point of view that is both natural and appealing.

The second example to consider is the problem of free will. This problem arises initially in the form of a threat to free agency from the hypothesis that actions are determined by antecedent circumstances. There have been many attempts to analyze agency in terms compatible with determinism – by reference to intentions, motives, second-order volitions, capacities, absence of obstacles or coercion. Real advances have been made in specifying necessary conditions of agency, but the possibility that these conditions are themselves determined seems still to present a threat to some element of the ordinary concept of action.[2] They may be necessary, but they do not seem sufficient.

---

[2] The literature on this subject is enormous. Three of the best recent articles are P. F. Strawson, 'Freedom and Resentment', *Proceedings of the British Academy* (1962); Harry G. Frankfurt, 'Freedom of the Will and the Concept of a Person', *Journal of Philosophy*, LXIII (January 14, 1971), 5–20;

The next step, however, is the discovery that free agency is not implied by the *absence* of determinism, even though it appears to be threatened by the presence of determinism. Uncaused acts are no more attributable to the agent than those caused by antecedent circumstances. One is therefore led to wonder what further factor, in addition to the absence of determinism, is required for free agency, and whether this further factor might not be sufficient for freedom by itself. The most difficult problem of free will is saying what the problem is, which seems to survive every attempt to specify sufficient conditions for free action.

The recent attempt to analyze action in terms of *agent* causation rather than event causation[3] is instructive because it reveals the true source of discomfort with determinism. The problem is that when one views an action as an event causally connected with other events, there is no room in the picture for someone's *doing* it. But it turns out that there is no room for someone's *doing* it if it is an event causally *un*connected with other events, either. Hence some philosophers have tried to capture this aspect by making an agent, rather than an event, the cause. I do not find the concept of agent causation intelligible, but I think I understand its motivation. While its positive content is obscure, its negative implications are clear. It removes action from the causal sequence of events by denying that it is caused by antecedent circumstances; and by substituting an agent as the cause, it avoids the alternative that action is something that just *happens*. It is a doomed attempt to capture the *doing* of the action in a new kind of causation.

But the problem is not that the idea of agency clashes with this or that particular conception of what happens in action, viewed externally as a type of event. It is not predictability that creates the problem, for I make many choices and do many things that are completely predictable. It is just that when I pick the shiny apple instead of the rotten one, it is *my doing* – and there is no room for this in an external account of the event, deterministic or not. The real problem stems from a clash between the view of

Gary Watson, 'Free Agency', *Journal of Philosophy*, LXXII (April 24, 1975), 209–20.

[3] Roderick M. Chisholm, 'Freedom and Action', in *Freedom and Determinism*, ed. Keith Lehrer (New York: Random House, 1966).

action from inside and *any* view of it from outside. Any external view of an act as something that happens, with or without causal antecedents, seems to omit the doing of it.

Even if an action is described in terms of motives, reasons, abilities, absence of impediments or coercion, this does not capture the agent's own idea of himself as its source. His actions appear to him different from other things that happen in the world, but not merely a different kind of happening, with different causes or none at all. They seem in some indescribable way not to *happen* at all (unless they are quite out of his control), though things happen when he does them. And if he sees others as agents too, their actions will seem to have the same quality. The tendency to express this conception of agency in terms of freedom from antecedent causes is a mistake, but an understandable one. When the act is viewed under the aspect of determination by antecedents, its status as an event becomes prominent. But as appears upon further investigation, no account of it as an event is satisfactory from the internal viewpoint of the agent doing it.

The connexion of this problem with moral responsibility is that when we view actions, our own or others', merely as part of the general course of events, it seems impossible to attribute them to individuals in a way that makes sense of the attitudes we take toward someone we regard as the source of an action. Certain attitudes toward the agent, rather than just about him, lose their footing. If an individual is destructive enough we may think it would be better if he did not exist; but if he is just a disastrous part of the world, blame directed at him or guilt he directs at himself make no sense, however causally or indeterministically complex his behavior and motives are.[4]

The true nature of the third problem I want to mention – that of personal identity – is also hidden in many discussions. The problem is usually presented as a search for the conditions that must obtain if two experiential episodes separated in time are to belong to a single person. Various types of continuity and similarity – physical, mental, causal, emotional – have been considered and they all seem to leave an aspect of personal identity unaccounted for. Given that any proposed set of condi-

---

[4] These points are discussed more fully in chapter 3 above.

tions is met, there still seems to be a further question as to whether the same *subject* or *self* is preserved under these conditions. This further question can be raised by imagining that you have the first of two experiences and asking about the other (which bears the candidate relation to it), 'Yes, but will it be *mine*?' As with free will, the real problem seems to be to identify the problem that always remains no matter how ingenious a solution has been proposed.

It may seem that this further question involves the assumption of a metaphysical ego which preserves personal identity. But this would be a mistake, for the ego, if it is a continuing individual with its own identity over time, would be just one more thing about which the same problem could be raised (will *that* ego still be me?). If on the other hand its *only* identity over time is that of still being me, then it cannot be the individual whose persistence *preserves* personal identity. For its identity would then simply consist in the fact that experiences had by it were all mine; and that cannot explain what makes them all mine.

The problem seems unreal when persons are viewed as beings in the world, whether physical or mental. They persist and change through time, and those are the terms in which they must be described. But as with the problem of free will, the persistent dissatisfaction with candidate analyses of this form derives from a submerged internal aspect of the problem which is left untouched by all external treatments. From the point of view of the person himself, the question of his identity or nonidentity with someone undergoing some experience in the future appears to have a content that cannot be exhausted by any account in terms of memory, similarity of character, or physical continuity. Such analyses are never sufficient, and from this point of view they may appear not even to supply necessary conditions for identity.

When someone poses inwardly the question whether a past or future experience was or will be *his*, he has the sensation of picking out something whose identity over time is well defined, just by concentrating on his present experience and specifying the temporal extension of *its subject*. The concept of the self is a psychological one, and it is characteristic of such concepts to give rise to the philosophical idea that their subjective essence, expressed most clearly in first-person applications, is detachable from more objective accompaniments and even to a considerable extent from necessary connexion with other psychological phenomena. (Another example: the conviction that it is a perfectly well-defined but in principle unanswerable question whether sugar tastes like *this* to other people.) This may be an illusion. It may have no sense to speak of 'the same self as this one' in complete detachment from all external conditions. But it is still the internal idea of the self that gives rise to the problem of personal identity. Any attempt to conceive persons completely as a kind of thing in the world persisting through time will come up against this obstacle. The self that appears to the subject seems to disappear under external analysis.

My fourth example is the mind–body problem. A particularly difficult aspect of that problem comes from the subjective character of experience. So long as mental states are looked at objectively, in their causal relations to stimuli and behavior, no special issues arise which do not arise about the physical analysis of other natural phenomena. Even problems of intentionality may seem to be soluble if one puts aside their subjective aspect, for then one may be able to describe certain kinds of computers as intentional systems. What seems impossible is to include in a physical conception of the world the facts about what mental states are like for the creature having them. The creature and his states seem to belong to a world that can be viewed impersonally and externally. Yet subjective aspects of the mental can be apprehended only from the point of view of the creature itself (perhaps taken up by someone else), whereas what is physical is simply there, and can be externally apprehended from more than one point of view.[6] Is there any way of including mental phenomena in the world as well, as part of what is simply *there*?

Here too the idea of impersonally comprehensible reality asserts its claim to dominance. We are not faced only with the problem of the relation between mind and body, or the inclusion of the mental in the physical world. The broader issue between personal and impersonal, or subjective and objective, arises also for a dualist theory of mind. The question of how one can include in the objective world a mental substance having subjective properties is as acute as the question how a physical substance can have subjective properties.

[6] See chapter 12 above.

The physical is an ideal representative for the objective in general; therefore much obscurity has been shed on the problem by faulty analogies between the mental–physical relation and relations between the physical and other objective aspects of reality. As determinism is a substitute for externality or objectivity in posing the problem of free will, so the physical is a substitute for objectivity in posing the mind–body problem. All the disputes over causal role, theoretical identification, and functional realization, while of interest in themselves, fail to give expression to the central issue that makes the mind–body problem so hard. And as with free will and personal identity, the internal element remains, even if ignored, as the true source of persistent dissatisfaction with all physical or other external theories of the mind. At the same time, the idea that persons (along with everything about them) must be parts of objective reality continues to exert its powerful appeal. Objectivity is naturally linked with reality; it is easy to feel that anything has to be located in the objective world in order to qualify as real, and that it must have as its real nature some character which, whether physical or not, can be regarded impersonally and externally.

The final example I want to discuss comes from ethics, and concerns the difference between consequentialist and more agent-centered views of right and wrong. A familiar type of objection to utilitarianism and other consequentialist views charges them with unjustifiably making questions about what to do subordinate to questions about what would be best overall. Such criticisms assert that an ethical theory should leave some room for each individual to pursue his own life without having to consider at every point how he is serving more comprehensive goals; or else they urge the need for certain restrictions or requirements on action that are not justified by their contribution to the general good. In other words, both what is permitted and what is required of a person can sometimes deviate from what would be best. I group these two rather different exceptions to consequentialism together because, while they can also be opposed to each other, they deviate from the consequentialist viewpoint in the same direction. This is clear in the case of permission to pursue one's own life, less clear in the case of general requirements or restrictions on action, whatever the goal.

Utilitarianism, or any other purely consequentialist view, is very demanding. It requires you to justify the pursuit of your own personal life and interests only as components of the general good, and does not permit reasons for action to *end* with a reference to what you want or are devoted to. Those considerations are completely encompassed by an impersonal point of view which accords you no special position, unless it can be impersonally justified. Resistance comes, naturally enough, from the point of view of the individual, who may be willing to accord impersonal considerations some weight, but who is also powerfully motivated by the independent claims of his own life – of the view from where he is in the world. But this does not remain a conflict between impersonal values and mere individual interest, because the resistance can be generalized. Someone who regards consequentialist requirements as unacceptable because of their claim to dominance over his own point of view will naturally extend this objection to others. He will gravitate toward a *general* exception to consequentialism in favor of the personal viewpoint, and this will constitute an alternative ethic, rather than merely a resistance to ethics. Such an ethic need be no less universal than utilitarianism, but it will be subjective in a way that consequentialist positions are not. Each person will be permitted, within limits, to concentrate on the pursuit of *his* life, and there will not be a single, objectively describable end by reference to which everyone's actions must be justified.

In this sense the deontological requirements that resist a consequentialist account are also subjective. Constraints against murder, lying, betrayal, assault, or coercion, though intended to apply universally, oppose the agent's specific relations to other people to the conception of a single end that everyone should exclusively promote. They are agent-centered, but in a different way. The real source of these restrictions, unlike that of the agent-centered permissions, is not the agent but the potential victim whose rights are protected. But the wrongness of violating those rights implies a constraint on each person against violating them, rather than a requirement that he try to minimize their overall violation (even if this means committing a few himself).[7] Deontological requirements are agent-centered because they instruct each person to determine the rightness or

7 See chapter 5 above.

wrongness of his acts solely from the point of view of his position in the world and his direct relation to others. The very idea that the basic moral concepts are right and wrong rather than good and bad entails that the character of one's actions rather than the world as a whole must be one's primary concern.[8]

If there is a difference in point of view between the two types of exception to consequentialism, it is that the first derives simply from the standpoint of the individual agent, whereas the second emerges when he considers in a certain way his own point of view together with those of the persons to whom he is directly related in action. Deontological constraints are intermediate between purely individual motives and completely impersonal values.

There are familiar disputes about whether utilitarianism really does have the consequences attributed to it by anti-consequentialist critics – aspects of the wider dispute between radical and moderate interpretations of utilitarianism. Likewise there are disputes about the formulation of alternative views: how absolutist they are, whether they should be stated in terms of individual rights, or liberty, or self-realization, or interpersonal commitment. But the essence of the conflict is clearer than the exact nature of the alternatives. The issue is how the individual position of the agent should enter into a decision about what he should or may do.

Obviously it cannot fail to enter in certain ways. Even on a consequentialist view, what one should do will depend on what one is in a position to do, and on the relative desirability of the possible outcomes. Nevertheless, the consequentialist judgment that one should do something is essentially the judgment that it would be best if one did it – that it ought to *happen*. The right thing to do is to turn oneself as far as possible into an instrument for the realization of what is best *sub specie aeternitatis*.

Agent-centered views, on the other hand, determine what is right, wrong, and permissible partly at least on the basis of the

---

[8] A moral theory of this type is developed by Charles Fried in *Right and Wrong* (Cambridge, Mass.: Harvard University Press, 1978). An intermediate view has been put forward by Samuel Scheffler, in 'Agents and Outcomes' (Ph.D. dissertation, Princeton University, 1977): he defends agent-centered permissions but rejects agent-centered requirements as having no intelligible basis.

individual's life, his role in the world, and his relation with others. Agent-centered morality gives primacy to the question of what to do, a question asked by the individual agent, and does not assume that the only way to answer it is to say what it would be best if he did, *sub specie aeternitatis*. It may also hold that the place for considerations of what would be best, in a decision about what to do, is not obvious and must be established by analysis of agent-centered choice and its grounds.

The real issue, therefore, is the relative priority, in regard to action, of two ways of looking at the world. On the one hand there is the position that one's decisions should be tested ultimately from an external point of view, to which one appears as just one person among others. The question then becomes, 'What would be best? Which of the acts within my power would do the most good, considering matters from out here, impersonally?' This point of view claims priority by virtue of greater comprehensiveness. The agent's situation is supposedly given its due in a larger perspective.[9]

On the other hand there is the position that since an agent lives his life from where he is, even if he manages to achieve an impersonal view of his situation, whatever insights result from this detachment need to be made part of a personal view before they can influence decision and action. The pursuit of what seems impersonally best may be an important aspect of individual life, but its place in that life must be determined from a personal standpoint, because life is always the life of a particular person, and cannot be lived *sub specie aeternitatis*.[10]

The opposition looks like a stalemate because each of the points of view claims dominance over the other, by virtue of inclusion. The impersonal standpoint takes in a world that includes the individual and his personal views. The personal

[9] In *The Possibility of Altruism* (Oxford: Oxford University Press, 1970) I defended a version of this position.

[10] This position is persuasively presented by Bernard Williams in 'A Critique of Utilitarianism', in J. J. C. Smart and Bernard Williams, *Utilitarianism For and Against* (Cambridge: Cambridge University Press, 1973). See also 'Persons, Character, and Morality', in *The Identities of Persons* ed. Amelie Rorty, (Berkeley: University of California Press, 1976), where he presses the claims not only of the view from within one's own life but of the view from the present time. This tendency of a subjective viewpoint to shrink into the present moment has been noted by Derek Parfit in his skeptical work on prudence (not yet published).

standpoint, on the other hand, regards the deliverances of impersonal reflection as only a part of any individual's total view of the world.

This list of problems could be extended. Obviously the difficulty of reconciling subjective and objective points of view arises with regard to space and time, death, and throughout the theory of knowledge. Perhaps the problem takes its purest form in a sense of incredulity that one should be anyone in particular, a specific individual of a particular species existing at a particular time and place in the universe. There is a pattern in these questions which justifies us in locating a common philosophical difficulty behind all of them, concealed by their diversity, and sometimes ignored in their treatment with unfortunate results. In what follows I shall discuss some strategies for dealing with the problem. But first let me discuss the parallels among its different forms.

Although I shall speak of the subjective viewpoint and the objective viewpoint, this is just shorthand, for there are not two such viewpoints, nor even two such categories into which more particular viewpoints can be placed. Instead, there is a polarity. At one end is the point of view of a particular individual, having a specific constitution, situation, and relation to the rest of the world. From here the direction of movement toward greater objectivity involves, first, abstraction from the individual's specific spatial, temporal, and personal position in the world, then from the features that distinguish him from other humans, then gradually from the forms of perception and action characteristic of humans, and away from the narrow range of a human *scale* in space, time, and quantity, toward a conception of the world which as far as possible is not the view from anywhere within it. There is probably no end-point to this process, but its aim is to regard the world as centerless, with the viewer as just one of its contents.

The distinction between subjective and objective is relative. A general human point of view is more objective than the view from where you happen to be, but less objective than the viewpoint of physical science. The opposition between subjective and objective can arise at any place on the spectrum where one point of view claims dominance over another, more subjective one, and that claim is resisted. In the dispute over consequentialism in ethics, it appears in the clash between internal and external views of human life, both fully admitting the importance of human concerns and ends. In the mind–body problem, it appears in the clash between an internal human view of human beings and the external view of physical theory. In the problem of personal identity, it appears in the clash between the point of view of a particular individual toward his own past and future and the view that others may take of him as a continuing conscious being, characterized by bodily and psychological continuities.

Another point I wish to emphasize is this. What is more subjective is not necessarily more private. In general it is intersubjectively available. I assume that the subjective ideas of experience, of action, and of the self are in some sense public or common property. That is why the problems of mind and body, free will, and personal identity are not just problems about one's own case.

I cannot here take up Wittgenstein's arguments about the publicity of rules and therefore of concepts.[11] I believe he is right, and that even our most subjective phenomenological concepts are public in a sense. But they are public in a very different way from that in which concepts used to describe the physical world are public. The coordination of the points of view of different individuals toward their own experiences is totally different from the coordination of their points of view toward the external world. Nothing in the former case corresponds to different individuals sharing a point of view toward the same object. Wittgenstein's position on sensations is that they just *are* appearances, so their properties are not the properties of objects which appear to whoever has them, and similarity in their properties is not similarity in the properties of such objects. Rather it is similarity in appearances. That is a similarity between irreducibly subjective phenomena. Only if we acknowledge their subjectivity – the fact that each is essentially an appearance *to* someone – can we understand the special way in which sensations are publicly comparable and not private. The private object or sense datum view is an instance of the false objectification of what is essentially subjective.

[11] Ludwig Wittgenstein, *Philosophical Investigations* (Oxford: Blackwell, 1953).

Since a kind of intersubjective agreement characterizes even what is most subjective, the transition to a more objective viewpoint is not accomplished merely through intersubjective agreement. Nor does it proceed by an increase of imaginative scope that provides access to many subjective points of view other than one's own. Its essential character, in all the examples cited, is externality or detachment. The attempt is made to view the world not from a place within it, or from the vantage point of a special type of life and awareness, but from nowhere in particular and no form of life in particular at all. The object is to discount for the features of our pre-reflective outlook that make things appear to us as they do, and thereby to reach an understanding of things as they really are. We flee the subjective under the pressure of an assumption that everything must be something not to any point of view, but in itself. To grasp this by detaching more and more from our own point of view is the unreachable ideal at which the pursuit of objectivity aims.

Some version of this polarity can be found in relation to most subject matter – ethical, epistemological, metaphysical. The relative subjectivity or objectivity of different appearances is a matter of degree, but the same pressures toward a more external viewpoint are to be found everywhere. It is recognized that one's own point of view can be distorted as a result of contingencies of one's makeup or situation. To compensate for these distortions it is necessary either to reduce dependence on those forms of perception or judgment in which they are most marked, or to analyze the mechanisms of distortion and discount for them explicitly. The subjective comes to be defined by contrast with this development of objectivity.

Problems arise because the same individual is the occupant of both viewpoints. In trying to understand and discount for the distorting influences of his specific nature he must rely on certain aspects of his nature which he deems less prone to such influence. He examines himself and his interactions with the world, using a specially selected part of himself for the purpose. That part may subsequently be scrutinized in turn, and there may be no end to the process. But obviously the selection of trustworthy subparts presents a problem.

The selection of what to rely on is based partly on the idea that the less an appearance depends on contingencies of this particular self, the more it is capable of being arrived at from a variety of points of view. If there is a way things really are, which explains their diverse appearances to differently constituted and situated observers, then it is most accurately apprehended by methods not specific to particular types of observers. That is why scientific measurement interposes between us and the world instruments whose interactions with the world are of a kind that could be detected by a creature not sharing the human senses. Objectivity requires not only a departure from one's individual viewpoint, but also, so far as possible, departure from a specifically human or even mammalian viewpoint. The idea is that if one can still maintain some view when one relies less and less on what is specific to one's position or form, it will be truer to reality. The respects in which the results of various viewpoints are incompatible with each other represent distortions of the way matters really are. And if there is such a thing as the correct view, it is certainly not going to be the unedited view from wherever one happens to be in the world. It must be a view that includes oneself, with all one's contingencies of constitution and circumstance, among the things viewed, without according it any special centrality. And it must accord the same detached treatment to the type of which one is an instance. The true view of things can no more be the way they naturally appear to human beings than the way they look from here.

The pursuit of objectivity therefore involves a transcendence of the self, in two ways: a transcendence of particularity and a transcendence of one's type. It must be distinguished from a different kind of transcendence by which one enters imaginatively into other subjective points of view, and tries to see how things appear from other specific standpoints. Objective transcendence aims at a representation of what is external to each specific point of view: what is there or what is of value in itself, rather than *for* anyone. Though it employs whatever point of view is available as the representational vehicle – humans typically use visual diagrams and notation in thinking about physics – the aim is to represent how things are, not *for* anyone or any type of being. And the enterprise assumes that what is represented is detachable from the mode of representation, so that the same laws of physics could be represented by creatures sharing none of our sensory modalities.

While there are problems about how to achieve this kind of transcendence, it is certainly one of the important ways of advancing our understanding. We cannot help wanting to extend it farther and farther, and to bring more and more of life and the world within its range. But the consistent pursuit of greater objectivity runs into trouble, and gives rise to the philosophical problems I have described, when it is turned back on the self, as it must be to pursue its comprehensive ambitions.

The trouble occurs when the objective view encounters something, revealed subjectively, that it cannot accommodate. Its claims to comprehensiveness will then be threatened. The indigestible lump may be either a fact or a value. The problems of personal identity and mind–body arise because certain subjectively apparent facts about the self seem to vanish as one ascends to a more objective standpoint. The problems about consequentialism and the meaning of life arise from a corresponding disappearance of certain personal values with the ascent to a more and more detached and impersonal point of view. The problem of free will combines both effects.

In either case it appears that something must give way, for two natural and necessary ways of thinking lead to a collision and cannot without adjustment be accommodated in a single view of how things are. But even allowing for adjustments, the options seem to be limited and unpalatable. If one wishes to insist that everything real must be brought under an objective description, there seem to be three courses available with respect to any recalcitrant subjective aspect: reduction, elimination, and annexation.

First, reduction: one may try to save the appearances as much as possible, by accommodating them under an objective interpretation. Thus one might offer a consequentialist account of rights or special obligations or the allowable forms of self-interest. Or one might analyze experience in terms of behavioral criteria, or agency in terms of certain kinds of causes, or personal identity in terms of physical or mental continuity.

Secondly, elimination: if no reduction seems plausible one may dismiss the deliverance of a subjective viewpoint as an illusion, perhaps offering an explanation of how it arises. For example, one might say there is no such thing as pure personal identity, or free agency. One might even say that there is no such thing as the subjective character of experience, that experiences can be adequately characterized by their causal roles and do not possess phenomenological properties in addition. And one might dismiss deontological requirements and other nonconsequentialist ethical intuitions as superstitious, selfish, or rulebound.

Thirdly, annexation: if one fails to reduce the subjective to familiar objective terms, and is unwilling to deny its reality outright, one may invent a new element of objective reality especially for the purpose of including this recalcitrant element: the will, the ego, the soul, or perhaps the command of God. Such metaphysical inventions, however, can seem to serve the purpose for which they were designed only because their obscurity prevents it from being obvious that the same problems of subjectivity will arise with regard to them, if they really belong to objective reality. It is no good trying to amplify our conception of the objective world to include whatever is revealed subjectively, for the problem is not that something has been left out. An objective conception of space and time cannot be faulted for *leaving out* the identification of the here and now. Any conception that included it would not be objective, and any objective realization would fail to capture it. This applies also to the prediction that mental phenomena will eventually come to be counted as physical, once we understand them systematically – even if they are not reduced to terms already admitted as physical.[12] We cannot solve these problems by simply annexing to the objective (or even physical) world everything that is not already in it.

The only alternative to these unsatisfactory moves is to resist the voracity of the objective appetite, and stop assuming that understanding of the world and our position in it can always be advanced by detaching from that position and subsuming whatever appears from there under a single more comprehensive conception. Perhaps the best or truest view is not obtained by transcending oneself as far as possible. Perhaps reality should not be identified with objective reality. The problem is to explain why objectivity is inadequate as a comprehensive ideal of understanding, without faulting it for not including subjective

[12] See Noam Chomsky, *Language and Mind* (New York: Harcourt, Brace & World, 1968), pp. 83–4

elements it could not possibly include. There is always room for improvement in our objective understanding of things, naturally, but the proposal I am considering is not that the objective picture is incomplete, but rather that it is in essence only partial.

This proposal is harder to accept than it may seem, for it implies that there is no single way things are in themselves. Even if one admits to the world facts or values involving a particular point of view, it is tempting to assume that something's being so from a particular point of view must consist in something else's being the case from no point of view. (The something else may of course involve some objective relations.) Those who believe there are no objective values may try to analyze the existence of subjective values in terms of objective facts about the individuals for whom they are values. Others have analyzed apparently subjective values in terms of objective ones.[13] And the philosophy of mind is full of refusals to admit that there may be no objective fact that is what *really* obtains when something looks red to someone.

The idealist tradition, including contemporary phenomenology, has of course admitted subjective points of view as basic, and has gone to the opposite length of denying an irreducible objective reality. I have concentrated on the tendency to resolve the conflict by objectifying everything because it has dominated recent analytic philosophy in spite of Wittgenstein. But I find the idealist solution unacceptable for the same reason: objective reality cannot be analyzed or shut out of existence any more than subjective reality can. Even if not everything is something from no point of view, some things are.

The deep source of both idealism and its objectifying opposite is the same: a conviction that a single world cannot contain both irreducible points of view and irreducible objective reality – that one of them must be what there *really* is and the other somehow reducible to or dependent on it. This is a very powerful idea. To deny it is in a sense to deny that there is a single world.

We must admit that the move toward objectivity reveals what things are like in themselves as opposed to how they appear; not just how they appear to one, relatively austere point of view as opposed to others. Therefore when the objective gaze is turned

---

[13] For example, G. E. Moore in *Principia Ethica* (Cambridge: Cambridge University Press, 1903), p. 99.

on human beings and other experiencing creatures, who are undeniably parts of the world, it can reveal only what they are like in themselves. And if the way things are for these subjects is not part of the way things are in themselves, an objective account, whatever it shows, will omit something. So reality is not just objective reality, and the pursuit of objectivity is not an equally effective method of reaching the truth about everything.

It is conceivable that everything has *some* objective properties. I do not know whether it makes sense to attribute physical and phenomenological properties to the same thing, but perhaps even experiences are events that can be in part described objectively, perhaps physically. But the properties that make them experiences exist only from the point of view of the types of beings who have them.

Since we are not the only creatures in the universe, a general conception of reality would require a general conception of experience which admitted our own subjective viewpoint as a special case. This is completely beyond us and will probably remain so for as long as human beings continue to exist.

It makes objectivity attractive by comparison. We can pursue a unified if very etiolated conception of reality by detaching progressively from our own point of view. We just have to keep in mind what we are leaving behind, and not be fooled into thinking we have made it disappear. This is particularly important in connexion with philosophical problems about free will, personal identity, agent-centered morality, or mind and body, which cannot be dealt with in detachment from the subjective point of view on which they depend for their existence.

The power of the impulse to transcend oneself and one's species is so great, and its rewards so substantial, that it is not likely to be seriously baffled by the admission that objectivity has its limits. While I am arguing for a form of romanticism, I am not an extremist. The task of accepting the polarity without allowing either of its terms to swallow the other should be a creative one. It is the aim of eventual unification that I think is misplaced, both in our thoughts about how to live and in our conception of what there is. The coexistence of conflicting points of view, varying in detachment from the contingent self, is not just a practically necessary illusion but an irreducible fact of life.

INDEX